Twayne's English Authors Series

Sylvia E. Bowman, *Editor*

INDIANA UNIVERSITY

James Beattie

TEAS 206

James Beattie

JAMES BEATTIE

By EVERARD H. KING

Memorial University
St. John's, Newfoundland

TWAYNE PUBLISHERS

A DIVISION OF G. K. HALL & CO., BOSTON

Library of Congress Cataloging in Publication Data

King, Everard H
    James Beattie.

    (Twayne's English author series ; TEAS 206)
    Bibliography: p. 181 - 86.
    Includes index.
    1. Beattie, James, 1735 - 1803. 2. Authors, Scottish
—18th century—Biography.
PR3316.B4K5   821'.6 [B]   76-54693
ISBN 0-8057-6653-7

To My Mother
and the Memory of
My Father

Contents

About the Author

Preface

Chronology

1. The Life and Times of James Beattie   15

2. Teaching Career   26

3. The Philosophy of Common Sense   38

4. Christian Apology   49

5. "The Castle of Scepticism"   60

6. Minor Poetry   75

7. *The Minstrel*   91

8. The Influence of *The Minstrel*   107

9. Literary Essays   134

10. Assessments of Writings   158

Notes and References   169

Bibliography   181

Index   187

About the Author

Everard H. King is professor of English at Memorial University of Newfoundland, where he specializes in teaching courses in English Romantic writers. As a Rothermere Fellow, he studied in the United Kingdom for two years and graduated from the University of London in 1965 with the degree of Doctor of Philosophy. Since then, he has published articles on eighteenth century education, thought, and literature, including several about Beattie, and on aspects of Romantic literature. At present, he is working on an edition of Beattie's *The Minstrel* and is also writing a book about *The Minstrel* and its place in the development of Romanticism.

Preface

James Beattie (1735 - 1803) was one of the most popular writers during the great period of eighteenth-century Scottish letters. In fact, he was regarded well into the nineteenth century as an outstanding poet, philosopher, Christian apologist, literary critic, and educational theorist. Beattie's work shows more clearly than that of any other writer the nature, scope, and achievement of contemporary Scottish writing; for he was an excellent example of the many Scots who, by choosing to write in English, exerted important influence throughout the English-speaking world. And, since he wrote in both prose and verse about many of the important topics of the time, his work has considerable representative value for its reflection of Scotland's role in shaping the transition from the neo-Classical to the Romantic period. This book about Beattie is, therefore, as much an attempt to see the waning of the Age of Enlightenment in Scotland and in England through a restatement and an analysis of his ideas and principles and of the preoccupations of his poetic life, as it is an assessment of Beattie's achievement, influence, and place as a writer.

Chapter 1 of this study of Beattie starts by describing the thriving intellectual life of eighteenth-century Scotland; it continues with a discussion of the important events, influences, and people in Beattie's life and of the widespread response to him as "a good man" that is found especially in the remarks of Dr. Johnson, Fanny Burney, and Thomas Gray; and it concludes with a brief account of the many editions of his publications during his lifetime as an indication of his great popularity. Chapter 2, which stresses the importance of Beattie's teaching career to his writings, shows the considerable influence of his relationships with his students on his books; and it also documents, through the use of unpublished manuscripts, the profound importance of the Scottish universities of the time. After Chapter 3 outlines the origin and principles of the philosophy of common sense, it presents Beattie's version of it in his *Essay on Truth* (1770) and discusses the remarkable contemporary reaction to the book. Chapter 4 presents an account of the Christian response to eighteenth century sceptical philosophy as a preparation for the discussion of the *Essay on Truth* as a work of Christian apology and of Beattie's later defense of Christianity in *Evidences of the Christian Religion* (1786). Chapter 5 analyzes "The Castle of Scepticism" (1767), a suppressed prose-satire about sceptical philosophers, as an important commentary on the *Essay on Truth* and on *The Minstrel* (1771, 1774), as well as an impressive work in its own right.

Most of Beattie's early poetry is shown, in Chapter 6, to be merely competent, neo-Classical verse, but "Retirement" (1761) and "The Hermit" (1766) are analyzed as influential early Romantic poems; and, in addition, a verse-satire about Charles Churchill (1765) is discussed as an important late Augustan satiric poem. Chapter 7 discusses *The Minstrel* as a significant transitional poem by showing its Romantic and its neo-Classical qualities, as well as its effect on eighteenth-century readers, its relationship to the *Essay on Truth*, and its importance as a Spenserian poem; and Chapter 8 demonstrates that the poem exerted an important seminal influence on the Romantic poets. Chapter 9 shows that Beattie was an important literary critic not only for playing a role in the evolution of Romanticism, and for publishing influential essays about such topics as the novel, satire, and the poetic imagination, but also for presenting a comprehensive and faithful reflection of current literary attitudes and ideas. Chapter 10 is an assessment of Beattie's writings which not only attempts to account for his great popularity and influence in his own time and for the decline in his reputation as an important minor writer but also stresses the need to pay attention to him if we are to claim that we fully understand the past.

Many people helped to produce this book, and I should like to record my thanks to them. Professors E. R. Seary and A. A. Macdonald encouraged me to undertake the research, and Professor J. R. Sutherland helped me to get started and offered many valuable suggestions. Professor Sylvia E. Bowman made many useful criticisms in editing the text for publication. My thanks are also extended to Lord Rothermere and the trustees of the Rothermere Fellowships Trust for generously supporting my research in Great Britain and to the administrators of the Central Research Fund of the University of London for giving me money to travel from London to Aberdeen on two occasions. I am grateful for the use of their resources to the librarians at the universities of Aberdeen and London and at the British Museum. My greatest debt, however, is to Joyce, who encouraged, criticized, and labored without complaint.

Preface

I acknowledge with thanks the kind permission to use quotations from the following sources: the Beattie papers at the University of Aberdeen, the manuscript "notes" taken by James Rennie at Beattie's lectures that are now in the library of the University of Glasgow, and the Clarendon Press for *The Correspondence of Thomas Gray*.

Everard H. King

Memorial University

Chronology

1735 James Beattie born on October 25 at Laurencekirk in the county of Kincardine, Scotland.

1742 Beattie's father died, leaving the family very poor.

1749 Became a student at Marischal College in Aberdeen.

1753 Graduated Master of Arts in March. Spent the next five years as the teacher in the village of Fordoun.

1756 First poems published in *The Scot's Magazine*.

1758 Appointed usher in the Aberdeen Grammar School.

1760 Became professor of moral philosophy and logic at Marischal College.

1761 *Original Poems and Translations* published in London and Aberdeen. Elected a member of the Philosophical Society of Aberdeen.

1763 First visit to London. Made pilgrimage to Alexander Pope's villa at Twickenham near the city.

1765 "Verses occasioned by the Death of the Rev[d] Mr. Charles Churchill" published in Edinburgh; "The Judgment of Paris" published in London.

1766 Second edition of collected poems. Began to write *The Minstrel* and the *Essay on Truth*. Met with Thomas Gray for two days at Glamis Castle. Wrote "The Hermit."

1767 Married Mary Dun on June 28.

1768 Edited and published Gray's poems. James Hay Beattie born on November 6.

1770 *An Essay on the Nature and Immutability of Truth, in Opposition to Sophistry and Scepticism* published in Edinburgh.

1771 Canto I of *The Minstrel* published in Edinburgh and in London.

1773 Visited London for four months and found himself a celebrity. Granted a pension of two hundred pounds for life by King George III.

1774 Canto II of *The Minstrel* published.

1776 "Essays: On Poetry and Music as they affect the Mind; On

Laughter and Ludricrous Composition; On the Utility of Classical Learning" published as a companion volume to the sixth edition of the *Essay on Truth*.

1778   Montagu Beattie born on July 8.

1783   *Dissertations Moral and Critical* published in London, Edinburgh, and Dublin.

1786   *Evidences of the Christian Religion* published in Edinburgh.

1790   Beattie's eldest son, James Hay, died on November 19. Volume I of *Elements of Moral Science* published in Edinburgh. Published his edition of Joseph Addison's *Prose Works* with preface.

1793   Volume II of *Elements of Moral Science* published.

1796   Beattie's only remaining son, Montagu, died on March 14.

1799   Published *Essays and Fragments of James Hay Beattie* with a memoir.

1803   Died on August 18.

CHAPTER 1

The Life and Times of James Beattie

I Scotland's "Age of Improvement"

JAMES Beattie (1735 - 1803) lived during the Scottish Renaissance of the eighteenth century. As the "Age of Improvement," the period was marked by the widespread desire for self-improvement in intellect and culture that generated great interest in spoken and written language, in economic and political theories, in history, and in the discussion of literary and philosophical principles. The cultivation of these diverse activities by many writers created in Scotland a reading public of a very high order of response and responsibility that ultimately produced "such notable results as the *Edinburgh Review* and *Blackwood's Magazine.*"[1] One can trace the evolution of these periodicals through the influence of such earlier publications in England as the *Tatler, Spectator, Guardian, Rambler,* and *World* in setting a standard of enlightened taste in Scotland. "They were the popular ways by which the public sought to improve its understanding of letters and philosophy."[2]

Since the literary and philosophical societies of the time were among the best results of this great outburst of intellectual life that placed Scotland at the center of the thinking world, the surviving records of such clubs, notably in Edinburgh, Glasgow, St. Andrews, and Aberdeen, provide important evidence of the fruits of the "critical" spirit that characterized the progress of the time.[3] The Philosophical Society of Aberdeen (1758 - 1773) was an outstanding example of the thriving spirit of inquiry that stimulated its members to publish many books, essays, pamphlets, and sermons.[4] The club's influence on Beattie was great, for the enlightened talk and the carefully prepared essays of the other members left their mark on his development, and he himself read many papers to them, including most of the installments of his philosophical treatment of common sense which grew into the *Essay on Truth*. Many of his attitudes and opinions were shaped by or for the club; and almost all of his principal works were written during the ten years after he became a member in 1760.

All except one of the members of the Philosophical Society were teachers at Marischal or King's College in Aberdeen; in fact, most of the important Scottish writers in Edinburgh, Glasgow, and St. Andrews, as in Aberdeen, were university teachers such as Adam Smith, "Jupiter" Carlyle, Adam Ferguson, Hugh Blair, Dugald Stewart, Thomas Reid, Alexander Gerard, and George Campbell. As teachers, they tried to satisfy the public desire for self-improvement by adapting their courses of study, by teaching their students to write in a simple and direct style, and by cultivating their taste and feelings on all aspects and problems of human life. They therefore helped to create in Scotland an interested and informed reading public: "We have the testimony of a succession of eminent men, to the effect that the chairs of mental philosophy, taken along with the essay-writing which the professors . . . demanded . . . sent forth a body of youths capable of thinking, and of expressing their thoughts in a clear and orderly manner."[5] The professor of moral philosophy (commonly called "mental philosophy" or "mental science") was the most effective teacher in training Scottish students, mainly because he was required to deal with a much wider range of topics than his colleagues. His lectures included "discussions of human nature, social forces, progress, marriage and family relationships, economic processes, maintenance of government, religion, international relations, elementary jurisprudence, primitive customs, history of institutions, ethics [and] aesthetics."[6]

At Marischal College, moral philosophy occupied the whole of the students' fourth and final year, so that the teacher always knew precisely what his students had been taught, and by whom, in their previous three years. As a result, he could easily adapt the curriculum at any time to meet the specific needs of his students or to satisfy special requirements such as the great desire of the public for improved spoken and written English. As the only professor of moral philosophy at Marischal College for nearly forty years, Beattie's influence on several generations of Scottish students was great, especially since he was by all accounts an outstanding teacher. A striking example of his ability to stimulate the intellectual curiosity of his students is the fact that over thirty of them published books in which several of them acknowledged indebtedness to his influence, and that sixteen of them are included in the *Dictionary of National Biography.*

Beattie's own prose works give a comprehensive idea of what he taught to his students, for they were all originally college lectures. In addition, a notebook written at his lectures by a student in 1767 - 1768 gives an important view of his performance in the classroom; and his own "Journal of Sessions," a detailed schedule of topics that he discussed in his classes from 1762 to 1793, completes the evidence of his work and influence as a teacher. Since Beattie's writings were profoundly affected by his teaching career, his achievements as a writer can be fully comprehended only when the reader is aware that the origins of his work almost always lie in his relationships with his students and with his reading public as an extension of his university classes. Beattie's writings provide, therefore, an excellent example of the public education that created Scotland's "Age of Achievement."

II   *Influences and Events in Beattie's Life*

Beattie was born on October 25, 1735, into the large family of a poor farmer and shopkeeper in the village of Laurencekirk near the eastern coast of Scotland. When his father died in 1742 and left the family destitute, Beattie experienced for several years physical privations that affected his attitudes for the rest of his life. But he was removed from these trying circumstances at the age of fourteen when he won a bursary to study at Marischal College in Aberdeen. He was such a good student that, when he received his Master of Arts degree in 1753, he was offered the post of schoolmaster in Fordoun, a village six miles north of Laurencekirk. Beattie accepted the offer immediately because he wished to give financial support to his mother and family who were still very poor. The next five years were the most formative of his life, for he took great pleasure in teaching his students and in reading widely. During this period also, he improved upon the schoolboy verses he had written at Laurencekirk, and he was delighted that several of his new poems were accepted for publication in *The Scot's Magazine* from 1756 to 1759. He spent his leisure time in playing musical instruments and in wandering alone for hours over the countryside. Years later, he recalled vividly his youthful preoccupations with the literal and imaginative landscapes of these walks; in fact he recreated them in the adventures of his minstrel, Edwin. Meanwhile, he moved to Aberdeen in 1758 to become a master in the grammar school until 1760 when he was appointed professor of moral philosophy and logic at Marischal College. During these early years in Aberdeen, Beattie's intellectual and social life was stimulated and enlarged by many new friends such as his colleagues at the colleges; and, apart from his journeys to London and to other parts of Scotland, he spent the rest of his life in Aberdeen.

In the 1760s, when Beattie was very busy preparing his college lectures and writing the *Essay on Truth, The Minstrel,* and other poems, his private life was one of turmoil because of his wife. He had married Mary Dun, the daughter of the headmaster of the Aberdeen Grammar School, on June 28, 1767; and, by 1770, as Beattie acknowledged years later, she was becoming physically ill more frequently and was falling more and more into fits of depression and emotional violence. For years, Beattie kept hoping that her periods of mental calm and clarity were signs of lasting improvement; but he was finally convinced by 1784 that she was too dangerous for him and their two sons to remain with them in Aberdeen; he therefore sent her to Edinburgh where her behavior could be controlled by his friend William Forbes. In 1793, Mary returned to Aberdeen to live with her aged father, and Beattie's fear and anxiety were renewed. The thought of their early happiness together and of her many later attempts to humiliate and injure him, as well as the threatening fact of her presence in Aberdeen, caused him constant concern almost to the end of his life. In addition, the mental anguish of his unfortunate marriage was aggravated by his own chronic illnesses. All his life he was frail and sickly, and he suffered often from vertigo and headaches. He frequently experienced stomach pains, and he was always susceptible to heavy attacks of influenza in the winter. In his old age, he endured the recurring pain of rheumatism and arthritis, and his sight failed. Finally, in April 1799, he suffered a stroke that left him paralyzed for the remaining four years of his life.

A good illustration of Beattie's many remarks about his own health and the effects of Mary's insanity upon him is found in his letter to Lady Newhaven of October 14, 1793:

With respect to my domestick concerns I am sorry I cannot give your Ladyship much agreeable information. In consequence of a long succession of horrors and sorrows my health is entirely broken down, and lowness of spirits, with a frightful dizziness of head, is my constant companion. This last complaint often deprives me of the power of commanding my thoughts, and disqualifies me for almost every sort of business. Yet I have hitherto, though under many discouragements, endeavoured to do my duty in the college, but cannot hope to do so much longer . . . . Mrs. Beattie's mind remains in the same melancholy condition in which it has been for many years. She now lives, in a very retired manner, in a house in this town under the inspection of her Father, who is hale, active, and indeed a strong man, of eighty-four. She is tolerably quiet, but like other persons in her unhappy circumstances, greatly dissatisfied, especially with me; and complains of the confinement in which she is kept; and that she is not permitted to appear in the world as she formerly did. I have not seen her these eight years. While she remained in lodgings near Edinburgh . . . I enjoyed tranquility; but since she was brought home I live in continued alarm.[7]

When he wrote this letter, Beattie was fifty-eight years old; but the trying circumstances of his life had aged him far beyond his years; in fact, "at forty-five he had the walk and manner and precautions that are usually observable at sixty."[8]

In view of these difficulties in his life, Beattie's achievements are remarkable, and especially so are his regular attention to his college lectures and other class work and his careful and prolonged preparation of the many editions of his poems and prose works. In addition, he often visited the sick and his friends, worshipped regularly in church, and attended as many social gatherings as possible, especially the weekly musical programs at which he often sang and played the violincello. Even though he allowed only extreme sickness to disrupt his busy schedule, his search for better health was always on his mind. After 1760, he exhausted himself every year at his teaching, and then he recuperated during the vacation in preparation for the next college session. During these periods of leisure, he traveled extensively on the advice of his doctor; and he also tried to improve his health by frequent walking, archery, mineral baths, and horseback riding. But his compulsive habit of intense and almost continuous study aggravated his physical and mental problems, even during his leisure time, and contributed greatly to his debility in his last years.

Meanwhile, Beattie took comfort from the usefulness of his books and from his many friends; and he doted on his two sons, James Hay and Montagu. He was therefore grief-striken when James Hay died in 1790 at the age of twenty-two, and he was completely overwhelmed by Montagu's death six years later at the age of eighteen. Beattie was an utterly broken man when he gazed on Montagu's body for the last time and was heard to whisper, "Now I have done with the world."[9] He continued to write letters to close friends and to teach his students for almost three more years; but he himself knew that his mind had been seriously affected, as he hinted to a friend on April 10, 1796: "I fear my reason is a little disordered, for I have sometimes thought of late, especially in a morning, that Montagu is not dead, though I seem to have a remembrance of a dream that he is."[10] Beattie's last seven years of life were so full of dejection and pain, that they were softened only a little by the visits and letters of friends and by medicinal alcohol.

Beattie's ideas and attitudes as a Christian were shaped and strengthened by the stern and often tragic circumstances of his life. His hope and his comfort sprang from the conviction that all things happen according to the will of God, whose justice and mercy are sometimes beyond man's comprehension. This belief did not soften his sorrow, but it did enable him to endure his suffering with patience, and it also endowed him with the dignity and the faith that are central to the Christian ideal of suffering. He was still able, therefore, to count his blessings only a month after Montagu's death: "A deep gloom hangs upon me, and disables all my faculties; and thoughts so strange sometimes occur to me, as to make me 'fear that I am not,' as Lear says, 'in my perfect mind.' But I thank God I am entirely resigned to the divine will; and, though I am now childless, I have friends whose goodness to me, and other virtues, I find great comfort in recollecting."[11] This noble courage, which enabled Beattie to sympathize with the weaknesses of others, especially if their intentions were good, was characteristic of him throughout his life. Even when he was a young teacher at Fordoun, he recorded in "Epitaph, Intended for Himself" the view that he hoped would be taken of him after his death:

> Forget my frailties, thou art also frail;
> Forgive my lapses, for thyself may's fall;
> Nor read, unmov'd, my artless tale,
> I was a friend, O man! to thee, to all.[12]

Beattie lived and died as an admirable Christian.

Throughout his lifetime, Beattie was liked, respected, and admired by all who knew him. "We all love Beattie," Dr. Johnson told Boswell in 1771,[13] and he wrote years later of Beattie as "a philosopher, a poet, and a good man" in his "Life of Gray"(1781).[14] In 1789, when William Creech wrote to Beattie from Edinburgh concerning his pride in being his publisher, he added, "I love the man, and I love his work."[15] Even as late as 1846, Thomas Miller wrote in a "Memoir" that few writers "have gone to the grave with a character so spotless as Beattie's. He was, in every sense of the word, a good and honest man."[16] Beattie's readers were most impressed, as Alexander Chalmers claims, because "his life and writings were in strict conformity. No man ever felt more strongly impressions of the value of the virtues he recommended than Dr. Beattie . . . . His zeal for religious and moral truth . . . originated in a mind fully convinced of the importance of what he prescribed to others, and anxious to display . . . that his convictions were sincere, and his practice resolute."[17]

Most readers readily perceived in Beattie's books the expression of his attitudes and of his personality that endeared him to his close friends and even to his acquaintances. He was both an astute judge of character and a patient observer of human frailty, and his sensitivity to affliction and distress were always expressed in compassionate understanding and generous gifts of money. Even though he had been quite shy as a youth, he developed into an able conversationalist and a witty punster. But, by nature, he was always a gentle, tender-hearted, cheerful man, whose greatest joy was found in the success of good men. He was, therefore, too level-headed to cultivate delusions of self-importance over his celebrity; but he was, nevertheless, equally at home in London's high society or in a humble cottage in Kincardineshire.

During all the difficulties of his life, one of Beattie's characteristic qualities was his sense of humor, which enabled him to perceive the funny aspects of experience, as well as its irony and tragedy; to find pleasure in overcoming problems; and even to laugh sometimes at adversity. On November 16, 1766, for instance, near the end of a severe attack of vertigo when he was finally "able to read a page, and write a sentence or two without stopping," he jokingly wrote of his illness to Charles Boyd:

My hopes and my spirits begin to revive once more. I flatter myself I shall soon get rid of this infirmity; nay, that I shall ere long be in the way of becoming a great man. For have I not headachs, like Pope? vertigo, like Swift? grey hairs, like Homer? Do I not wear large shoes, (for fear of corns,) like Virgil? and sometimes complain of sore eyes, (though not of *lippitude*,) like Horace? Am I not at this present writing invested with a garment, not less ragged than that of Socrates? Like Joseph the patriarch, I am a mighty dreamer of dreams; like Nimrod the hunter, I am an eminent builder of castles (in the air.) I procrastinate, like Julius Caesar; and very lately, in imitation of Don Quixote, I rode a horse, lean, old and lazy, like Rozinante. Sometimes, like Cicero, I write bad verses; and sometimes bad prose, like Virgil . . . . I am small of stature, like Alexander the Great; I am somewhat inclinable to fatness, like Dr. Arbuthnot and Aristotle; and I drink brandy and water, like Mr. Boyd.[18]

The valuable evidence of contemporary reaction to Beattie as recorded by writers in England is typified by his relationship with Dr. Johnson. The two writers first met in the summer of 1771 when Beattie arrived in London with a letter of introduction to Johnson from James Boswell. In September, Mary Beattie wrote from London to her father in Aberdeen that James "has been often wt Dr. Johnson since I wrote you. The Dr. has taken an extraordinary attachment to him; he is not satisfied wt seeing him at his own house, but he has introduced him to all his favourites that are near London."[19] Later that year, Johnson thanked Boswell for arranging the meeting with Beattie; and, on July 5, 1773, during Beattie's next visit to London, he complained to Boswell that "Beattie is so caressed, and invited, and treated, and liked, and flattered, by the great, that I can see nothing of him."[20]

In fact, Johnson spent as much time as possible with Beattie whenever he came to the city; and, although they saw each other infrequently and corresponded only occasionally in later years, Johnson always remembered Beattie with affection. Johnson therefore invited him to revisit London on August 21, 1780:

More years than I have delight to reckon have passed since you and I saw one another. Of this, however, there is no reason for making any reprehensory complaint, *sic fata ferunt:* But, methinks, there might pass some small interchange of regard between us. If you say, that I ought to have written, I now write; and I write to tell you, that I have much kindness for you and Mrs. Beattie, and I wish your health better, and your life long. Try change of air, and come a few degrees southward; a softer climate may do you both good. Winter is coming on, and London will be warmer and gayer, and busier, and more fertile of amusement than Aberdeen.[21]

Johnson's warm regard for Beattie was strongly supported by his admiration for Beattie's writings, especially for the *Essay on Truth* and *The Minstrel*.

Aside from Johnson's views, Fanny Burney's impressions of Beattie which were recorded in her diary for 1787 are vivid and lengthy.[22] Since she had long approved of the *Essay on Truth* and *The Minstrel*, she invited the author to her home on July 13: "I kept my appointment with Dr. Beattie, and was much gratified by so doing. I found him pleasant, unaffected, and full of conversible intelligence; with a round, thick, clunch [stumpy, thickset] figure, that promises nothing either of his works or his discourse; yet his eye, at intervals, and when something breaks from him pointed and sudden, shoots forth a ray of genius that instantly lights up his whole countenance. His voice and his manners are particularly and pleasingly mild, and seem to announce an urbanity of character both inviting and edifying." On the following day, Beattie again visited Burney, who wrote a long account of their conversation that ends with this admission: "I like Dr. Beattie extremely. I am quite happy he made this visit. My dearest Mrs. Delaney told me he had been formerly amongst the first men in his social powers; but family calamities had greatly altered him. I was truly sorry to hear of his sad fate, but as I had not known him in his happier days, I found him now all I could wish."

On July 17, Beattie kept another appointment with Burney: "I was just dressed when Dr. Beattie arrived . . . . He was very cheerful and very charming. He seems made up of gentleness and benevolence, yet with a disposition to decent mirth, and an enjoyment of humour and sport, that give an animation to his mildness truly engaging. You would be surprised how soon you would forget that he is ugly and clumsy, for there is a sort of perfect good-will in his countenance and his smile, that is quite captivating." Finally, on the next day, she made this simple, sad notation: "I saw no more of him, to my great regret. He left Windsor the next day." Fanny Burney was enthusiastic about Beattie's books, appreciative of his reputation, and charmed by his personality and conversation. Mrs. Montagu, the Duchess of Gordon, Hannah More, the Dowager Duchess of Portland, Mrs. Thrale, Mrs. Delaney, and many other fashionable ladies reacted in a similar manner. Many, especially Mrs. Montagu and the Duchess of Gordon, were frequent correspondents and confidants almost to the end of his life.

Even though Beattie's relationships with such women were important in his personal life, they were not nearly so valuable to him as a writer as were the friendship and advice of Thomas Gray. Beattie first met Gray in August 1765 at Glamis Castle, where the two poets spent two days together. Before this meeting, Beattie had long been an admirer of Gray's poetry; and Gray was acquainted with Beattie's *Original Poems and Translations*(1761). During their long conversations about poetry, Gray became a tutor to Beattie's compositions; and he offered additional advice about the poetic life in a letter of October 2, 1765, after he had returned to Cambridge:

It is a pleasure to me to find, that you are not offended with the liberties I took, when you were at Glames. you took me too literally, if you thought I meant in the least to discourage you in your pursuit of Poetry. all I intended to say was, that if either Vanity (that is, a general & undistinguishing desire of applause) or Interest, or Ambition has any place in the breast of a poet, he stands a great chance in these our days of being severely disappointed: and yet after all these passions are suppress'd, there may remain in the mind of one, *ingenti perculsus amore* (and such a one I take you to be), incitements of a better sort strong enough to make him write verse all his life for his own pleasure, & that of all posterity.[23]

Thereafter, Beattie sent copies of all his new works to Gray, from whom he always received helpful criticisms and high praise. On March 8, 1771, for instance, Gray wrote to Beattie concerning the *Essay on Truth:* "I am happy to hear of your successes . . . because I think you are serving the cause of human nature, and the true interests of mankind. Your book is read here too, and with just applause."[24] This letter also contains praise for Canto I of *The Minstrel* and detailed criticisms of "Minuitiae" in it, all of which led Beattie to make changes in the second edition. To show his gratitude for such advice, Beattie had suggested in 1767 that he would like to publish an edition of Gray's poems to be printed by the Foulis brothers of Glasgow who were then famous for their beautiful printings of the classics. Gray, who was flattered by the proposal, sent his poems to Beattie on December 24, 1767; and Beattie personally supervised the production of a magnificent edition which pleased Gray greatly.

Gray's death on July 30, 1771, ended the useful criticisms that Beattie had always expected from him; but it is nevertheless clear from his letters that Gray, even before Beattie became well-known, thought he recognized extraordinary talent in his friend's poetry; in fact, he regarded Beattie as an equal: " . . . you see Sr, I take the liberty you indulged me in when first I saw you [of criticizing his poems] & therefore I make no excuses for it, but desire you would take your revenge on me in kind."[25] Beattie's good fortune in gaining Gray's interest and support was not only of importance to his writing but it also helps to explain his popularity and influence as a writer.

III *Popularity as a Writer*

Beattie achieved instant celebrity as a philosopher and poet in the early 1770s by publishing *An Essay on the Nature and Immutability of Truth, in Opposition to Sophistry and Scepticism*[26] (1770) and

Canto I of *The Minstrel; or, The Progress of Genius* (1771). These two major works remained in great demand long after Beattie's death in 1803; there were sixteen editions of the *Essay on Truth* by that date, including translations into French, Dutch, and German, and almost thirty editions of *The Minstrel*. Meanwhile, to satisfy the great demands for more writing from him, Beattie published his first literary essays in 1776 in conjunction with a new edition of the *Essay on Truth*. The success of this literary book produced seven more editions by 1803 and also prompted Beattie to print more literary essays in 1783 in *Dissertations Moral and Critical* which was reissued at least three more times before his death.

In the mid-1780s, the controversy concerning the *Essay on Truth* as the definitive answer of the Christian philosopher to the agnostic metaphysician had died down, for Beattie's book had been decisive in settling the issue. Beattie was, therefore, very much pleased to write about his favorite subject, the joy of the Christian life, without the need to establish its validity on the battlefield of empirical philosophy. When he published his celebration of "true religion" in *Evidences of the Christian Religion* (1786), the book met with an enthusiastic audience, which was large enough to produce at least six new editions by 1803. Beattie's readers, who regarded *Evidences* as a sequel to the *Essay on Truth*, believed that he was the great Christian apologist of his time. The enduring power of his reputation as a writer is indicated in the reception given to his last major publication, *Elements of Moral Science* (1790 - 1793), which went into three editions during the last ten years of his life. But perhaps the best indication of the extent of Beattie's popularity is the fact that all his major works were not only well known in North America in the eighteenth century but were also published in American editions during his lifetime.

CHAPTER 2

Teaching Career

A large number of Beattie's students wrote tributes to his teaching which often seem, by their extravagant praise and expressions of gratitude, to be sanctimonious flattery. Since, however, very few teachers have received so many published testimonials, one concludes that such praise was genuine and indicative of Beattie's great skill in the classroom. Such accounts, therefore, show him to be an excellent teacher who liked his subject and knew it well, who liked his students, and who was loved and respected in return.[1] He was a fluent, clear, and precise lecturer who always took great pains to give a unified, coherent view of his subject. The illustrations that he used of his principles were often imaginative and striking, but they always served as transitions from one thought to the next. Beattie stimulated his students to think for themselves, and he never missed an opportunity to challenge them to excel in studying and in living the Christian life. His intellectual honesty, patience, and sincerity enabled him to create a stimulating atmosphere for learning by winning the confidence and trust of his students; and his sense of humor helped to maintain good rapport in the classroom.

Outside the classroom, Beattie's relationships with his students were characterized by kindness, gentleness, and frequent encouragement. He was generous in giving due praise, time, advice, and money to them, sometimes long after they had left the college. But, while they were still his students, he cultivated in them good handwriting, strong memories, adaptibility in the face of problems, a taste for literature, a good prose style, a reverence for the Classics, and a sense of responsibility. His greatest joy, however, was to emphasize beautiful things and to give positive, practical advice. Since he himself continually revised his lectures and his course of study, his devotion to the principles of hard work and Christian living was an example and a challenge to his students. Because Beattie practiced what he preached, he was much admired and often emulated.

I *A Student's Record of Beattie's Lectures*

James Rennie's record of Beattie's lectures in 1767 - 1768 consists of almost six hundred closely written pages which reveal the extent and nature of Beattie's course of moral philosophy and logic early in his teaching career.[2] Rennie's notes give, therefore, valuable evidence of the growth of Beattie's ideas and technique over the years, especially when they are compared with the version of Beattie's lectures that he published. Rennie was so affected by Beattie's thoughts that he used many of them, often verbatim from his notebook, in a series of essays that he published in the *London Magazine* after he had moved from Aberdeen to London. While Rennie's apparent dishonesty in publishing such ideas as if they were his own is of little importance to this study, his act does indicate a significant reliance on Beattie's authority as a teacher, just as Rennie's notes themselves reveal Beattie's concern and respect for his students. Beattie carefully states the aim of his course in his introductory lecture: "True Philosophy lays no restraint upon human sentiment; its glory is to teach man rather how to think than what to think"(Rennie, p. 14). As a teacher, therefore, Beattie believes that he has no right "to impose upon [his students] a system of doctrine, and require [their] belief in them"; instead, he hopes to convince them of the soundness of his principles: "The prosecution of this science has led men sometimes into the principles of libertinism and Scepticism . . . but it is certain and I hope to convince you by experience that this science may be prosecuted so far as to produce a contrary effect"(p. 13).

Beattie wishes to allow each student not only to ponder the teacher's arguments and illustrations but also to reach his own conclusions. He therefore urges them to work diligently and not to be discouraged at the start if the course is more complicated than they had anticipated: "I do not mention these things wt a view to discourage in the beginning; I mention them only to show you that the strictest attention will be necessary if you want to understand the science of human nature. This science like all others is more difficult at the beginning than after one has made any progress in it; if you be attentive at first, you will soon find it becomes easier, and fields of delightful and important speculation will soon open upon your view w: will amply repay your labour"(p. 13). But Beattie believes so strongly that he should help his young, inexperienced students to avoid "useless speculation" that he openly tries to guide them into a positive, practical approach to his subject:

. . . our design is not to advance paradoxes, but to enforce the dictates of common sense and the genuine sentiments of nature. Our design is not to meddle wt matters w: cannot be understood, nor tho they were understood could be of any use. We shall therefore avoid all intricate speculation and all vain and useless disputes. It will be our care to accustom you to a habit of self attention and of free sentiment, to lead you to admire the nature and perfection of the Supreme Being, to make you sensible of your relation to him as his creatures and of your relation to one another as participants of the same nature, members of the same society, subjects of the same government, and expectants of the same happiness.(pp. 13 - 14)

There are many exhortations throughout Rennie's notebook to work diligently and systematically: "In studying we ought to cherish all those affections w: produce a liking to the subject, and render it of importance in our eyes, such as a generous emulation, hope of success, curiosity and a sense of the advantage we may reap from knowledge"(p. 501). To aid his students' private study, Beattie often refers them to authors to whom he has made only a passing reference. When, for example, he states that logic is divided into judgment, memory, and communication, he also informs his students that some philosophers add a fourth division called invention; and he asks them to read "Some curious observations" about it "in the Novum Organum of Lord Bacon and his treatise de Augmentis Scientiarum"(p. 436). Beattie later refers to Bacon as the man to whom "Phil[osoph]y is more indebted than to any other person," and he urges the study of his works.

Likewise, after Beattie explains that there is not enough time for him to consider fully Locke's theory of "clear and obscure perceptions," he recommends that his students peruse "the 29th, 30th, 31st, & 32nd Chap[ter]s of the 2nd book of Locke's Essay on human understanding," and he also gives them a hint about studying them: " . . . observe that his notion . . . of all modes being complex objects, & of all complex modes being arbitrary creations of the mind makes him run into several mistakes w: it will be easy for an attentive reader to rectify"(p. 135). With an eye to his students' future reading, Beattie ends his lectures as recorded by Rennie with the sincere wish that they will all lead intellectually stimulating, happy lives: "The sciences w: you have now gone through are to be considered not as the accomplishment but only as the foundation of human knowledge. And as a foundation without a superstructure is of little use and if neglected soon becomes a heap of rubbish so what you have now learned will avail you nothing if you aim at no further acquisitions"(pp. 544 - 45).

II *"Journal of Sessions"*

Beattie's "Journal of Sessions"[3] is a neatly written, systematic account of his lectures and class work from January 6, 1762, to April 2, 1793. He records the exact dates and times of class periods, topics of lectures and discussions, and periods used for questioning and examining his students; and he even notes such information as the nature and duration of his illnesses and the periods of his fasting. The "Journal" is an index to Beattie's scholarly activities for thirty-one years which gives, in conjunction with his published and unpublished lectures and with James Rennie's notebook, a remarkably complete notion of Beattie's work and of the Scottish educational system. One can also trace in the "Journal" the considerable influence of the Philosophical Society of Aberdeen relative to the ideas and techniques used by Beattie in the classroom. For many of the topics discussed with his students and the subjects summarized in his *Elements of Moral Science* (1790 - 1793), the resumé of his college lectures not already published as separate essays, are also noted in the "Minutes" of the club. In recording these concerns, therefore, Beattie chronicles closely the cultural and intellectual growth of the period, for the "Journal" is in effect a kind of schema of Scotland's "Age of Improvement." But for the purpose of this study, it is most valuable for its confirmation of Beattie's excellence as a teacher.

A good example from the "Journal" of Beattie's competence is his use of "recapitulation and questions." This technique involved reviews with questions and answers that tested by written and oral examinations units of work at regular intervals. In this way, the students' learning was consolidated by repetition and testing; and, as a consequence, they were encouraged to work steadily over the whole college year and thereby to enable Beattie to make accurate and regular judgments about their progress. On October 15, 1773, Beattie explained this method of teaching in a letter to Mrs. Montagu:

I will venture to affirm, from experience, that if a professor does no more than deliver a set of lectures, his young audience will be little the wiser for having attended him. The most profitable part of my time is that which I employ in examinations, or in Socratic dialogue with my pupils, or in commenting upon ancient authors, all which may be done by a tutor in a private apartment, as well as by a professor in a public school. Lectures indeed I do . . . give . . . but I have always found the other method, particularly the Socratic form of dialogue, much more effectual.[4]

The "Journal" not only confirms Beattie's use of "the Socratic method" in the classroom but also indicates the growth of his skill in modifying it from year to year. Early in his career, for instance, Beattie spent very little time in examining his students; but, having discovered the great benefits of the technique, he used it more and more. In fact, he devoted as many as sixty periods a year to Socratic dialogue during the last twelve years recorded in the "Journal."

III   Influential Views of the Teacher

Since all of Beattie's published essays were derived from his college lectures, he probably would not have written any of them had he not been a teacher. In fact, the "preparation for the instruction of his class was . . . considered by Beattie to claim the first place in his studies. He spared no pains on the composition of his lectures at the first delivery, and he subjected them to much careful rewriting and correction in after years."[5] As a result, the ideas and attitudes that Beattie tried to impart to his students became such a shaping influence on his writing that even his literary essays are marked by a strong didactic tone and point of view. All of his essays were often admired because they had been college lectures. William Rose, for instance, in reviewing *Dissertations Moral and Critical* in 1783, wrote that those practical rules "for the conduct of life which [Beattie] mingles with his speculations [are] a valuable part of the work, and [I] heartily wish that the instructors of youth, instead of resting contented with forming mere scholars and philosophers, would imitate Dr. Beattie in teaching their pupils to act as well as to *speculate*, and to conduct themselves with honour, probity, and resolution in the different departments of life."[6] Rose's praise indicates that Beattie's published essays were enjoyed and valued by the reading public in the same way that his students had been entertained and instructed by them.

The influence of the Scottish universities in stimulating public opinion is exemplified by Beattie's role in the movement that led to the abolition of slavery in the British possessions in 1833. As a hotly debated issue in the eighteenth century, slavery was made to appear more and more as monstrously immoral through many books, pamphlets, newspapers, and periodicals. But the most effective arguments against the slave trade were probably propagated from the pulpit and in the college lecture. Beattie's "Journal of Sessions" shows that every year in his classes he denounced slavery as an evil abomination that is antithetic to all principles of human decency and to the spirit of Christianity. "There is something in the nature of slavery w: human nature recoils from wt abhorrence," James Rennie noted in 1767 (p. 388) as he filled ten pages of his notebook with Beattie's propaganda against the slave trade. In 1770, Beattie used five pages of his *Essay on Truth* to announce his views on slavery to the public. And the immediate and prolonged success of the *Essay* made him a popular spokesman for abolition as is indicated also by the many letters he received and wrote on the subject. William Wilberforce, for instance, wrote to him several times and finally asked him on behalf of the leading Abolitionists in England to help to organize the campaign against slavery in the north of Scotland. Meanwhile, Beattie continued year after year to impress upon his students the urgency of the cause. Of the seventy-four pages of *Elements of Moral Science* (1793) that he devoted to economics, for example, fifty-two of them deal with the history of slavery and the need for its abolition.

As public dissatisfaction with slavery grew stronger, Beattie wrote a petition concerning it in 1788. After it was signed by all the teachers at Marischal and King's colleges, he sent it to the House of Commons in London with the official approval of both colleges. At the same time, he started to revise for publication "A Discourse on Slavery," which he had written ten years earlier. But this essay was never published, for, as Beattie wrote to Mrs. Montagu on June 28, 1788:

My papers on the slave-trade would now appear too late. The legislature . . . will undoubtedly bring on such regulations, as would make my zeal and my arguments both unnecessary and unseasonable. In fact, several of those abuses, which I had attacked with most severity, are already in part redressed, or in a fair way of being so; particularly the horrid cruelties perpetrated upon the poor negroes in their passage across the Atlantic, and the cruel laws to which they are subjected in some of the West Indian islands, particularly Barbadoes and Jamaica. If one may believe the newspapers, considerable reformations have already taken place in both those islands, as well as in North America. As to the final abolition of the traffic, I pray for it as earnestly as anybody; but I do not think it can be accomplished soon, though in a few years it may, and I trust it will.[7]

But three years later the prospect of abolition seemed brighter when he wrote to William Forbes on June 7, 1791: "I read yesterday the debate on the slave-trade, which fills a two-shilling pamphlet. The speeches of Mr. Wilberforce, Mr. Pitt, Mr. W. Smith, and Mr. Fox, are most excellent, and absolutely unanswerable. The friends to the abolition are very sanguine in their hopes, that this diabolical commerce will in two or three years be at an end."[8]

While Beattie was too optimistic at this time, the movement was gaining the kind of support that led to its eventual success. Meanwhile, in a letter of May 25, 1789, to Mrs. Montagu, he wrote an accurate estimate of his own contribution to the movement: "I have been collecting materials on that subject for upwards of twenty-five years; and, as far as my poor voice could be heard, have laboured, not altogether unsuccessfully, in pleading the cause of the poor Africans. This, at least, I can say with truth, that many of my pupils have gone to the West Indies; and, I trust, have carried my principles along with them, and exemplified those principles in their conduct to their unfortunate brethren."[9] Beattie was justifiably satisfied with his efforts; for, as almost all writers of his "Memoirs" claim, he helped greatly in forming the climate of public opinion that led to the reformation of slavery.

Beattie's views about slavery were closely associated with the common sense philosophy which he and his colleagues in the Philosophical Society created as a solution to the appalling effects of scepticism and sophistry on their students. As a result, the students in Aberdeen had been exposed to the principles of common sense long before the publication of books about it; in fact, as is clear from Rennie's notebook, Beattie's students played a role in the writing of the *Essay on Truth*, the book that made the philosophy of common sense popular. Beattie himself openly acknowledged that he wrote the *Essay* primarily for their benefit. On March 2, 1767, for example, he wrote to Robert Arbuthnot that the composition of the book "has rivetted my conviction of the insignificance of metaphysics and scepticism; and I hope it will be of some use to the young people under my care; for whose principles (at least as far as they depend on me) I hold myself accountable to my own conscience and the public."[10]

Likewise, in the introduction to the *Essay,* Beattie asserts that he will be satisfied if "these pages . . . shall suggest, to the young and unwary, any cautions against that sophistry, and licentiousness of principle, which too much infest the conversations and compositions of the age"(*Truth,* p. 19). In addition, many of the arguments of the *Essay* may be observed in their formative stages in Rennie's notebook. As an emotional attack on sceptical philosophy, the *Essay* contends, for example, that the common sense appeal to Christian principles could refute any sceptical argument. James Rennie notes: "Common Sense and Religion approve themselves to all the world, and will continue in repute among people of sense as long as mankind exists"(p. 548). Since the time "is fast approaching, when all the ornaments of human life shall disappear for ever and when nothing shall be found of any moment, except divine approbation & the testimony of a good conscience," Beattie advises his students to read "Butler's Analogy, Ditton on the Resurrection & Campbell's dissertation on Miracles" and to do so with a view to keeping "God's commandments" (p. 551).

Parts of Rennie's notebook read, therefore, like a rough draft of the *Essay on Truth,* for it contains the same ideas, the same style of emotional belligerency, the same application of Christian principles, and the same appeal to practicality; in fact, the two works differ essentially in one way only. In the *Essay,* Beattie confidently aims at the swift destruction of current metaphysical thought; in Rennie's notebook, he is seemingly content to issue a friendly warning to any student who is tempted to read sceptical books:

. . . metaphysical systems last for a very short season; they are admired perhaps for a few years and then they perish forever. Never therefore let the subtleties of metaphysicians wheedle you out of your senses or Religion. Be assured that Sceptics have neither your interest nor the interest of truth, nor any interest at heart but their own. If therefore you commit yourself to their guidance you act as absurd a part as the traveller who resigns himself up to the Robber, knowing him to be such, and is by him conducted to a precipice, from whence the other throws him headlong that he may make himself master of his purse.(pp. 548 - 49)

Beattie's concern for his students not only inspired him to write the *Essay on Truth* but also contributed to the book's highly emotional and practical nature. As Rennie noted, Beattie's view was that "false Phil[osoph]y is founded not in fact but in theory; and that useless philosophy [is that] w: tends not to assist practice but only to gratify curiosity" (p. 6).

IV   *Development of the Critic*

Beattie's "Journal of Sessions" also gives valuable insights into his development and influence as a literary critic. After translating Horace's *Ars Poetica* every year with his students, he devoted several periods to the explanation and discussion of its ideas. In addition, he always reviewed most forms of literature; and he paid particular attention to poetry and rhetoric. With only one exception, Beattie assigned at least twenty-two periods a year to rhetoric and belles-lettres and sometimes as many as eighty-four periods. In the beginning of his career, he spent most of his time on psychology and very little on literature and language. In the "Journal" for 1762 - 1763, for instance, 116 periods (40 percent) were given to psychology; but only thirty-seven (13 percent) were devoted to rhetoric and none to belles-lettres. But by 1776 - 1777, he was spending sixty-one periods on psychology (23 percent), forty-three on rhetoric (17 percent) and twenty-three on belles-lettres (9 percent). Much later, however, in 1792 - 1793, thirty-six periods were assigned to psychology (13 percent) and sixty-seven to rhetoric and belles-lettres (26 percent). The "Journal of Sessions" shows, therefore, that Beattie learned to organize his materials better; by confining himself to the essentials of psychology, he used the time saved to concentrate on his true bent, the teaching of literature and language.

But these notations of Beattie's progress as a teacher are even more important for the indication that they give of one of the most important literary developments in eighteenth century Scotland. Before Beattie became a professor in 1760, there had been successful attempts to teach polite literature in the Scottish universities. At the University of Glasgow, for example, in addition to regular teaching, the professors of philosophy, "for the purpose of public instruction . . . gave every week, on different, but stated days, two additional hours; at which time they prelected, or delivered discourses on subjects not necessarily connected, yet so much connected with the immediate duty of their profession as to be very useful to those who attended them."[11] Adam Smith used these two hours to deliver the lectures on rhetoric and belles-lettres that he had used at the University of Edinburgh from 1748 to 1751.[12] When Smith moved to Glasgow in 1751, Robert Watson continued to give similar lectures at Edinburgh. From 1759, three years after Watson had moved to St. Andrews as professor of logic, Hugh Blair followed the practice. "Blair's success in turn led to the creation of the Regius Chair of Rhetoric and Belles Lettres—the first of its kind in Britain—on 27 April 1762."[13]

But, in relation to Beattie's treatment of literature and language in his regular classes, it is significant that all of these lectures given at Edinburgh, Glasgow, and St. Andrews were public discourses; in fact, before Beattie's second year at Marischal College (1762) when the chair of rhetoric and belles lettres was established at Edinburgh, the famous Professor Stevenson seems to have been the only teacher to deal at any length with literary topics during the normal university course. A compendium of professors' lectures of the time "contains digests of the lectures in logic given by Stevenson at Edinburgh, Reid at Aberdeen . . . Watson at St. Andrews, and . . . Clow at Glasgow;"[14] but none of them was nearly so lengthy or so comprehensive as was Beattie's literary course by 1772.

In addition to Beattie's regular classes, he, too, gave many public lectures to large audiences every year. His reputation as an excellent teacher and his fame as a writer attracted students and the public to his lectures and aided him in his attempts to stimulate their compositions and their appreciation of literature. While Beattie's published essays contain many of the ideas that he expressed in the classroom, Rennie's notebook indicates much more clearly his technique and its effects on his students. In addition, the notebook includes literary discussions never published by Beattie. For example, Rennie records a detailed examination of Homer, Vergil, Shakespeare, and Milton (pp. 151 - 81) as an illustration of Beattie's analysis of literary taste and its effects. Having commented on characteristic passages from each author, Beattie gives his students an outline of what other critics have written about them and concludes with his own views about literary criticism itself. His final comment urges his students not only to consider ways of improving their taste but to read extensively. This considerable body of criticism was delivered in 1767 - 1768 when, according to Beattie's "Journal of Sessions," he spent only 14 percent of his time on rhetoric and belles-lettres. He dealt much more extensively with these subjects in the last twenty years of the "Journal," when the time he devoted to them rarely dropped below 20 percent and when it reached as high as 34 percent in 1782 - 1783.

While Beattie stressed that his students should be well versed in the study of literary works as models of esthetic contemplation and of the proper use of language, he also placed great emphasis on teaching them to write well. James Rennie recorded the following exhortation in his notebook:

I would earnestly recommend it to each of you to study the english language; a language w: very few of the inhabitants of Great Britain do understand but w: is of great importance to every British Scholar to be well acquainted with. Study it as it is to be found in the best english writers, in our common translation of the Bible, in the works of . . . Raleigh, Milton, Dryden, but especially in those of Swift, Pope, and Addison. Exercise yourself in it by frequent compositions w: you may make on any subject that occurs and w: will at once improve you in thinking and speaking.(pp. 550 - 51)

Beattie's preoccupation with the difficulty of teaching literature and composition grew out of his dissatisfaction with his own experiences as a student: ". . . all the while I was at school and college, I never received one single advice on the subject of composition, except in the matter of syntax alone; and, though I heard every day, that Homer, and Virgil, and the rest of them were excellent authors, there was no reason assigned for that assertion; so that in forming my judgment of the classicks I had nothing to trust to, but my own feelings, and some critical remarks which I met with occasionally in books."[15]

Beattie's own theory of language, which he called "universal grammar," was an attempt to relegate syntax to a minor role in the study of language and to emphasize instead the cultivation by each student of a precise, clear, and coherent prose style. In this way, he hoped that all of his students would learn to emulate the energy, imaginative insight, and fineness of expression of the best writers. After Beattie announced his ideas about language to the public in "A Dissertation on the Theory of Language" as part of *Dissertations Moral and Critical* (1783), he became such a popular educational theorist that the essay was published several times "for the use of seminaries of education" and to comply "with the wish of many readers and critics."[16] Beattie's own fine prose style in essay after essay provided striking proof to his students and his readers alike that his theories about literature and language were not only pedagogically sound but, when applied intelligently and diligently, could enable a writer to shape his own notable style.

In Beattie's view of moral philosophy and logic, rhetoric is the subject that records and analyzes the most eloquent written expression of the best thoughts of the great minds throughout history. Almost always he selects his principles and illustrations of rhetorical excellence from literature. Rennie's notebook contains a large body of literary criticism that is not noted in Beattie's "Journal of Sessions" for 1767 - 1768 but which must have been delivered under "the art of judging" in his treatment of rhetoric. In addition to much material about prose style, Beattie's *Elements of Moral Science* (1790 - 1793) includes forty-two pages on "the general nature of Poetry" that are quite different from the lectures that he had published as "An Essay on Poetry and Music" (1776). Similarly, his "On Laughter and Ludicrous Composition," (1776), "On Fable and Romance" (1783), "Of Memory and Imagination"(1783), and "On Illustrations of Sublimity"(1783) are all specialized literary essays which developed from his general discussions of literature.

By allowing his fascination with great writing to influence increasingly over the years the matter and the manner of his teaching, Beattie created and delivered to his students, and later to his readers, one of the most important courses of rhetoric and belles-lettres of the period. Beattie's achievements in this matter exemplify the important role played by the eighteenth-century Scottish universities in teaching rhetoric and belles-lettres when other English-speaking universities in the world paid little significant attention to English language and literature. Beattie and his colleagues thereby laid the foundations for the creation of modern university departments of English.

CHAPTER 3

The Philosophy of Common Sense

I *Origin and Principles*

MANY essays, sermons, and books published by members of the Philosophical Society of Aberdeen show that they developed the philosophy of common sense as a solution to the alarming moral degeneracy and "irreligion" of the times. Since these Scottish philosophers were convinced that the decline of moral standards had been caused by the rise of modern scepticism expressed in the books of such writers as George Berkeley and David Hume, they formulated their theories on the premise that the development of sceptical philosophy was an illogical thesis about human nature and understanding that had to be refuted if human decency and common sense were to be restored to society. They argued, therefore, that the seventeenth century philosophers, Descartes and Locke, had built their systems of thought on the erroneous notion that the mind perceives ideas only from external reality. In rejecting these theories in the early eighteenth century, Berkeley, the common sense philosophers claimed, had argued himself into the untenable belief that ideas are the only reality. Finally, Hume had demonstrated in his *Treatise on Human Nature* (1739) the logical absurdity of sceptical reasoning by denying the existence of both ideas and reality. According to the principles of common sense, such nonsense had to be disproved before philosophy could be restored to a firm foundation.

Thomas Reid's *An Inquiry into the Human Mind upon the Principles of Common Sense*(1764) is by far the most impressive treatment of common sense philosophy, especially since its principal tenets were accepted as basic by later writers in the school such as Beattie and William Hamilton. Reid believed that, in writing about the principles of common sense, he was identifying and explaining ancient truths that had been obscured by modern scepticism. This tenet provided the main opportunity for elaboration by his disciples: Hamilton cites forty-eight authorities who had adhered to common sense beliefs before Reid; and Beattie often supports his arguments in the *Essay on Truth* by references to such writers as Aristotle, Plato, Socrates, Shakespeare, Bacon, Milton, Johnson, and Montesquieu. The Scottish brand of common sense, therefore, purports to be the reversal of scepticism, which is immoral and impractical, and to be the revival and final statement of true philosophy, which is moral and practical.

For that reason, Beattie defines philosophy as "the knowledge of nature applied to practical and useful purposes."[1] His arguments in the *Essay*, therefore, are clear, easily followed, and free from doubt and idle speculation. For Beattie, common sense is "that power of the mind which perceives truth, or commands belief, not by progressive argumentation, but by an instantaneous and instinctive impulse; derived neither from education nor from habit, but from nature; acting independently on our will, whenever its object is presented, according to an established law, and therefore not improperly called *Sense;* and acting in a similar manner upon all mankind, and therefore properly called *Common*" (*Truth*, pp. 35 - 36). The vividness and clarity of this definition and its great claim for the indisputable validity of common sense are characteristic of Beattie's thought in the *Essay on Truth*.

Beattie makes an important distinction between common sense as the "power by which we perceive self-evident truth" and reason as the "faculty by which we perceive truth in consequence of a proof" (*Truth*, p. 289). At best, the two concepts are mutually dependent, differing only in the mode of obtaining belief: common sense shows truth through instinctive perception; reason requires logical argument and proof. At worst, they seem independent of each other, resulting inevitably in the abuse of reason and in the denial or disregard of common sense and thereby of truth. Many metaphysical philosophers have fallen into this trap, Beattie claims, so "that too much reasoning hath made them mad" (*Truth*, p. 40); for, when reason is the ultimate judge, truth is variable, and conviction is achieved only through tedious and repetitious argument. But, when reason supports common sense, the mind operates naturally and properly: "In the laws of nature, when thoroughly understood, there appear no contradictions: it is only in the systems of philosophers that reason and common sense are at variance" (*Truth*, p. 132).

Common sense, therefore, assures men by the law of their nature that "things are as our senses represent them" (*Truth*, p. 50) and that the working of the mind in using memory and imagination is accurate and reliable. But consciousness, the "internal sense," is more important than the external senses; for, as "the clear, the intelligent, the irresistible voice of Nature," it indicates fixed and eternal truth (*Truth*, p. 58). The moral standard of common sense that is established through investigation and experience is the accurate reflection of this ultimate vision of truth. As a consequence, common sense is the truth of reality as revealed through natural instinct and the senses and as regulated by reason and judgment. Beattie tests this theory by discussing in turn mathematical reasoning, external senses, internal sense or consciousness, the evidence of memory, reasoning from the cause to the effect, probable or experimental reasoning, analogical reasoning, and faith in testimony. In every case, the conclusion is identical: some things may be proved by reason, others must be accepted on faith, but all must conform to the principles of common sense. There is, therefore, only one sound philosophical method: "To common sense . . . all truth must be conformable; that is its fixed and invariable standard. And whatever contradicts common sense, or is inconsistent with that standard . . . is not truth but falsehood" (*Truth*, p. 122).

II *Beattie's Version of Common Sense*

Beattie openly declared his reliance on Reid's theory of common sense: "My principles, in the main, are not essentially different from Dr. Reid's."[2] But, since Reid's demonstration of the nonsense of sceptical writings had been read by very few, Beattie decided to rewrite it in a different style. Whereas Reid's *Inquiry* is a logically argued and intellectually respectable book, Beattie's *Essay on Truth* is by design bitterly polemical in its intolerance and abhorrence of sceptical philosophy. Consequently, the immediate success it received helped to make it a bestseller for many years. It was, therefore, Beattie's emotionally charged, simplistic view of philosophy that was almost solely responsible for the remarkable propagation of the philosophy of common sense throughout the British Isles, Europe, and North America: "In face of the authority of Hume, and despite the attacks of Priestley, the philosophy of common sense spread itself rapidly . . . it penetrated into the universities, among the clergy, into the bar, among men of letters and men of the world; and, without producing a movement so vast as that of the German philosophy, it exercised an influence of the same kind within narrower limits."[3] The extent of this propagation may be seen in the popularity of the *Essay on Truth* in American universities: "In his lectures [Samuel Stanhope Smith, president of Princeton from 1795], draws explicitly upon the work . . . of Beattie . . . in addition to that of Thomas Reid," and the "*Essay on the Nature and Immutability of Truth* . . . [was] very important at Yale during the late eighteenth century."[4] This remarkable achievement cannot be fully understood, however, without an assessment of the influences under which Beattie wrote the *Essay*.

Since Beattie knew very little about metaphysics when he became professor of moral philosophy in 1760, he began to prepare his lectures by reading the writings of Locke, Berkeley, and Hume concerning "moral and human nature."[5] But he was so "surprised to find them . . . replete with absurdities" and experienced such great difficulty in following their arguments that he began "to suspect [his] own understanding." He was given a new perspective, however, by listening to papers and by joining in the discussions about metaphysical writings in the Philosophical Society. When Thomas Reid read his latest essays concerning his theories about common sense, which were to grow into his *Inquiry* (1764), Beattie began to understand why the world seemed to be so impressed by the absurdities that he found in Locke, Berkeley, and Hume. As his confidence in his own judgment returned, he reread their works and decided confidently that sceptical philosophy was "a frivolous, though dangerous, system of verbal subtility" and that "its most extravagant state" appeared "in the works of Mr. Hume."

Beattie therefore agreed with Reid's theories and with the refutation of Hume's ideas about human nature in George Campbell's *A Dissertation on Miracles* (1763), which also grew out of the discussions in the Philosophical Society. By 1767, as Rennie's notebook shows, Beattie had not only incorporated many of their ideas into his lectures on moral philosophy but had also reached his own firm opinions of the effects of sceptical philosophy: "I am convinced, that this metaphysical spirit is the bane of true learning, true taste, and true science; that to it we owe all this modern scepticism and athesism; that it has a bad effect upon the human faculties, and tends not a little to sour the temper, to subvert good principles, and to disqualify men for the business of life."[6]

Beattie could not reconcile his own unequivocal views with the "extraordinary adulation" of Hume that Reid and Campbell had expressed in their books; for he wished that they had written with "more firmness and spirit." He had begun to write his *Essay on Truth* in 1766 to correct their mistaken admiration for Hume and to create a more appropriate style of attack, especially since their books had been largely unnoticed. He was particularly encouraged to do so by John Gregory, one of the founders of the Philosophical Society, who had moved to Edinburgh in 1764 and who was shocked by the moral decadence of the city. Reading this situation as evidence of advanced scepticism, Gregory wrote many letters to Beattie in which he stressed the urgent need for reform and begged him to publish his refutation of sceptical philosophy as quickly as possible:

. . . if the present spirit is not very speedily checked, I am confident it will give the finishing stroke to that corruption of heart and principles which makes such an alarming progress. It is not worth while to say, after this, that it will as certainly and speedily suppress all great efforts of genius and imagination. You are the best man I know to chastise these people as they deserve; you have more philosophy, and more wit, than will be necessary for the purpose, though you can never employ any of them in so good a cause."[7]

In addition, Gregory often offered advice about the style that he knew Beattie was trying to develop to gain a popular audience: ". . . to be read, you must not be satisfied with reasoning with justness and perspicuity; you must write with pathos, with elegance, with spirit, and endeavour to warm the imagination, and touch the heart of those, who are deaf to the voice of reason."[8]

Beattie therefore worked very hard to formulate a new style of philosophical argument by searching for striking illustrations of common sense theories: ". . . he who makes these sciences the study of his life, may perhaps collect particulars concerning their evidence, which, though known to a few, are unknown to many; may set some principles in a more striking light than that in which they have been formerly viewed; may devise methods of confuting new errors, and exposing new paradoxes; and may hit upon a more popular way of displaying what has hitherto been exhibited in too dark and mysterious a form" (*Truth*, p. 13). As indicated by this passage, Beattie sought to establish philosophy as a useful as well as a popular mode of intellectual inquiry by endowing it with clarity of principle and with simplicity of design and expression. This concept of "true philosophy" is mirrored remarkably in Beattie's prose style, which enables him to present the study of human nature as "easy and obvious" to every man of common capacity": "Truth, like virtue, to be loved, needs only to be seen" (*Truth*, p. 17). The *Essay* itself is a classic model of practical common sense, for it is organized as a paradigm of the method for avoiding the pitfalls of scepticism that Beattie wishes to promote: Part I presents the principles of common sense; Part II illustrates them; Part III anticipates and answers objections; and the book ends with a test for detecting scepticism and with hints for resisting it. In this way, Beattie helps his readers to improve their intellectual judgment, their moral perception, and their taste, and thereby to repudiate the ambiguous formulations of metaphysical reasoning that by its very nature negates the principles of common sense. The main point he makes about Hume's philosophical writing, for instance, concerns his "notable talent at puzzling his readers and himself" (*Truth*, p. 227); Berkeley's "non-existence of matter" theory is reduced to "the ambiguous use of a word" (*Truth*, 132); and Locke is personified as "the first to declare [some of his theories] absurd" when compared to the common sense standard (*Truth*, p. 9).

Even though Beattie wrote the *Essay* explicitly for the common reader, he had little hope before publication that it would be widely read; for he believed that "a scheme like this . . . cannot be popular, far less can it be lucrative."[9] But he had not realized the power of the wide spread rumor that an obscure philosopher in Aberdeen had written a biting, personal attack on David Hume, the most popular and esteemed metaphysician of the time. Consequently, many people who bought the book in the hope of reading a polemical diatribe were not disappointed; but, in addition, they discovered it to be so well argued and so well written that it seemed to most of them to demolish sceptical reasoning and thereby to forecast a new era of enlightenment. As word of Beattie's triumph spread, the book became "required reading" in all circles; and its early popularity led to its phenomenal sales for the rest of the century. Beattie had, therefore, the unique distinction of publishing a book about metaphysical philosophy that gained instant, wide-spread success and that was still being reprinted occasionally almost a hundred years later, and even once in the 1970s.

III   *Contemporary Reaction to the* Essay on Truth

Beattie was surprised and delighted by the enthusiastic response to the *Essay on Truth,* especially since the only adverse criticism came from Edinburgh, the home of David Hume, the "Great Infidel." For several years after 1770, writers in Edinburgh made many attempts to refute or discredit Beattie's book; and he was also much vilified there by the newspapers and by gossipers. While the good-natured Hume was not involved in this disreputable campaign against Beattie, he was upset by the book; for, as John Gregory reported to Beattie in 1770, " . . . the hero of the piece is extremely angry, and so are all his friends, who are numerous."[10] Hume was also so concerned, because the book had affected the sales of his own essays, that he decided to publish a retraction of his *Treatise on Human Nature;* and he then resolved never to write again about religion. When he sent his statement of retraction to William Strahan, his publisher in Edinburgh, to be included with his latest book, Hume added a note that indicates his frustration with the popularity of the *Essay on Truth* and his amazement at the incredulity of Christian apologists and their readers: "This . . . is a complete Answer to Dr. Reid and to that biggotted silly Fellow Beattie."[11]

Hume's public retraction of his ideas about religion was not a denial of their validity or of their importance; but it does illustrate the great influence at the time of the *Essay on Truth.* Perhaps Hume even suspected that his work would be associated with Beattie's book by the common reader for some time to come. At any rate, as N.K. Smith claims, the *Essay* did determine well into the nineteenth century "the popular conception of the character and consequences of Hume's philosophical teaching."[12] The popularity of the book also had other perhaps even more important effects, for it sometimes directed important philosophical thinkers to consider English empirical thought; in the 1780s, for example, Emmanuel Kant discovered Hume's work by reading about it in a German translation of the *Essay on Truth.*

While reaction to the *Essay* outside Edinburgh was almost always very favorable, its greatest support was in London, where Oliver Goldsmith was one of the very few to oppose it. "Everyone," Mrs. Thrale wrote to Dr. Johnson in 1773, "loves [Beattie] but Goldsmith, who says he cannot bear the sight of so much applause as we all bestow upon him. Did he not tell us so himself, who could believe he was so amazingly ill-natured?"[13] Years later, when Beattie read this remark in Mrs. Thrale's published letters, he commented to William Forbes in his letter of July 10, 1788, that

> what she says of Goldsmith is perfectly true. He was a poor fretful creature,
> eaten up with affectation and envy. He was the only person I ever knew
> who acknowledged himself to be envious. In Johnson's presence he was
> quiet enough; but in his absence expressed great uneasiness in hearing him
> praised. He envied even the dead; he could not bear that Shakespeare
> should be so much admired as he is. There might, however, be something
> like magnanimity in envying Shakespeare and Dr. Johnson; as Julius
> Caesar's weeping to think, that at an age at which he had done so little,
> Alexander should have done so much. But surely Goldsmith had no occa
> sion to envy me; which, however, he certainly did, for he owned it (though,
> when we met, he was always civil); and I received undoubted information,
> that he seldom missed an opportunity of speaking ill of me behind my back.
> Goldsmith's common conversation was a strange mixture of absurdity and
> silliness; of silliness so great, as to make me sometimes think that he
> affected it. Yet he was a genius of no mean rank; somebody, who knew him
> well, called him *an inspired idiot.*[14]

Beattie's recollection of Goldsmith's peculiar temperament and
provocative speeches during the summer of 1773 is verified by
many contemporary accounts; in fact, Goldsmith once expressed his
petulance even within Dr. Johnson's hearing by scorning the *Essay
on Truth:* "Here is much ado about nothing . . . why the Man has
written but one Book, and I have writ several." Johnson immediately defended Beattie with a sharp rebuke: "So you have Doctor . . .
but there go many Halfpence remember—to one Guinea."[15]

Goldsmith was not only envious of Beattie's recent success as a
writer but he was also annoyed that Beattie's petition for a pension
from King George III was actively supported by many influential
people when his own long-standing application for a similar pension
had apparently been forgotten. Beattie, well aware of Goldsmith's
ill-feeling toward him at the time, often wrote about it in the diary
that he kept of his trip to London. On Monday, June 14, 1773, for
example, Beattie noted that "Miss Reynolds told me to day some
particulars of Goldsmith. He, it seems, not only is, but even
acknowledges himself to be, envious of all contemporary authors
whose works are successful, and has several times spoken wt. some
peevishness of the attention that has been shown to me in
England."[16] When, however, the newspapers reported in July that
Goldsmith's pension was to be granted, his feelings toward Beattie
changed; for example, shortly after Beattie had returned from Ox-

ford where he had received an honorary Doctor of Laws degree on
July 9, he noted in his diary: "In my way to Covent garden I met
Goldsmith; who congratulated me on my late honour, & told me
the news-papers had it lately that he and I were both to receive pen-
sions; I told him, that I sincerely wished it might be so" (p. 74).

But, when Beattie was granted a pension and Goldsmith was not,
his bitterness was renewed. The crowning frustration, however, was
yet to come: Goldsmith soon learned that his friend, Sir Joshua
Reynolds, had laid aside an unfinished portrait of him in order to
complete the allegorical painting, "The Triumph of Truth, with the
Portrait of a Gentleman."[17] Since the gentleman in the picture was
Beattie, Goldsmith angrily expressed his displeasure to Reynolds:
"It very ill becomes a man of your eminence and character, Sir
Joshua, to condescend to be a mean flatterer, or to wish to degrade
so high a genius as Voltaire before so mean a writer as Dr. Beattie;
for Dr. Beattie and his book together will, in the space of ten years,
not be known ever to have existence, but your allegorical picture
and the fame of Voltaire will live for ever to your disgrace as a
flatterer."[18] While these peevish outbursts were probably much less
related to Beattie than to the difficult emotional problems that, according to his biographers, were bothering Goldsmith at the time,
they certainly illustrate the fine response given to Beattie and to his
Essay on Truth in England.

Aside from such anecdotes about the reaction to Beattie as a person and a writer, the most important published treatment of the
Essay on Truth at the time was contained in Joseph Priestley's *An
Examination of Dr. Reid's "Inquiry into the Human Mind on the
Principles of Common Sense," Dr. Beattie's "Essay on Truth," and
Dr. Oswald's "Appeal to Common Sense in Behalf of Religion"*
(1774).[19] When Priestley had first read the *Essay on Truth* in 1770,
he had been pleased with Beattie's "good intention" in writing it,
even though "his principles appeared . . . to be very wrong."[20] But
the idea of examining the school of common sense did not occur to
him until he later read David Hartley's *Obervations on Man* (1749)
which seemed to offer him a much more reasonable view of human
nature. As a result, Priestley's book starts with a long refutation of
Reid's *Inquiry* which also serves as a preparation for the discussion
of the *Essay on Truth* and of Oswald's *Appeal*. Apart from
Priestley's demonstration that common sense is an illogical system
of thought, he censures both Beattie and Reid for their spirited style
of argument which, he is convinced, will not allow validity to any

ideas that are different from their own. Priestley claims that this type of inflexible thinking led them to the greatly exaggerated belief that scepticism was the cause of the then modern display of licentiousness. Even though he concedes that the *Essay on Truth* in its own way "has done a great deal of good to the cause of religion," Priestley nevertheless thought that it had done so only for "*superficial thinkers*, who are satisfied with seeing superficial objections answered in a lively, though superficial manner."[21]

For this reason, Priestley fears that "other persons of greater penetration, finding Dr. Beattie argues on fallacious, unphilosophical principles, should reject at once, and without further examination, all that he has built upon them."[22] For these readers, Beattie performs a disservice; for, by implying that religion cannot be defended with rational argument, the *Essay on Truth* is actually very similar to the type of emotional, illogical scepticism that it purports to overthrow. On the other hand, Priestley himself is convinced that scepticism has a good effect on religion and society: "Now I, for my part, am truly pleased with such publications as those of Mr. Hume, and I do not think it requires any great sagacity, or strength of mind, to see that such writings must be of great service to religion, natural and revealed. They have actually occasioned the subject to be more thoroughly canvassed, and consequently to be better understood than ever it was before."[23]

While Priestley's book was viewed by Beattie and his supporters as the predictable and dangerous sophistry of a dissenting clergyman, his work was, in fact, an able demonstration that the *Essay on Truth* could not be regarded as a legitimate philosophical work. And not long after Priestley's publication, the great philosopher Emmanuel Kant pronounced in 1783 a just verdict on Beattie's views of philosophy: " . . . seen in its true light, the argument is nothing better than an appeal to the verdict of the multitude; a clamour before which the philosopher blushes, and the popular witling scornfully triumphs." To have done "the problem justice," Kant claims, Beattie should have "penetrated deeply into the nature of Reason, in so far as it is occupied solely with pure thought."[24] Both Kant and Priestley were correct in their assessments, for Beattie cannot be defended as a philosopher because he deliberately avoided the intricacies of pure thought in order to make philosophy practical and useful. Since it is also futile to argue that the *Essay on Truth* was popular and influential largely because it did not fit the Kantian model of true philosophy, it is important to stress that Beattie modeled his philosophical writing on the method for propagating ideas that had been suggested by Joseph Addison.

In the tenth issue of *The Spectator*, which was published on Monday, March 12, 1711, Addison informed his readers that he was aiming at their instruction and diversion, by attempting "to enliven Morality with Wit, and to temper Wit with Morality," in order to rescue "them [from] that desperate State of Vice and Folly, into which the Age is fallen." He was determined, therefore, to save the mind "that lies fallow but a single Day, [for it] sprouts up in Follies that are only to be killed by a constant and assiduous Culture."[25] Addison's ambitions as a popular philosopher are quite evident in his pronouncement: "It was said of *Socrates*, that he brought Philosophy down from Heaven, to inhabit among Men; and I shall be ambitious to have it said of me, that I have brought Philosophy out of the Closets and Libraries, Schools and Colleges, to dwell in Clubs and Assemblies, at Tea-tables, and in Coffee-houses."[26] Beattie's remarkable accomplishment in the *Essay on Truth*, his attempt to achieve such goals by teaching his readers how to combat vice and by making philosophy accessible to the common man, is a testimony to Addison's influence on his life. Beattie not only modeled his prose style on Addison's but also often used his ideas in his own lectures and continually recommended his essays to his students and to his readers. As the direct descendent of *The Spectator* papers, therefore, the *Essay on Truth* may be viewed as a supreme manifestation of Addison's wish that philosophy might be made popular as well as useful to mankind.

CHAPTER 4

Christian Apology

I   *The Christian Reaction to Scepticism*

BY the time Beattie started to write the *Essay on ˙Truth* in the 1760s, the Christian religion had long been under attack and its influence undermined throughout Britain by sceptical writers who claimed that modern Britain would not become completely enlightened and civilized until the unthinking, superstitious belief in the tenets of Christianity was put aside. Many clergymen argued against this view by preaching and publishing sermons about the current public degeneracy that they considered to be the obvious consequence of the unbridled, sceptical criticism of Christianity. While more impressive rational arguments seem to have been published by writers such as Joseph Priestley and David Hume than can usually be found in such sermons, the published sermon was in the eighteenth century a popular form of literature as well as a means of moral instruction. The immorality and the irreligion depicted in such sermons were, therefore, the latest manifestation of the evils of the flesh, the world, and the devil that Christianity had always opposed. Consequently, the sceptical writer was deliberately cast in the role of infidel and atheist by Christian apologists, especially in their published sermons. Such irreligious writers were regarded as saboteurs of the public morality who had to be identified and chastised in public.

A typical description of the results of such sabotage in Scotland is found in a sermon preached by Beattie's teacher and colleague at Marischal College, Alexander Gerard, in the High Church of Edinburgh on May 31, 1761, which was published under the title, "The Influence of piety on the public good":

One age is distinguished from another by no circumstance more remarkably, than by the particular vices which are predominant, and the particular virtues which are fashionable in it. There is no vice which marks the character of the present age more strongly than irreligion. Piety is very generally disregarded, or allowed to have only a small degree of worth; the most unaffected expressions of it are studiously avoided by many, and professedly ridiculed by some. Yet the most natural sentiments of the human heart proclaim, in very intelligible language, that piety is the first and noblest of the virtues, and has a peculiar prerogative above all the rest.[1]

Since Gerard's sermon was preached to the converted, his remarks do not convey the alarm and the overflow of defensive emotionalism that typify the writings of many Christian apologists of the time. The English clergyman, John Brown, for instance, denounced scepticism violently in *An Estimate of the Manners and Principles of the Times* (1757 - 1758): "Enthusiastic Religion leads to *Conquest:* rational Religion leads to rational *Defense;* but the modern Spirit of *Irreligion* leads to *rascally* and abandoned *Coward-ice.* It quencheth every generous Hope that can enlarge the Soul; and levels Mankind with the Beasts that perish."[2] Brown concluded that "we are rolling to the Brink of a Precipice that must destroy us," and he placed the blame for the impending catastrophe on the fact that "the clergy have lost their influence."[3] This kind of ex-aggerated view of the effects of scepticism was prevalent because clergymen often chose the abuse of sceptical ideas as a stimulating topic for their sermons; and they thereby did their part in keeping the controversy alive. The books they read while preparing their sermons probably convinced them that, in spite of a few notable successes by Christian writers, the present deplorable situation was the result of the increasing popularity of sceptical writers throughout the eighteenth century. Such clergymen viewed with alarm the lesson that they learned from the great debate between Christianity and Deism in the early 1700s.

By proposing the establishment of a natural religion based on reason, the early Deistic thinkers openly attacked the traditional Christian beliefs in immortality, in supernatural revelation, and even in moral distinctions. In the most popular Christian answer to Deism, the *Analogy of Religion* (1735), Joseph Butler argued that, on the contrary, human reason demonstrated that the Christian claims about God and man were analogous to and proved by natural phenomena. But, while Butler's ideas were read by many Christians long after Deism ceased to be popular, the *Analogy of Religion* was not a proper philosophical answer to David Hume's contention in his *Treatise on Human Nature* (1739) that the existence of God as the creator of the universe could not be proved by reason. By the 1750s, therefore, any clergyman who read Hume's book was bound to find himself at a loss for a reply; he was therefore very likely to beg the question entirely and to resort, instead, to the emotional charge that writers like Hume were the corrupters of society whose books should never be read. That many clergymen did so is amply illustrated by their published sermons.

Hume and other sceptical philosophers were also attacked in several books which had a style of argument and a belligerent tone similar to the sermons of the time. Hume's opinion of these books, as recorded in the autobiography that he wrote shortly before his death in 1776, provides an excellent view of the Christian attempts to refute his opinions.[4] "Never literary attempt was more unfortunate," Hume writes, "than my Treatise on Human Nature. It fell *dead-born from the press*, without reaching such distinction, as even to excite a murmur among the zealots."[5] But by 1750, as the *Treatise* and his other books became better known, "answers by Reverends, and Right Reverends, came out two or three in a year; and I found, by Dr. Warburton's railing, that the books were beginning to be esteemed in good company."[6] William Warburton, who was the first to attack Hume in print, expressed himself in a belligerent, offensive style that was later adopted by Richard Hurd in his *Remarks on Mr. D. Hume's Essay on the Natural History of Religion: addressed to the Rev. Dr. Warburton* (1757).[7] Consequently, Hume remarks in his autobiography that his own book, which was published in the same year as Hurd's, "was rather obscure, except only that Dr. Hurd wrote a pamphlet against it, with all the illiberal petulance, annoyance, and scurrility, which distinguish the Warburtonian school."[8] Hurd's remarks provide a good example of the type of virulent treatment given to Hume, especially since Hurd openly admits the pleasure he took in castigating him as an atheist. Hurd writes, for example, that he "hath not scrupled to adopt [Warbrburton's] manner of composition, as well as [his] Arguments . . . . [h]e [Hurd] is not one of those cool opposers of Infidelity, who can reason without earnestness, and confute without warmth. He leaves it to others . . . to combat the most flagitious tenets with severity. . . . For himself, he freely owns, he is apt to *kindle* as he writes."[9]

In this way, Hurd struck the public pose of treating Hume as beneath contempt by stressing that he himself had merely published with little correction the thoughts that he had jotted in the margins of Hume's essay when first reading it: "[The author] never designed the following animadversions for an elaborate piece of instruction or entertainment to the learned reader. He would employ only a vacant hour in exposing to the laughter of every man, that can read, the futility, licence, and vanity of Mr. David Hume."[10] Hurd's contemptuous dismissal of Hume's ideas as if they were the ravings of a lunatic is typical of the response of Christian apologists to him in England.

While the published answers to Hume in England may have been biased somewhat by nationalistic animosity, his works were always more favorably received in Scotland, even by those who believed them to be dangerous to the common good. About the time that Hurd was abusing Hume, for instance, both Thomas Reid and George Campbell were submitting the manuscripts of their refutations of his philosophical system to him for his comments; and both acknowledged their indebtedness to his ideas and their admiration for his fine mind. In the preface to A *Dissertation on Miracles* (1763), for example, Campbell praises Hume warmly: "I have not only been much entertained and instructed by his works; but, if I am possessed of any talent in abstract reasoning, I am not a little indebted to what he has written on *human nature*, for the improvement of that talent."[11]

But such an enlightened, tolerant view of Hume's work belies the fact that the Scottish philosophers were quite disturbed by the deleterious effects that they were certain his writings had on society. In another context, for example, Campbell describes Hume's attacks on religion in terms of the wind buffeting a giant oak tree: ". . . they shake it impetuously and loudly threaten its subversion; whilst in effect they only serve to make it strike its roots the deeper, and stand the firmer ever after."[12] Hume's Scottish opponents were deeply concerned that the reputation he had rightly gained for his great intellect might persuade unthinking people to disregard religion and their duty to society and to become fashionable infidels because they believed his books to have sanctioned such behavior. For this reason, Alexander Gerard published a sermon in 1770 that makes precisely that point concerning Hume's very great talent: "This will gain him attention from the inquisitive; and will render his reasonings on every subject, more specious than those of many others, and on that account more dangerous when, at any time, he happens to mistake."[13]

But the reputable philosophical answers to Hume that were

published in the 1760s by Reid, Campbell, Gerard, and others did not gain a popular audience; and Hume was still much admired as the Great Infidel. In this respect, these Scottish philosophers were much like the earlier Christian writers in England who had used pure philosophical arguments to fight scepticism but who had received very little attention from the reading public. This comparison also points up the fact that Beattie's *Essay on Truth* was very much like Butler's *Analogy of Religion* as a work which received great support because it was more a restatement of orthodox beliefs than a philosophical argument. But this view of Beattie's book explains its success only in part; for he also managed to bridge the gap between the Scottish and English responses to Humian scepticism by combining a reproduction of Reid's ideas with the "warmth and spirit" of the Warburtonian School. Beattie's philosophical roots are to be found as much in English as they are in Scottish intellectual soil. The *Essay on Truth* stands, therefore, not only as the culmination of a long line of Christian apologia, but also as a remarkable amalgam of attitudes and ideas and as a style of argument that mark it as an important document of the Scottish contribution to English thought.

II *The* Essay on Truth *as a Christian Apology*

In spite of Beattie's claim that the *Essay on Truth* was a philosophical treatise, the book was viewed from the beginning primarily as a work of Christian apology. Clergymen were particularly pleased with it, for it presented them with the means of renewing their battle against scepticism and irreligion in much the same way that Butler's *Analogy* had been used as an authoritative demolition of Deistic beliefs. Beattie's book provided an exciting incentive for them to continue their incessant fight against the materialistic views associated with scepticism, just as it yielded many illustrations and arguments for their sermons. Beilby Porteus, the bishop of London, for example, in a sermon on irreligion published in 1772, expressed the wish that Beattie, "who has lately done such essential service to the cause of religion, by utterly subverting Mr. Hume's uncomfortable and intelligible system," would also publish a refutation of "the other two fashionable infidels," Voltaire and Rousseau.[14] The *Essay's* growing popularity may be attributed directly to the recommendation of its devotees that it should be read as a Christian answer to corrupt philosophical principles; and, as a consequence, it became a kind of devotional book. Fanny Burney, for example, wrote in her diary on July 13, 1787,

that the "*Immutability of Truth* is full of religious instruction, con-
veyed with such a rare mixture of precision and of wit as to carry
amusement hand in hand with conviction."[15] As Margaret Forbes
claims, therefore, Beattie's contemporaries "judged his 'Essay on
Truth' . . . by the heart it had put into the party of religion at a
time when it was considered the mark of superiority in talent and
enlightenment to be an unbeliever."[16] Even in the nineteenth century, the book was published in a series called *Evidences of the
Christian Religion* (1816).

But the *Essay on Truth* was not regarded as a Christian apology
merely because it attacked scepticism; it is in effect a restatement of
New Testament doctrines for the common reader in the guise of
philosophical argument. Beattie's most important conclusion is that
natural impulse is "the voice of God" (*Truth*, p. 59) by which He
reveals Himself when man's reason is convinced by the evidence
revealed through the common sense process of instinctive and instantaneous perception; in this way, the philosophy of common
sense provides the pattern whereby man may learn to control his
thoughts and actions and eventually to gain knowledge of the truth.
Since Beattie's common sense argument is founded on the belief
that the God of Christianity is the omnipotent creator and preserver
of all things, Beattie affirms the Christian religion to be the divinely
ordained expression of God's love and mercy, as well as the principal means of salvation for man. Common sense is, therefore, a
natural gift that gives intimations of immortality to the true
believer.

For this reason, Beattie's proof that scepticism is always a form of
falsehood, which makes man miserable, is based on the assertion
that Christianity propagates the kind of truth that brings lasting joy
to man. God's will is done, therefore, when man deliberately avoids
scepticism and trusts instead in the principles of common sense; and
this trust in "true religion . . . tends to make men great, and good,
and happy" (*Truth*, p. 127). But, since man's natural tendency is to
be complacent and easily led, scepticism is thriving, Beattie claims,
because it offers an easy alternative to the rigors of true Christian
living. Beattie tries, therefore, to impress upon his readers the error
of the sceptic's style of life by using a sustained metaphor in which
the debilitating metaphysical sickness of the age is cured by its antidote, belief in common sense, so that the patient—the im-
pressionable common reader—is restored to robust intellectual
health and to grace in the practice of true religion.

Directing the full force of his thoughts and feelings against Hume's claim that no rational conclusions may be reached concerning the cause of the universe, Beattie demonstrates by his own rational argument that the universe was made by the very Christian God who is so studiously ignored by Hume. In the section of his argument that Beattie calls "Reasoning from the Effect to the Cause," he insists that God endowed man with sensory perception so that intimations of the divine presence in the world could be recognized in the grandeur of nature: "That the whole sensible universe hath to us the appearance of an effect, of something which exists not by any necessity of nature, but by the appointment of some powerful and intelligent cause different from and independent on it . . . cannot be denied. . . . We offer violence to our understanding, when we attempt to believe that the whole universe does not proceed from some cause; and we argue unphilosophically, when we endeavor to disprove this natural and universal suggestion of the human mind" (*Truth*, p. 97).

Beattie's argument is not essentially different from Joseph Butler's in the *Analogy of Religion* where the author wills his belief to be true, and then makes it so by describing certain effects of nature as if they were manifestations of a divine will; but, on the rational ground of philosophical thought, such a response really begs Hume's question. It is characteristic of Beattie's argument, therefore, that he concludes his answer to Hume's claim with the confident assertion that the union of true religion and true philosophy is effected only when common sense is allowed to reveal God's truth: ". . . truth is something fixed and determinate, depending not upon man, but upon the Author of Nature" (*Truth*, p. 120). Beattie's insistence on the divine authority for his brand of philosophy was its most appealing quality for most eighteenth century readers: for, as was indicated by his friend, Mrs. Montagu, in 1773, "Philosophy is a holy thing, should keep erect, look up to heaven, contemplate the stars, and adore their Maker. . . . Dr. Beattie will give a voice to all the mute objects I now admire, and lead me further in virtue and wisdom than I can advance by myself."[17] As the only common sense philosopher to insist on the divine origin of his theories, Beattie hit upon the single most important element in his book that made him the most popular Christian apologist of his time.

III *Evidences of the Christian Religion*

The composition of *Evidences of the Christian Religion* (1786) was a labor of love for Beattie, as he told Mrs. Montagu in a letter of April 26, 1786: "I never wrote anything with more pleasure, and I would fain hope it may do some good."[18] Even though Beattie's great reputation as a Christian apologist at the time indicated a good sale for the book, he must have been surprised at its outstanding success; for it was reprinted twice in the first year alone and was reissued for many years after. For this reason, William Forbes in his biography of Beattie considered the book to be "the most popular, as it is certainly among the most useful of [his] prose-writings."[19] During Beattie's lifetime, the book achieved impressive success as a practical guide to living the Christian life: it was credited, for example, with several conversions to Christianity; it was assigned by the bishop of London as an aid in converting the Negroes of the West Indies; and it became a classbook at Christ's Hospital, the London Charity School. In addition, many readers made a point of informing Beattie that they felt *Evidences* to be very effective in promoting the Christian faith. Consequently, Beattie learned to regard it as his favorite book, especially for its "closeness of matter and style."[20]

Beattie was pleased with *Evidences* for another reason, for it was the fulfillment of the ambition that he had formed as a young university teacher to write a definitive treatise about the evidences of Christianity and morality. Since the *Essay on Truth* was his first attempt to follow that plan, the two books may be regarded as companion volumes that are closely linked by their attacks on a common enemy, the modern spirit of scepticism. The *Essay* was so well known by 1786 that Beattie assumed familiarity with it in the readers of *Evidences*. The two books share the same principal aim of illustrating the absurdity of scepticism, but they differ in format and material: the *Essay on Truth* develops principles for living the Christian life; *Evidences* provides hints for following those principles. Since the argument of the *Essay* that the God of Christianity was the author of common sense was widely accepted, Beattie concentrates in *Evidences* on his proof of the superiority of Christianity to scepticism and on answers to sceptical questions. In fact, the only significant dissimilarity between the two books is the fact that *Evidences* drew no recorded response from the defenders of scepticism. David Hume had been dead for ten years, and the controversy stirred up by the *Essay on Truth* had spent itself with the popular victory being claimed by the supporters of Christianity. With the need to deal with metaphysical speculation in relation to the Christian life apparently satisfied, Beattie therefore took great joy from writing pure Christian apology; but his was, nevertheless, a unique kind of apology, since the assumption of common sense as the perfect union of philosophy and religion is as basic to *Evidences* as it is to the *Essay*. In a word, Beattie uses philosophical argument to preach Christian doctrines in the *Essay;* in *Evidences*, he defends Christianity with common sense philosophy.

Since Beattie wrote *Evidences* as a kind of reader's guide to the Bible and to the books of Christian writers whom he wished to recommend, he announces at the start that the book is aimed at the person "who may be in danger from the books, or from the company, of infidels, and is candid enough to desire to be informed, in a few words, whether the evidence on the other side be so plausible, as to deserve the notice of a rational mind."[21] Beattie therefore presents his readers with a short summary of the historical development of philosophy in which he emphasizes the practical uselessness of philosophical thinking to the vast majority of people who find it incomprehensible. Even at its best, philosophy has always been "very incomplete as a system of natural religion and moral duty" (p. 10), Beattie claims; while, at its worst, as it is found in writers like Hume, it becomes the idle absurdities of "a few speculative men" (p. 11).

Even in the ancient world, the tendency of philosophy toward impractical reasoning was often prevalent: the abstruseness of the Stoics, for example, made their teaching useless; Socrates, on the other hand, was a public teacher, but he never claimed to be a reformer; and Cicero was an ineffectual intellectual. Beattie stresses his belief that all ancient philosophy was incomplete because it was far removed from the common people. But this serious defect of philosophical thought was corrected, Beattie argues, by the life and teaching of Jesus as found in the New Testament, which records the culmination of the best impulses in ancient philosophical writing. As God in human form, Jesus fulfilled his divine mission in life by becoming "the Teacher of the Poor" and by offering the means to satisfy the yearning after immortality that had been expressed by ancient philosophers. As a result, his "doctrine was distinguished from that of all other teachers not only by its intrinsic truth, and by those mighty works that bore testimony to its truth, but also by its being in so peculiar a manner addressed to the poor, and consequently to all the rest of mankind" (p. 15).

Having established in this way the validity and historical importance of Christianity, Beattie then considers the problems that face his contemporary readers. Common sense philosophy, he claims, provides for modern man the ultimate interpretation of the meaning of Christ's life and divinity; thus God's twin gifts of common sense and reason unite to justify the Christian's faith and hope in Christ's promise of the good life that will be followed by eternal life. The common sense reading of the Bible, and of other books by Christian writers, is therefore the basis for the most enlightened form of Christian apologia; for from "true philosophy" and "a right use of reason," Beattie insists, "our religion has nothing to apprehend": "The more carefully and candidly it is studied, the more conspicuous will its truth and beauty appear. Wherever it and human nature are understood, they are found so admirably suited to each other, that the believer needs not fear, and it is vain for the adversary to wish, their final separation. God has joined them, and it is not in man's power to put them asunder" (p. 131).

In addition to this kind of argument, Beattie uses common sense principles throughout *Evidences* to support his view of Christianity. The book is, therefore, the definitive statement about the divine origin of the philosophy of common sense. As a consequence, the most important part of the book deals with common objections to Christianity. The third objection cited by Beattie, for example, states that biblical and doctrinal obscurities prove the human origin of Christianity. On the contrary, Beattie argues that such obscurity, which is always caused by human error, is part of God's plan by which man may choose either to live according to the clear dictates of his God-given conscience or to drift into immoral habits by following the corrupting suggestions of metaphysical writers. Man's inventive powers are quickened and his moral perception sharpened when he struggles with his inability to comprehend fully difficult biblical passages or complex doctrinal precepts; but, on the contrary, man's blind admiration for the perverted obscurity of metaphysical reasoning deadens the innate moral sense and breeds irreligious behavior. Since sceptical speculation hardens the heart against God's will and impedes man's ability to perceive the truth clearly, man must learn to think and act according to the dictates of common sense, Beattie concludes, because such obedience to the word of God is the most practical way of living the Christian life:

" . . . is it not infinitely to the honour of our religion, that the more firmly it is believed, and the less it is corrupted, by human invention, the more powerful it is in improving and purifying the human soul?"(p. 131). The philosophy of common sense, therefore, confirms and explains God's plan for the growth of man's intellectual and spiritual life that is revealed in the Bible and in the Christian religion throughout history.

CHAPTER 5

"The Castle of Scepticism"

SINCE "The Castle of Scepticism" (1767) is a prose-satire about the same sceptical writers that Beattie treats in the *Essay on Truth,* the work is an important commentary on the writing of the *Essay* and on the response that it received from the reading public.[1] The value of "The Castle" as a contrast to the *Essay* is underscored by the note that Beattie jotted on the first page of the manuscript in 1773 when he was at the height of his fame as a poet and philosopher: "This was written about six years ago, in the year 1767 & before the Essay on Truth was finished. It was never intended for publication." This remark seems to indicate not only that Beattie was under some pressure to publish the work but also that he deliberately suppressed it; in fact, his reasons for not publishing it are to be found in his experiences with writing the *Essay* and in the nature of "The Castle" itself. In spite of the bitter, polemical temper of the *Essay,* Beattie was not a vindicative person; for he allowed anger to rise in him only over published ideas that he felt to be deleterious to society and especially to the young. In fact, his strong sense of duty to mankind forced him to spend over four years writing and revising the *Essay,* even though he detested metaphysics and suffered the physical and mental effects of the labor for the rest of his life.

When Beattie sent the manuscript of the *Essay* to the printer in 1769, therefore, the relief that he experienced was so great that he felt "like a man who has escaped from the mines"[2]; and ten years later, after the *Essay* had gone through twelve editions, he still could not bear to read the book "without some degree of horror" because it recalled the long evenings passed "in those severe studies."[3] The *Essay on Truth* was his considered, public opinion of the horrific consequences of popular scepticism; but "The Castle of Scepticism" was his private, literary response in which he translated the nightmarish terrors of his personal fight against evil into a satirical dream allegory. The compelling need to escape from time to time from his "metaphysical speculations" is seen also in *The Minstrel,* in which there are several references to his public career as a moral philosopher. "The Castle of Scepticism", however, not only gives insight into the *Essay on Truth* and *The Minstrel,* but is also a respectable work in its own right.

I   The Dream Allegory

"The Castle" is "an account of a vision" that came to Beattie in a deep sleep induced by reading one of Hume's essays. In it, Beattie finds himself hurrying along with a great crowd of excited people who appear eager to reach some very desirable destination. As the journey proceeds over different kinds of landscape, Beattie engages several of his companions in conversation and learns much about them and their attitudes and especially about the purpose of the pilgrimage. They are going to pay homage to the "Great Oracle of modern times" who is the "Governor of the Castle of Scepticism"; in this way, Hume is introduced as the supreme commander of the sceptical forces. Meanwhile, they arrive at the gates of the castle, where every pilgrim is expected to worship at one of the shrines and to sacrifice his common sense at an altar before going in. All the pilgrims perform these rites except Beattie who, in the hope of his later conversion, is permitted to enter, even though he is still in possession of his common sense. Inside, he is allowed to wander at will to see the many activities and experiments in progress.

From the beginning of the journey, Beattie had found himself in conflict with the ideas expressed to him; and, after listening for a long time in silence, he had begun to argue against them. But the mild debates during the journey with the allegorical figures of the unthinking followers of sceptical writers and with some who should know better become inside the castle uncontroled harangues against him by confirmed sceptics who threaten him with physical violence. The growing hysteria of the dream reaches its climax in the meeting of Beattie and the governor (Hume) at the very end when Beattie is saved from destruction and awakens in the bright sunlight of the Scottish countryside.

II   Allegorical Figures

From the start, Beattie concentrates on presenting and exploring the extreme, irreconcilable opposition between the God-given common sense view of life as represented by his own speeches and the evil sceptical view as seen in all the other figures in the allegory, ranging from the pilgrims' blind, unreasoning adulation of sceptical writers, through the mildly ludicrous ambivalence of Thomas Reid, to the hellish insanity of David Hume. At first, Beattie's studied naiveté provides the opening which introduces Hume's ideas without actually bringing him on stage. As Beattie hears the words "Ideas, Priestcraft, Sceptick, Quality, [and] Entity," he thinks the pilgrims will soon attend "a dissertation on the nature of things" ("Castle," p. 2). Meanwhile, they are walking through very beautiful countryside called "The Land of Truth" by the vulgar and "The Den of Prejudice" by the learned. When Beattie remarks that "Den" doesn't seem quite the proper word to describe such a fine region, he is called "a fool and a pedant" (p. 2). Dissatisfied with the silly answers to his questions, he asks where they are going. A very well-dressed "person of great rank, and consequently of great abilities," tells him very politely, "You are going to learn wisdom from the Great Oracle of modern times" (p. 4).

Consquently, the allegorical figure representing Hume is named as "the deepest genius and wisest philosopher ever known," for he far surpasses "the acumen of Aristotle, the eloquence of Plato, the learning of Theophrastus, the taste of Quintillian, and the imagination of Lucretius" (p. 4). The gentleman adds that his works "are obscure, and perhaps require more thought and attention than people of fashion have to bestow; but this I take to be only a proof of their depth; for the gentleman is none of your superficial thinkers" (p. 4). In the last age, Addison, Steele, and some other "pretended philosophers," who "found fault with their betters in everything," were very different from this "charming philosopher" whose "sentiments coincide with ours so exactly that they seem to be borrowed from us" (p. 5). These ideas are related to Beattie "very gracefully", but, since he finds them unconvincing, he concludes that "the world admired the philosopher because good judges did so; and good judges admired him because the world did" (p. 6). The way is thereby prepared for the conflict between the ideas of Beattie and Hume to intensify throughout the satire and for their inevitable confrontation at the end.

One of the most effective minor confrontations is between Beattie and Thomas Reid, who, Beattie felt, had been much too gentle and fawning in his book against Hume. When Beattie meets Reid before entering the castle, he asks him his opinion of the governor (Hume):

His abilities are astonishingly great, and justly entitled to the highest praise: though it must be confessed, that his doctrines exceed all that were contrived in absurdity and folly. . . . His penetration seems to surpass the measure of human capacity: but the most glaring absurdities pass upon him, when disguised by technical words, and recommended by his favourite authors. . . . It is equally to his honour, and to that of the age, that his philosophy, notwithstanding its subtility and obscurity, has obtained so much credit with people of all rank: and it is no less remarkable, that, those who read it least admire it most and none so much as they who have never read it at all (pp. 6 - 7).

This speech, an exaggerated version of the arguments of Reid's *Inquiry*, concentrates on Reid's ineffectiveness in communicating the truth of common sense; but it also suggests a possible reason for his ineptness: ". . . the speaker from time to time looked to the listening multitude with much timidity in his countenance, which tempted me to think, that it was partly for fear of giving offence, that he thus blended his censure with compliment" (p. 7).

But Reid's nonsense is soon forgotten after Beattie enters the castle and sees how densely it is populated by sceptics, infidels, and heretics. Scepticism is thriving under Hume, and many of his devotees are eager to convert Beattie to their cause. For example, a doting sceptic describes Hume's system of reason as a remarkable machine:

To show that all inferences of reason are false or uncertain; and that the understanding acting alone does entirely subvert itself, and prove by argument that by argument nothing can be proved, he has contrived a puppet of mushrooms, cork cobwebs, gossamer, and other fungous and flimsy materials, to which he gives the name Reason. He performs with it several dextrous feats to the surprise of every spectator; and at last, by a wonderful apparatus in the machinery, he makes it open its mouth, and with a sudden jerk throw its whole body, feet, head, trunk, legs and arms, down its throat, where it totally disappears. He has published a full account of the whole affair in a very elaborate Treatise in three volumes, which has given us all the most perfect satisfaction. The method by which this operation is performed is too subtle to be understood, and he never performs it except in the dark, or behind a screen; but as he himself has assured us that it is plain to a demonstration, every body is convinced (pp. 19 - 20).

This kind of reasoning has made them all mad, Beattie believes; and he finds ample evidence of insanity everywhere he looks in the castle. The many nameless experimenters are, of course, merely following the examples of the well-known "philosophers" who also live in the castle. For example, Bernard Mandeville attempts to prove "that private vices are really public benefits" by using the corpses of criminals as "manure to improve agriculture"; and he therefore invites everybody "to promote felony and encourage the hangman" (p. 27). Voltaire, "with his face screwed into a strange sarcastick grin," boasts that he has "laughed and sneered at every thing sacred and serious, proved Shakespeare to be a madman, Milton an idiot, and Homer a dreaming old woman"; indeed, he plans "to exterminate that Scoundrel Religion from the face of the earth" (pp. 28 - 30). Thomas Hobbes, "armed cap-a-pie in the Gothic fashion," with a cocked blunderbuss in each hand, spouts ideas from his *Leviathan* and cringes in terror of every shadow because he fears a "mutiny or plot going forward." While claiming that he had taught the governor (Hume) "some ideas which he had not acknowledged," (p. 31) Hobbes skilfully pilfers all of Beattie's possessions from his pockets; but he playfully returns them when he sees that they are of little value.

The description of Pyrrho, the ancient philosopher who denied his own existence, conveys very well Beattie's disgust and scorn toward advanced scepticism. When he first sees Pyrrho in a magnificent "old-fashioned apartment," Beattie mistakes him "for an Egyptian mummy . . . a vegetable in human shape." He is informed, however, that the great philosopher "awakened four times a day, half an hour each time, and then ate and drank voraciously, but never spoke a word." Many attempts had been made "to engage his attention" during the waking periods, including "counterfeited convulsions" and "mock hangings," but to no avail. "As this extraordinary indifference was judged to be the effect of scepticism and philosophy, he was regarded as a most respectable personage, and as one who, by attaining to Indisturbance, had improved human nature to its highest pitch of perfection. Many worshipped him as a God: and all agreed, that if Wisdom herself were to visit earth, she would certainly assume the form and character of Pyrrho" (pp. 13 - 14).

Beattie puts many pointed questions to sceptics and allows them to condemn themselves and their theories with their own words. Having asked Hobbes for an explanation of his theory of morality, for example, Beattie counters with a common sense question that indicates his diametrically opposed view. "This question disconcerted the Sage in armour so much, that instead of returning any answer, he began to survey me from head to foot with a most furious look; on which I thought it high time to be going, and accordingly took to my heels, and ran a full quarter of a mile before I ventured to take breath" (pp. 35 - 6). The common sense notion that moral sentiment is universal and immutable is thus presented as superior to Hobbes's opinion. Faced with such wisdom, Hobbes's silence and his menacing manner prove that he sees the truth of common sense. Having defeated Hobbes in argument, Beattie sees no point in battling with him physically.

Since Beattie is the only sane person in the castle, his common sense speeches fall on deaf ears. This rejection is the most horrible aspect of the whole ghastly dream. His sanity is assured because he had refused to deposit his common sense at the temples outside the gates that are dedicated to affection, ignorance, self-conceit, fashion, licentiousness, ambition, avarice, and hypothesis. The power of common sense aids him immediately after entering the castle when a very alluring woman "in a masque" offers the travelers "a cordial of her own preparing." Almost all of the pilgrims drink to her good health; but, when Beattie puts the glass to his lips, "the liquid of its own accord flew off in the opposite side, and besprinkled all the lady's rich stomacher and tucker" (p. 12). Immediately, she curses him for not having offered a sacrifice; and, in her anger, she reveals herself as Modesty. Meanwhile, the aphrodisiac in the drink diverts the attentions of the others elsewhere. Beattie's common sense protects him even without his knowledge.

After many such adventures, Beattie finally meets Hume in the darkest part of the castle amid the terrible noises of a Medieval torture chamber.

Close by the postern, stood the Governour, in gorgeous apparel, attended by a numerous company of priests, lawyers, and fine gentlemen; and with a show of extreme politeness, yet methought very officiously, invited the travellers to the threshold, and then pushed them out headlong; smiling at the same time with a mixture of contempt and self-complacancy; and now and then putting his hands in his pockets, and clinking his money. Seeing me a little shy, he addressed me in a most soothing manner in the English tongue; but there seemed to be something exotick in his pronunciation, for he spoke through his teeth like a Scotsman, and through his nose like a Frenchman. He spoke much about ideas, and doubts, and impostures, and

parsons, and machinery; and concluded a long harrangue with a few cor-
ollaries, plausible indeed and well-disguised, but of such blasphemous im-
port that my hair stood on end with horror (pp. 36 - 37).

Beattie's fascination with Hume's macabre performance overcomes
his repulsion and draws him closer to hear him the better.
     When Hume spots the intruder near him, he stretches out his
"huge hands" to grab him. Suddenly,

a peal of thunder burst over our heads, so loud and so terrible, as if the
frame of nature had been going to pieces. The orator fell on his knees, and
began to repeat the Apostles' creed with the utmost vehemence and
gesture; the crowds and castle vanished; the darkness was dissolved and the
sun shone out with the most delightful brilliance. But my attention was
now wholly engrossed by a shrill and sweet voice, which seemed to come
from a distance, and spoke these words "Turn, ye mortals, from the paths
of the destroyer, and now listen to the words of Truth." I was wonderfully
affected with this address, and fixed myself in a posture of the most devout
attention, when methought, the voice grew less and less articulate; and the
next moment I found myself broad awake, and listening to the bell of the
parish-church that now summoned me to prayers. (p.37).

This apocalyptic vision shows the believer (Beattie) rewarded and
the sceptic (Hume) cowering before God. Hume's hypocrisy in dis-
believing his own theories is revealed; and fear makes him a last
minute penitent who seeks refuge in the Apostles' Creed, the
traditional recitation of Christian beliefs, when an angelic voice tells
of damnation and salvation. The nightmare is dissipated by the
revelation of God's truth, and the "shrill and sweet voice" is discovered to be the saving grace for humanity as it blends with the
sound of the church bell that summons all to forsake evil and to
welcome the certainty of the Christian religion. This prevision of
judgment shows the bright sun of Christian revelation penetrating
the foggy darkness of scepticism and lighting the path to the reunion of philosophy and religion. The main plea of the "Castle,"
therefore, is for man to live by God's will as revealed in the Bible
and true religion.

III   *Classic Tradition*

     The "Castle" is set in the classic tradition of John Bunyan,
Samuel Butler, John Dryden, Alexander Pope, and Jonathan Swift,
all of whom Beattie mentions by name or alludes to in the satire.

Like these predecessors, Beattie also relies heavily on his readers' knowledge of Greek and Roman writers which would enable them to understand his extensive use of Classical allusion. In addition, he makes use of scenes from other English writers, notably Spenser and James Thomson, to support his allegory. But his greatest debt in the use of sources is to Vergil, for Beattie's satire is a direct adaptation of the descent of Aeneas into the underworld in Book VI of the *Aeneid*. Beattie indicates in the opening sentence the studied nature of his reliance on Vergil by stressing his dream as a "vision" which so affected his imaginative "fancy" that he is compelled "to lay before the world an account of [it]" (p. 1). The opening sentence also adds the Homeric to the use of the Vergilian mode by noting Beattie's denial of "ambition to be thought a dreamer of dreams" and of any pretense to conjecture "whether [the vision] issued through the gate of ivory, or through that of horn." Beattie and many of his readers were well aware of the current controversy over Book VI of the *Aeneid* in general and over the gates of horn and ivory passage in particular. Beattie himself joined in the public debate in his "Remarks on some passages of the sixth Book of the Eneid" which was read before the Royal Society of Edinburgh in 1788.[4] In fact, these remarks are an excellent gloss on the use of Classical allusions in "The Castle of Scepticism."

Beattie claims in this lecture that all the critics have been led astray by interpreting Vergil's gates with Book XIX of Homer's *Odyssey* in which false dreams are transmitted to the upper world through a gate of ivory and where true dreams arrive through a gate of horn. "But Virgil's account differs from Homer's more than the commentators seem to be aware" (p. 52), Beattie writes, for Vergil's gates are specifically associated with sleep, not with dreams. Beattie claims that the word "umbrae" that is translated as "dreams" by the critics really means "ghosts" in the Vergilian context. They are "those who, after having been a thousand years in Elysium, and taken a draught of Lethe, were sent back to the upper world to animate new bodies" (p. 53). These shades are so substantial that they are capable of being liberated; and the result is their passage through a gate to this world. Similarly, Aeneas and the Sybil, who are flesh and blood, must pass through a gate to leave the underworld or remain there forever. Consequently, Beattie has it both ways in his satire: the vision of the realm of scepticism which came to him in his sleep is, in the Homeric sense, an account of a dream about truth and falsehood; and, in the Vergilian sense, it is an extended metaphorical allegory in which the figures actually incorporate in a poetic way the qualities assigned to them. The polarity of this situation is expressed in Beattie himself as the embodiment of virtue and in Hume, of evil.

Even the landscape of the work is Vergilian as it suggests in turn Aeneas' journey through the pleasant fields of Elysium and then through the "melancholy plains" approaching the rocky, tortuous region of Tartarus and its river of fire. Similarly, Beattie starts his pilgrimage on a sunny day in beautiful countryside; proceeds through an area of "precipices" and troublesome "stones, brambles, and underwood" (p. 8), and finally arrives at the castle where Hume is found pushing his victims into a dark pit amidst "the thunder of temptestuous fire bursting" forth (p. 36). Clearly the castle itself is a kind of Tartarus in Beattie's vision. In fact, his picture of the horrors of the pit is in large part his own translation into English of appropriate parts of Vergil's descriptions of Tartarus. The adaptation of such allusions to modern scepticism is made plain at the start by Beattie's denial that he has "any pretensions whatsoever to Second Sight" (p. 1). As he wrote to Mrs. Montagu in 1772, the popular belief in second sight was "an excess of folly and wickedness"[5]; and Beattie obviously intends the readers of his satire to equate its vision of scepticism with such ignorance and superstition. Yet, as he remarks in the same letter, he does not "mean to deny the existence of ghosts, or to call in question the accounts of extraordinary revelations."[6] The power of the allusions is imposed on the satire by Beattie's vision of modern life, so that the work is both an ironic picture of the world as it actually is and a hopeful vision of the better world that it might become.

Even though the parallels between eighteenth century philosophical controversy and the Homeric-Vergilian context are not exact, they would certainly have provided a reader with considerable scope for amused conjecture. As a result, the horror expressed throughout at the follies and vices of scepticism is softened somewhat, and one's perspective on the satire is enlarged by the realization that Beattie is presenting himself in mock-serious fashion as the heroic, patriarchal traveler who is the incarnation of the collective wisdom of his race. Part of the pleasure in reading the satire, therefore, lies in speculating how far one may legitimately read Classical allusions into it. Is Beattie's common sense, for instance, anything like the golden bough, the Vergilian symbol of wisdom and the passport into the underworld?

One must emphasize that the mock-serious aspect of the satire has the remarkable effect of supporting and verifying the totally serious presentation of the evils of modern scepticism. It is, of course, this serious element that is closest to the central Vergilian theme of the descent as the figurative expression of the manner in which wicked impulses turn man away from God and from the control of reason. This view of reality is also a precise statement of Beattie's complaint against scepticism as it is reinforced in the satire by the association with such ancient symbolic concepts as spiritual darkness, the abyss of chaos, and the descent into hell. The landscape and the figures of Beattie's allegory are thereby infused with the powerful sense of the vitality and order of a better world as it imposes itself on the fallen world of reality.

IV The Satiric Tradition in English

Like the works of Homer and Vergil, Spenser's *The Faerie Queene* (1590) and Thomson's *The Castle of Indolence* (1748) had an influence upon Beattie's satiric technique. He studied both poems and deliberately adopted many aspects of their style into "The Castle of Scepticism." One is meant to view the figure of Beattie, therefore, as a Spenserian questing knight who gains victory by enduring the most severe and fundamental test of his knighthood, thereby earning the perfection of his virtue and a return to the world of sanity. He is also like Thomson's Knight of Arts and Industry who by his magic reveals the surroundings of the Castle of Indolence to be a terrible wasteland and who can save its inhabitants from corruption if they will follow him. In borrowing the castle from Spenser and Thomson as his setting, Beattie was aware that it had long been used as a symbol for attacks on virtue or vice by the powers of evil or good. His satire, therefore, is so full of the echoes of the Christian knight's duty to combat evil that Beattie even includes the traditional attempt at seduction by a voluptuous harlot. As part of the allegorical landscape, the castle indicates the need for the Christian to protect his soul from the external dangers that lurk all about him. In Spenser, Thomson, and in Beattie, these dangers are associated with the corrupt religious ideas of atheists who perplex the judgment and stir the emotions of the people.

Many symbols in the work that are associated with Homer, Vergil, Spenser, and others are also distinctly Christian, especially such concepts as that of common sense as the spirit of God that works in the world, of the journey of the Christian soul through life,

and of the hellfire at the end. All these elements of Beattie's satire
are unified to sustain the central theme concerning the modern battle between Christianity and scepticism. Since Beattie had little
hope at this time of getting the *Essay on Truth* into print and none
for it to become popular, it is interesting, nevertheless, that he had
visions of himself as the champion of the established church as the
means of restoring order and contentment to a beleagured world.
Like Don Quixote, Beattie may not have realized that he was tilting
at windmills. In fact, his description in *Dissertations* (1783) of the
effects of *Don Quixote* in destroying the "wild dreams of chivalry"
is remarkably similar to the conclusion of the "Castle": "Mankind
awoke as from a dream. They laughed at themselves for having
been so long imposed on by absurdity; and wondered that they had
not made the discovery sooner" (*Dissertations*, 563).

The "Castle of Scepticism" is a cleverly formed amalgam of
allegory, allusion, and personal diatribe in the mode of Pope's *The
Dunciad* (1728) and Swift's *Gulliver's Travels* (1726) that enlivens
and gives an interesting perspective to the philosophical controversy
of the time. One of the strengths of Beattie's satiric technique is the
way in which he quietly aligns himself with Butler, Pope, Dryden,
and Swift, either by having infamous sceptics attack them or by
mentioning them himself. The effect is a clear demarcation
between Beattie and the great English satirists on one side and on
the other the unregenerate sceptics who are the proper objects of
censure and scorn. At the time, Butler's *Hudibras* (1663 - 1678) was
well known as a burlesque of the *Aeneid,* so that Beattie's readers
would probably recall it in recognizing Vergilian allusions in the
"Castle." Consequently, Beattie needs merely to refer to two
squabbling "philosophers" as being "like Hudibras and the Con-
jurer" to direct attention to his Hudibrastic, mock-heroic style and
to his grossly exaggerated images. The great reliance of *Hudibras*
upon *The Faerie Queene* confirms the aptness of Beattie's
references.

As with the similarities between Butler and Spenser, Beattie's
allusions are effective because they bear only a superficial
relationship to their sources. Like Butler, therefore, Beattie assumes
his audience will catch the allusions and then quite deliberately
tries to shape them to suit his own purposes. Similarly, Beattie uses
Pope by having Voltaire ridicule him as an answer to Beattie's simple faith in the Christian God: "And so . . . you believe, with one
Pope, an English poet, that *Whatever is is right,* and think

Providence, no doubt a mighty sort of thing': here he interrupted his speech with a second fit of laughing much more violent then the first, in which he was joined by the whole company" ("Castle", pp. 27 - 28). This simple reference is sufficient to bring the devasting power of *The Dunciad* to bear against Beattie's tormentors, at once confirming his belief and condemning their insolence.

But the best example of this aspect of Beattie's satire is his use of Swift's *Gulliver's Travels*. His descriptions of the experiments that he sees inside the castle are clever imitations of those of the projectors that Gulliver observes in Balnibarbi; and, in addition, he calls on Swift directly when ridiculing Hume:

A person who called himself the Genius of Metaphysick was continually busied in turning a large engine, like that described in Gulliver's travels, which threw up an endless variety of combinations of words and letters, out of which were framed sentences and paragraphs, sections, chapters, and treatises. He told me, he was much employed, and had the custom of all the literati of the place, particularly of the Governour, who (he said) was his very good friend; adding, that if I had any job on hand in the bookmaking way, he would furnish me with materials in the neatest and newest fashion, and on the most reasonable terms (p. 21).

As the reader recalls Swift's myriad master strokes, the effect is the confirmation of Beattie's censure of sceptics and the affirmation of his technique. For one's memories of *Gulliver's Travels* reiterate Beattie's echoing of the Homeric and Vergilian worlds, the effects of reason gone mad, the journey of the mock-epic hero, and above all the abuses of spiritual pride. There is yet another respect in which Beattie is like Swift. In 1710, Swift visited Gresham College, the home of the Royal Society, where he found ample materials to assign to his projectors in Balnibarbi. Having studied the writings of many metaphysical philosophers, Beattie's best response was not his philosophical answer in the *Essay on Truth* but his literary condemnation in "The Castle of Scepticism" where by means of his allusive technique he enlists as his champions many of the most admired writers from Homer to Swift.

V   *Beattie's Audience*

It is important to repeat that Beattie never intended to publish the satire. Apart from its therapeutic effect on Beattie himself, it was written to amuse his friends in the Philosophical Society who, as a highly intelligent, well-read audience, would immediately catch most of the personal and eccentric references as quickly as the literary allusions. Beattie therefore created the satire for the kind of specialized élite for whom Pope had written, thereby making the world of *The Dunciad* as a symbolic vision of what happens when standards are allowed to deteriorate. Consequently, Beattie's readers in the society would recognize, for example, the literal as well as symbolic nature of the landscape in the allegory as they recalled the fact that, every time they walked to the Old or New Town of Aberdeen to attend the monthly meetings, they passed by the Castlegate at Castle Hill. "In very early days, the Kings of Scotland had a castle on this hill, but it having, at one time, fallen into the hands of the English, who burned the town, the townsmen retook it, razed it to the ground, to prevent its ever again being used against them, and in its place built a chapel to St. Ninian."[7] In Beattie's satire, the sound of a churchbell attends the destruction of the castle of scepticism, so that the real and the allegorical buildings are associated with the subversion of the Christian ideal of protecting the flock and with the triumph of evil forces. Both must be destroyed to preserve those they were intended to guard. The power of Beattie's allegory is greatly strengthened by this literal assocation of sceptical philosophy with such a castle in the Scottish countryside.

VI   The Achievement of "The Castle"

Traditionally, the English satirist makes no attempt to play fair with his opponent's performance; in fact, he usually feels compelled to make the enemy appear as ridiculous as possible. As Beattie himself wrote in *Dissertations Moral and Critical*, "A candid account of facts is not to be expected in an allegorical tale, written with the express design to make a party ridiculous" (p. 512). One should not find fault with Beattie's satire for showing little comprehension of the ideas of Hume, Hobbes, and other great philosophers. One should not even permit oneself to scoff at the fact that Beattie literally believed the sceptical writings of such philosophers to be so insane. Instead, his performance must be judged solely as a literary lampoon; and its success or failure must be based upon an assessment of Beattie's satiric intent. In this light, Beattie's satire is merely mildly polemical when compared to the viciously accentuated creatures who haunt the footnotes of Pope's

The Dunciad or to the brutally formed projectors of Swift's Balnibarbi. The only considerable weakness of Beattie's satiric method lies in the way he makes himself preach common sense at his created caricatures of Hume, Hobbes, and company; as a consequence, he does not let his own views appear by implication in his treatment of the figures themselves and in their distorted speeches.

In spite of this defect, however, the "Castle" is lively and vigorous in style and is faithful in its statements to Beattie's own beliefs. In the shaping of its vision of the intellect driven mad by sceptical reasoning, it is sensitive to the English tradition of satire which often superimposes its view of current life onto the heroic backdrop of the Homeric and Vergilian mode in order to accentuate the follies and vices of the modern world. This technique is supported by Beattie's use of English writers such as Spenser, Swift, and Addison, thereby creating the impression that he is the latest in the long line of angry prophets of truth that stretches back to the time of Greece and Rome and of the Old Testament. Consequently, the powerful presence of Beattie's character as a man of integrity, intelligence, knowledge, and common sense pervades the satire, unifies its rambling diversity, and enlivens its allusive dependence on other writers for support. As a contrast to the *Essay on Truth*, the vehement expression of disgust and frustration in the "Castle" indicates the extent to which the arguments and language of the *Essay* are controlled and directed; for Beattie permits himself to use in the *Essay* only the right amount of emotion and invective to appeal to popular audiences.

There is evidence in a well-known anecdote about Hume that the effects of Beattie's satire were felt by people who had never seen the manuscript or even known of its existence: "One dark night, as [Hume] walked along a footpath over a boggy ground behind the Castle, his ponderous frame fell and stuck fast in the mud. His calls brought a woman to the spot, who unsympathetically asked, 'Are ye Hume the infidel?' 'Well, well, my good woman, but Christian charity bids us help our enemies,' he pleaded. 'I'll dae naething for ye if ye dinna say the Lord's Prayer and the belief, but leave ye where I fand ye.' The philosopher readily obeyed, and the body of the Deist was laboriously extricated from the mire by the Christian."[8] Since this story was circulated after Hume's death in 1776, it is interesting that in 1767 the concluding scene of Beattie's satire shows Hume escaping from a bog in precisely this way. It is clear that the popular anecdote was spread so widely through oral transmission by those who had read the manuscript to those who had not that it finally became a popular belief about the famous atheist. Just as the *Essay on Truth* affected the popular interpretation of Hume's philosophical writings for a long time, so, it seems, Beattie's "The Castle of Scepticism" provided the public with allegorical stories that it propagated as truth. If Hume actually had such an experience, the similarity is even more remarkable.

CHAPTER 6

Minor Poetry

I Early Poems

MOST of the poems in *Original Poems and Translations* (1761), the first volume of poetry to be published by Beattie, were enthusiastically praised for their originality and fineness of execution by the periodical reviewers and by such readers as John Wesley and Thomas Gray. While many of the poems in this collection are worthy of note as highly skilled exercises in the popular modes of the time, they are otherwise without distinction, a fact that Beattie himself acknowledged by excluding them from editions of his poems after 1766 and by destroying all copies of *Original Poems* that he could find. Among the few poems that Beattie wished to preserve from the volume is "Retirement," a poem that had gone unnoticed by the reviewers and by almost all readers but that is, nevertheless, "one of the finest fragments to be found among the minor Romantic poets of the day."[1] This poem is about a "pensive youth" who searches for the truth about life in the solitude of nature. In the midst of nature's grandeur, he experiences a vision that brings knowledge of the inherent sorrow of life and that convinces him of the necessity for man to seek "retirement" in nature as the only possible means of avoiding the care, distrust, and envy of the world. Such traditional themes and images are combined in the poem with an imaginative and original setting to create a remarkable fusion of the neo-Classical and the Romantic views of thoughtful solitude. The youth's familiar "tender theme" therefore attains new significance from a more closely observed and realistically shaped setting than any poet other than perhaps Thomson had yet achieved.

Beattie's new view of nature as the means of promoting the growth of knowledge is introduced in the opening stanza where the

youth begins to recite his lugubrious meditation amid the hypnotic
sights and sounds of a solitary sunset:

> When in the crimson cloud of even
>   The lingering light decays,
> And Hesper on the font of heaven
>   His glittering gem displays;
> Deep in the silent vale, unseen
>   Beside a lulling stream,
> A pensive youth of placid mien
>   Indulg'd this tender theme (1 - 8).

In these lines, the traditional image of "Hesper" combines with a
new use of metaphor to create a new setting for the poetical figure
of youthful contemplation. As the youth wonders how to woo
"matchless fair" retirement and win her "heavenly smile" that
"smooths the brow of Care,/And stills the storm within" (25 - 28),
the theme of the vanity of human wishes grows stronger, reinforc-
ing the knowledge and consequences of the inevitable fall from innocence into experience:

> Ah, why did Fate his steps decoy
>   In stormy paths to roam,
> Remote from all congenial joy!
>   O take the wanderer home (45 - 48).

The youth's yearning is for the return in peace to "the gay dreams
of fond romantic youth" (*The Minstrel*, II, xxx). As a result, the last
stanza shows him, aged before his time, as accepting the sad fact
that "man to man acts a betrayer's part," and as thereby giving
witness to the death of his "romantic youth":

> For me, no more the path invites
>   Ambition loves to tread:
> No more I climb those toilsome heights
>   By guileful Hope misled;
> Leaps my fond fluttering heart no more
>   To Mirth's enlivening strain;
> For present pleasure soon is o'er,
>   And all the past is vain (73 - 80).

The inevitable, hopeless despair of the poem's ending, however,
belies the youth's earlier hymn of praise for nature:

> Thy shades, thy silence now be mine,
>   Thy charms my only theme;
> My haunt the hollow cliff, whose pine
>   Waves o'er the gloomy stream (49 - 52)

The rest of this stanza is a particularly fine Romantic image, which Beattie himself says "was drawn after real nature"[2]:

> Whence the scar'd owl on pinions gray
>   Breaks from the rustling bough,
> And down the lone vale sails away
>   To more profound repose (53 - 56).[3]

But the suggestion of elusiveness in the image finds its counterpart in the youth's disturbed mind; his "only theme," the charms of retirement in nature, is therefore soon interrupted:

> O while to thee the woodland pours
>   Its wildly warbling song,
> And balmy from the bank of flowers
>   The Zephyr breathes along;
> Let no rude sound invade from far,
>   No vagrant foot be nigh,
> No ray from Grandeur's gilded car
>   Flash on the startled eye (57 - 64).

This wish is a hopeless one, for such intrusion is inevitable; indeed, even the youth is an intruder. The "perfection" of nature's solitude mocks at imperfect man's desire for perfect peace and joy, for man's lot in life is to endure with patience and to seize momentary joy when he can. The youth therefore prays for solace in the faith that conquers earthly sorrow:

> But if some pilgrim through the glade
>   Thy hallow'd bowers explore,
> O guard from harm his hoary head,
>   And listen to his lore;
> For he of joys will tell
>   That wean from earthly woe,
> And triumph o'er the mighty spell
>   That chains this heart below (65 - 72).

Thus the poem rolls to its ponderous, Johnsonian conclusion: the vanity of human wishes pervades even the solitude of nature.

The originality of "Retirement" is demonstrated by the extent to which it records Beattie's own observations about man and nature. For, by his own admission in a letter to Mrs. Montagu on July 26, 1773, he intentionally recreated in the poem experiences that he remembered from his youth: "In my younger days I was much attached to solitude, and could have envied even 'The shepherd of the Hebride isles, placed far amid the melancholy main.' I wrote odes to retirement; and wished to be conducted to its deepest groves, remote from every rude sound, and from every vagrant foot. In a word, I thought the most profound solitude the best."[4] Beattie's recollection in verse of his early experiences as colored by his reading of the melancholic poetry of such poets as Thomson is very like "that phase of gloomy dreaming" contracted by all the young Romantic poets as "a sort of poetic measles."[5] Like them also, Beattie wrote that he had learned to control those "solemn and incessant energies of imagination" to fit himself "for the business of life."[6] And yet, like them, he was grateful for the experiences, as he writes in commenting on the pleasure that he found in reading Edward Young's poems: "I used to devour his 'Night Thoughts' with a satisfaction not unlike that which, in my younger years, I have found in walking alone in a church-yard, or in a wild mountain, by the light of the moon, at midnight. Such things may help to soften a rugged mind; and I believe I might have been the better for them."[7]

As a Romantic poem, then, "Retirement" shows the distinctive qualities of the close observation of nature that brings both joy and fear, of personal experience as the poem's informing principle, of the contrasting themes of the world's vanity and nature's splendor, of the lingering over "the sad vicissitudes of life," and of a new use of metaphor that transcends the poem's eighteenth-century diction. These original qualities were not recognized in 1761 when the poem was first published because readers had not yet been prepared to find them. Eighteenth-century readers could not be expected to realize that the poem's most important value lies in its pointing to and perhaps even in its helping to shape future poetic development

II   *"The Hermit"*

"The Hermit," which Beattie wrote in the autumn of 1766, is a more distinguished early Romantic poem than even "Retirement." In addition to its Romantic qualities, it is unique among Beattie's poems in that he did not publish it until long after *The Minstrel* had made him a famous poet. Meanwhile, "The Hermit" had been circulated widely in manuscript, and had been reprinted many times in periodicals and in newspapers without Beattie's sanction; indeed, it appears to have fascinated many readers in much the same way that *The Minstrel* was later to be admired. The sudden renown that *The Minstrel* brought to Beattie probably added greatly to the vogue that "The Hermit" had attained by its own merits. The great success of these two poems in the late 1760s and the early 1770s, in contrast to the lack of response in 1761 to the Romantic elements of "Retirement," indicates an apparently rapid change in literary taste that records the nature of and the extent to which incipient Romanticism was taking shape.

With greater skill and self-assurance than he had used in "Retirement," Beattie begins "The Hermit" with the sudden revelation of a new Romantic view of the world that is reflected in his accurate and sensitive poetic picture of a calm, peaceful evening in autumn:

> At the close of the day, when the hamlet is still,
> And mortals the sweets of forgetfulness prove,
> When nought but the torrent is heard on the hill,
> And nought but the nightingale's song in the grove (1 - 4).

Since this passage is as much an imaginative as a literal landscape, it marks a clear advance in the poetic use of natural objects. Man is not at the center of the scene, as he had to be in previous nature poetry if it was to be taken seriously; the scene itself demands attention and creates its own validity as worthy of observation. When man does enter, in the figure of an old recluse, a fusion of the neo-Classical and the Romantic views of nature occurs that indicates not only that Beattie was aware of the original qualities of "Retirement" but also that he was learning to improve them. When the hermit intrudes into the evening solitude, therefore, his speeches stress the tension between man's desires and his inevitable failure to achieve them; and, as a consequence, they emphasize the need for man to seek atonement in nature. The hermit himself has become a sage because, in receiving the joy and the perfect recompense of nature's solitude, he has acquired a balance between intellect and emotion. His faith has made him whole; his being is at one with the unified, imaginative world of the poem; and his words therefore have prophetic power.

For this reason, Beattie is able to breathe new poetic life into old

themes and ideas. Although the hermit echoes the common
eighteenth century theme of the vanity of human wishes, the poet
presents it in a form that is very much like the Wordsworthian concept of "earth's diurnal round," for a remarkable transmutation is
achieved in the poem's best stanza where Beattie's images of light,
darkness, and natural generation are used to present death as the
central fact of life:

> 'Tis night, and the landscape is lovely no more:
> I mourn, but ye woodlands, I mourn not for you;
> For morn is approaching, your charms to restore,
> Perfum'd with fresh fragrance, and glittering with dew:
> Nor yet for the ravage of winter I mourn;
> Kind Nature the embryo blossom will save:
> But when shall spring visit the mouldering urn!
> O when shall it dawn on the night of the grave! (25 - 32).

The hermit is speaking for all men, but his words and indeed the
whole movement of the poem were conceived by Beattie who was a
thoroughly convinced Christian. The next stanza therefore presents
the Christian pilgrim on life's "stormy path" as he should
be—stripped of his vanity and pride, well aware of the futility of
following material goals, he prostrates himself before God, the only
salvation and the only source of true freedom and joy:

> 'Twas thus, by the glare of false science betray'd,
> That leads, to bewilder, and dazzles, to blind,
> My thoughts wont to roam, from shade onward to shade,
> Destruction before me, and sorrow behind.
> "O pity, great Father of light," then I cried,
> "Thy creature, who fain would not wander from thee;
> Lo, humbled in dust, I relinquish my pride:
> From doubt and from darkness thou only canst free" (33 - 40).

When Beattie's images of travel, darkness, and light are drawn
together in the concluding stanza, the different rebirths in nature
become symbols of man's resurrection. The hermit sees a prophetic
vision of life after death, and therefore by implication of the second
coming of Christ, as the poem ends in a manner that is reminiscent
of the climax of Shelley's *Prometheus Unbound:*

And darkness and doubt are now flying away;
No longer I roam in conjecture forlorn.
So breaks on the traveller, faint, and astray,
The bright and the balmy effulgence of morn.
See Truth, Love, and Mercy, in triumph descending,
And nature all glowing in Eden's first bloom!
On the cold cheek of Death smiles and roses are blending,
And Beauty immortal awakes from the tomb (41 - 48).

"The Hermit" presents an intensely religious, sacramental view of man and nature. Moved by the power of Beattie's own belief, the poem captures with deep sincerity the spendor of Christian faith and revelation; but it also stresses the terrible finality of physical death. It therefore appealed greatly to a generation so fascinated by death that it called forth a large number of night pieces on death; treatments of the "pleasures" of melancholy, and elegies, epitaphs, and countless monuments. Dr. Johnson, for example, whose colossal melancholia was almost entirely centered on death, was intrigued and yet repelled by any form of oblivion. The fact that Boswell saw him in tears over "The Hermit" is therefore very significant. "Such was his sensibility," Boswell reports, "and so much was he affected by pathetic poetry, that, when he was reading Dr. Beattie's 'Hermit' in my presence, it brought tears to his eyes."[8] Johnson was particularly moved, Boswell continues, by the fourth stanza, which begins, " 'Tis night, and the landscape is lovely no more," and which ends, "But when shall spring visit the mouldering urn!/O when shall it dawn on the night of the grave!" (25 - 32). The poem undoubtedly evoked tears of both fear and joy, for it presents an unusually fine blending of emotion and thought about life and death within its newly conceived natural setting. The hope of eternity emerges full-blown, imaginatively achieving the fruition of its promise. The poem's most distinctive quality, then, a new Romantic rhythm and material, gave expression to the deepest fears and hopes of many readers.

This new form of poetry was to be much-used by the next generation of poets and was to reach perfection with Lord Byron. In fact, the evidence in "Retirement," "The Hermit," and *The Minstrel* of Beattie's ability to view human experience in a new way indicates that he made an important contribution to the growth of a new type of perception, especially since he learned to focus more and more

on the difficulty of being a poet in the world of men. This developing concept may be seen in the speeches of the youth in
"Retirement," of the recluse in "The Hermit," and of the two
figures in *The Minstrel* who are used as the prototypes of the
minstrel and the hermit. The faint beginnings of the Romantic
preoccupation with individual poetic identity and its relationship to
the universe are to be found stirring in these two early Romantic
poems; they progress in *The Minstrel*, as will be shown in Chapter
8, to the vision of the poet who struggles to know himself and his
place in life; and they culminate in poetry like Wordsworth's *The
Prelude*, the record of the poet's imaginative and psychological
journey into the universe of his own soul. Beattie's "Retirement"
and "The Hermit" therefore show the Romantic conscience beginning to grapple with the considerable problems of human life.

III   *"Verses occasioned by the Death of the Rev^d Mr. Charles Churchill"*

Beattie's verse-satire on Charles Churchill has been noted in
twentieth century criticism only by the very few writers who show
an interest in this eighteenth century social and political satirist. In
1927, J. M. Beatty dismissed Beattie's poem by quoting ten lines
from it "to indicate the scurrilous tone of the whole,"[9] and Douglas
Grant's only comment in his introduction to the Oxford edition
(1956) of Churchill's poems notes that Beattie "attacked the
proposal [to erect a monument to Churchill in Westminster Abbey]
in some verses, which he rightly omitted from his collected
works."[10] Meanwhile, in 1953, in the only full scale life of
Churchill, W. C. Brown cites Beattie's poem as his example of the
most extreme attacks on Churchill in the age and quotes two lines
from it.[11] Today, one has the impression that the poem is worthy of
note only as an abusive, vindictive satire of no literary value.

There are indications, however, that the poem was regarded more
highly in its own time. When first published anonymously in
January 1765, it had such a rapid sale that Beattie was persuaded to
include it in the second edition of his poems in 1766. Many of his
literary friends called it "one of the best and most spirited satires
that was ever written," and Hugh Blair considered it Beattie's best
poem to date.[12] From the beginning, however, it was condemned as
too severe by many readers, and little attention was given to it after
Beattie decided to exclude it after 1776 from his collected poems.

But its memory was kept alive by nineteenth century writers of memoirs, most of whom perpetuated the myth of its extreme severity and worthlessness.

With such a disparity between the early and modern views of the poem, one may wonder where the truth about it lies. In fact, the poem not only offers an interesting perspective on the political, literary, and religious ideas that marked the waning of the spirit of Augustan satire but is also a better poem than the modern commentators on Churchill allow it to be. In the context of Beattie's own life and writings, it provides an oblique but valuable commentary on the transition from the neo-Classical to the Romantic mode.

Churchill's reputation at the time of his death in 1764 was the main reason that Beattie wrote his poem. According to W. C. Brown, the great publicity that Churchill received in the 1760s and later was "a tissue of fact, rumor, and prejudice, for which there were ample reasons but dubious justification."[13] The anonymous *Memoirs of the Reverend Mr. Charles Churchill* (1764), the only life that Beattie could have read before writing his poem, is described by Douglas Grant as "a partisan and inaccurate sketch whose tone and matter were too frequently and uncritically adopted by later biographers."[14] Consequently, Beattie's claim in vindication of his poem in the preface of 1765 that he had "said nothing of Churchill's manners that is not warranted by the best authority" (Beattie's *Poems*, pp. 146 - 47) was probably based entirely on the opinion of his literary friends in Scotland, one of whom had suggested that he write a poem of protest against the proposal to honor Churchill. There is no doubt that Churchill's reputation for sexual promiscuity and political amorality was widely accepted as true in Scotland. The many scathing attacks on Lord Bute, the Scottish prime minister of England, and on Scotland itself that had been written by Churchill and by John Wilkes in *The North Briton* had made him the object of national hatred. In addition, the anger of Scotsmen was greatly aggravated by Churchill's scornful delineation of Scotland as a barbarous land in his satire *The Prophecy of Famine* (1763).

Beattie's poem undoubtedly added to Churchill's reputation as a lecher and political hack writer; in fact, by striking a blow for Scotland's honor, Beattie became the kind of prejudiced, opportunistic critic that W. C. Brown condemns in his complaint that "no reliable friend came forward to write about [Churchill] after his death."[15] The fact is that Churchill the man was known to Beattie only by his public reputation; and the thought that such a scribbler might be sanctified with the great writers in Westminster Abbey aroused Beattie's disgust and scorn. Seen in this light, his poem is much more than a scurrilious attack that is characterized solely by personal abuse. It is a formal, public poem that demonstrates by direct statement, allusion, and personal conviction that Charles Churchill, the public person renowned as a sensational libertine and inflammatory writer, has no right to a public place of honor and posthumous prestige. The changes that Beattie made in the second edition and the fact that the proposed monument had been forgotten by then show clearly that he regarded the poem as a satiric exposé of universal literary and political vices and follies. He therefore changed the title to "On the Report of a Monument to be erected in Westminster Abbey, to the Memory of a late Author" and substituted "Bufo" for Churchill's name and asterisks for Wilkes's name.

Of the seventy-three heroic couplets in the poem, forty-seven are directly concerned with Churchill's writings and reputation. This concerted barrage of controled invective builds to a final burst of vehement frustration at the possibility of high honors being paid to a hack:

> When to the grave descends the sensual sot,
> Unnam'd, unnotic'd, let his carrion rot
> ....
> But when a ruffian, whose portentous crimes
> Like plagues and earthquakes terrify the times,
> Triumphs through life, from legal judgment free,
> For hell may hatch what law could ne'er foresee;
> Sacred from vengeance shall his memory rest?
> Judas though dead, though damn'd, we still detest. (135 - 46)

In contrast to Churchill's performance, the rest of Beattie's poem provides a vision of order and stability through the elegant and impassioned invocation of the great English writers who had established a standard of literary brilliance and of moral worth:

> Is this the land where Gray's unlabour'd art
> Soothes, melts, alarms, and ravishes the heart;
> While the lone wanderer's sweet complainings flow
> In simple majesty of manly woe;
> Or while, sublime, on eagle-pinion driven,

> He soars Pindaric heights, and sails the waste of heaven?
> Is this the land, o'er Shenstone's recent urn
> Where all the Loves and gentler Graces mourn?
> And where, to crown the hoary bard at night,
> The Muses and the Virtues all unite? (29 - 38)

The presentation of Beattie's studied schism between Churchill and the republic of English letters is sustained to the very end where "Britannia" weeps "o'er her sullied fame" and where "the Muse, with honest zeal possess'd," seeks to "avenge her country by [Churchill's name] disgrac'd" (128 - 130).

Beattie's poem grows out of a thorough knowledge of Churchill's satires in general and of *The Prophecy of Famine* in particular. Starting with the defiant dismissal of Churchill and his writings ("Churchill, begone!") and with the fervent wish that "Faction's fire" may "expire" with his death (1 - 2), the poem then demonstrates the irreparable damage that has been done to the common good by the writer's obscene propaganda. The informing principle of Beattie's satiric technique entails the presentation of the world of English letters in terms of the very worst and the very best in literature. Churchill alone represents the extreme in bad writing; but Milton, Spenser, Shakespeare, Pope, Gray, Shenstone, and Akenside are named as the greatest writers in the language. But, even before he uses them to belittle Churchill, Beattie prepares at the beginning to support his denigration by alluding directly to Churchill's own writings. Dr. Johnson had called Churchill a blockhead; in Book II of *The Ghost* (1762), therefore, Churchill had satirized Johnson as "Pomposo, —insolent and loud, [the] vain idol of a scribbling crowd" (653 - 54).[16]

In the third line of Beattie's poem, he turns this portrait against Churchill and to his own purpose by describing Churchill's "Fame" as the "dirty idol of the brainless crowd," thereby declaring himself to be on the side of Dr. Johnson as the great arbiter of morality and literary taste. The polarity of the situation is clearly defined in the sixth line by the equating of Churchill to "Cromwell, and Catiline [and] Guido Faux." Beattie thereby prepares the way for his specific reference in the next verse-paragraph (7 - 18) to Churchill's self-portrait in *The Prophecy of Famine* (79 - 92).[17] In this ironic picture of himself, Churchill claims no inspiration from a "heavenly Muse" and "no judgment" to temper the "fires" of his "rash genius." Rather, his only "merit" is in having the "mere knack of

rhyme/Short gleams of sense, and satire out of time" (79 - 82).
Churchill also indicates that he has not the "fancy" to write of
nature nor the wit to "Coin fine epithets, which mean no ill" (88).
He is too "uncouth" to be fit "For pacing poesy, and ambling wit"
(90). As a result, "Taste" beholds him with contempt, judging him
to be unworthy of a place even "Amongst the lowest of her favour'd
race" (91 - 92).

The point of Churchill's mock disparagement of his poetic ability
is to declare the impossibility of his writing pastorals so that he may
call upon real nature to help him to compose an ironic-heroic poem
about Scotland. But Beattie, who deliberately misreads the passage
as a statement of the truth, claims that Churchill was "uninspir'd by
nature, [and] untaught by art"[7]; and he stresses the lies and
lewdness of his verses, not even granting him "one pure un-
prostituted line"(10). Consequently, in Beattie's poem, "bawling
blackguards" mistake Churchill's "Coarse virulence in coarser
doggerel writ" for "conscience, honour, slighted, spurn'd,
o'erthrown" (16 - 17). In this way, Beattie demonstrates how far
beneath "the lowest of her favour'd race" true taste places
Churchill: "Lo! Churchill shines the minion of renown!"(18). From
the implied superior satirist in Churchill's self-portrait, Beattie has
created a servile follower of the unthinking mob. At this point, as
the word "shines" makes one recall "Faction's fire" of the opening
line, one realizes that Beattie has completed his equation between
the burning ardor of unlawful dissenters and the shining reputation
of Churchill among them as a disturber of the peace. To advance
the extreme contrast between Churchill and the great writers, Beattie introduces in the very next line (19) the celestial fire of the
English imagination as hinted at earlier in the allusion to Johnson
and in direct contrast to the hellish fire of Churchill's influence: "Is
this the land that boasts a Milton's fire."

The metaphor is extended into the "one strong blaze" by which
Pope's "energy divine bade wit and fancy shine" (24) and into the
"bold yet temperate flame of ancient days" (40) in Akenside. In
fact, the metaphor defines the limits of Beattie's vision to the end of
the poem; and its implications for Churchill are reiterated often
since the poem's overriding purpose is to make plain the evil of
Churchillian political propaganda. "Faction's fire" is repeated, for
example, in "rebellion's brand" that is tossed by "Discord the
fiend" (63); in Churchill's "incendiary train" (86); and in the
"hell" to which Beattie returns Churchill at the end. By contrast,

"Milton's fire" is reflected in the "lovely spark/Of wit" that brightens the dark and shows "the gloom more hideous" (99 - 101); in "the pure diamond's flame" of truth (120); and in "Heaven's indulgent smile" (50).

Beattie's system of derived symbols and allusions belies the poem's apparently simplistic movement toward the correction of the public view of Churchill. Having alluded to Churchill's treatment of Johnson at the beginning, for example, Beattie subtly recalls Churchill's later attack on him in Book III of *The Ghost* where Pomposo's "Fame around should tell/How he a slave to interest fell" (797 - 98).[18] Consequently, Beattie compares Churchill's fame to a contemptuous Irishman who "own'd his soul to liberty enslav'd" (96), thereby reversing the roles that Churchill had assigned to himself and to Johnson. Such references are supported by Beattie's use of common satiric personifications that Churchill had also used: Discord, who is disguised as Peace in *The Prophecy of Famine* (539 - 46),[19] becomes in Beattie's poem "Discord the fiend"(62), who violently disrupts the peace of society. The liberty that Johnson stood for is ratified by Beattie, but Churchill's concept of liberty is equated to anarchy.

The dichotomy between great and bad writing is expressed by Beattie through an implied vision of heaven and hell in which writers like Gray soar to "Pindaric heights [in] the waste of heaven" (34) and in which Churchill is in league "with Wilkes and Hell" (61). Beattie begins by banishing Churchill from the civilized world that is implied in his poem and ends by pronouncing him worthy of the damnation inflicted on Judas as the most detestable of betrayers. The symbolism is supported by the use of the land of Milton, Shakespeare, and the others as a kind of mythological kingdom in which good triumphs and evildoers get their just desserts. In this way, Beattie makes it obvious that to erect a monument to Churchill in Westminster Abbey would be to ratify bad writing and to degrade the great writers already commemorated there.

By the implication of Beattie's Scottish birth and of his English writings, Scotland becomes a part of this "green and pleasant land" where the justice of earlier times is in danger of perversion by Churchillian hacks. Beattie draws the hint of Scotland's role in his poem from Churchill's *The Prophecy of Famine* where it is "the home . . . of all that is low, mean, base, and brutish."[20] In becoming the champion of Scotland, Beattie combines his native country with England into the land of ultimate civilization where great writing sets the standard of proper human behavior. His Scotland is therefore presented as the direct opposite of Churchill's Scotland. Just as Churchill's Goddess of Famine foretells the conquest of England by the Scots, Beattie shows that the real enemy to civilization is within the community itself, identifies the enemy with Churchill and his followers, and preaches the urgent need to be vigilant against him. Beattie's poem is therefore concerned with a unified Britain that is in deliberate opposition to the warring states of England and Scotland of Churchill's poem.

Beattie's vision of the land overrun by the mob, burning and looting as it runs wild, owes a great deal to Alexander Pope. In addition to such Popean images as the sight of Churchill as he teaches prose to stagger and to "limp on stilts of rhyme around the land" (82), the world of Beattie's poem is in part a parody of *The Dunciad* in which the actions and speeches indicate the effects of the spreading of stupidity and insanity throughout the land by the Goddess of Dulness, thereby putting out the light of intelligence and imagination. Beattie expects his readers to recall that Pope's goddess is shown casting "a healing mist before the mind" throughout the whole of Britain (I, 151 - 55).[21] The inevitable result is the symbolic destruction of true taste and the creation of ultimate mediocrity at the end of Pope's poem where Dulness lets "the curtain fall,/And universal Darkness covers all" (III, 339 - 56).[22] The most horrible aspect of this vision is the fact that it must occur if proper standards are not maintained: "Still her old empire to confirm, she tries,/For born a Goddess, Dulness never dies" (I, 16 - 17).[23] The conclusion of *The Dunciad* merely marks the goddess's return to her ancient realm of "Chaos and eternal Night" (I, 9 - 19).[24]

Beattie's Popean allusions show Churchill as a disciple of Pope's goddess, and Churchill's own Goddess of Famine is revealed as a new embodiment of dullness: "Hard-fated Churchill! could not dulness save/Thy soul from sin, from infamy thy grave!" (74 - 75). This reprimand is introduced by Beattie's comparison of Churchill to Milton's Satan who had "turn'd abbhorrent from the hated light" (72), and the poet thereby brings the power of the Miltonic struggle between good and evil to support the allusions to Pope. Consequently, the value one puts on Beattie's poem depends on the extent to which one catches such echoes of Milton, Pope, and others in it. Beattie's lines about rebellion's triumphing "in the miseries of man," for instance, not only contain a literal picture of mob violence and echoes of the biblical, Miltonic apocalypse but even recall the "Conflagration" which marks the absurd stage effects of productions of *Dr. Faustus* in Pope's time (III, 229 - 36).[25] But the equation of Churchill to Popean dunces is best served by verbal echoes of Pope's poem. When the Churchill in Beattie's poem is said to be "By nature uninspir'd, untaught by art" (7), for example, the reader is meant to recall Pope's lines, "Dulness and her sons admire . . . the charms, that smite the simple heart/Not touch'd by Nature, and not reach'd by Art" (III, 226 - 28)[26] As a consequence, the concept of dullness in *The Dunciad* is brought to bear against Churchill as "the blind zeal of a misjudging crowd" (108), and similar lines reiterate the Popean indictment of hack writers.

Beattie's character in the figure of the satirist dominates throughout; for he literally speaks his poem, and thereby he sets himself up as the public prosecutor who makes his appeal to the literary taste and the sense of public morality of his readers. The satirist thereby pays them a gracious compliment by assuming that they have sufficient knowledge and acumen to judge for themselves. In effect, Beattie loudly proclaims his own reputation in opposition to Churchill's; and, while Churchill literally becomes in the poem the public figure he was reputed to be in life, Beattie is presented as a writer of integrity and good sense who after long silence is moved to speak because of his exasperation at public gullibility. Beattie's role is an interesting parody of that played by Churchill himself in his own poems and of the whole satiric treatment of Scotland in *The North Briton*. In *North Briton*, Number 4, for example, Wilkes satirizes the Scottish people as if he were a Scotsman defending his country; Beattie the satirist is actually such a champion, who aims the thrust of his rhetoric at the false prophets Churchill and Wilkes.

As the spokesman for enlightened society, Beattie's aim was a high one: first, to preserve the balance between reasoned restraint and flights of imaginative joy associated with himself in the company of Milton, Shakespeare, Pope, and the rest; second, to show without fear of contradiction that Churchill's proper place was with the Colley Cibbers and the hated enthusiasts of earlier times. Aiming for the tone and authority of an Old Testament prophet, Beattie's poem sounds more like the impassioned pulpit oratory of a George Whitefield. Whitefield's sermons were often condemned as marking a revival of enthusiasm; Beattie's poem has been dismissed as an artless diatribe. Both judgments are inaccurate.

Whether one can agree with W. C. Brown that Churchill was "a major figure in the tradition of Neo-classic satire,"[27] there is no doubt that he was one of the best satirists of his time. It is clear also that, just as his poetry "has been over-praised,"[28] Beattie's satire has been undervalued. In addition, there are similarities between Churchill and Beattie that give an interesting perspective on the final resurgence of the heroic couplet as the effective vehicle of Augustan satire. In a sense, Churchill's poetry provides the justification for the severity of Beattie's poem; for, as James Laver suggests, it is "difficult . . . not to be slightly horrified by Churchill's ridicule of Scottish poverty [in *The Prophecy of Famine*], or to gloat with him over the shepherd's five brothers who had perished in the Rebellion of '45."[29]

But the most significant similarity between Beattie and Churchill lies in the way in which both poets show the clear signs of the creation of a new mode of poetry, and thereby signify the end of neo-Classicism. Most of Churchill's verse is under the direct influence of the great Augustan satirists, and only *Gotham* (1764) has "couplets . . . less like those of Dryden and Pope, and more like those of Keats, Tom Moore, and Shelley in the early nineteenth century." Thus *Gotham* "anticipates the breakdown of the neo-Classic couplet fifty years later."[30] Beattie's poems offer a much more important view of the transition of neo-Classicism to Romanticism. For he cultivated his satiric abilities only on the infrequent occasions when the need arose, and he concentrated instead on the traditional ode and elegy and especially on adapting the Spenserian stanza to the growing preoccupation with poetic identity. In fact, he created in *The Minstrel* the fundamental, simple pattern for this new nature poetry that the Romantic poets transformed into great statements about the poetic life. The relationship between his satiric verse and his nature poems therefore shows an important early attempt to cope with the tensions between neo-Classicism and Romanticism which helped to shape the poetry of the young Romantic poets.

CHAPTER 7

The Minstrel

I As a Romantic Poem

The Minstrel; or, The Progress of Genius is a Spenserian poem about the early life and training of a Medieval poet and musician named Edwin. In Canto I (1771), Beattie describes Edwin's exciting Wordsworthian experiences with nature; and, in Canto II (1774), he records Edwin's disturbing encounters with an old recluse who reveals the cruelty, folly, and vice of humanity and who tries to compensate for the consequent disillusionment and sadness in the young poet by guiding him into intellectual considerations. The poem is the first deliberate attempt in English to trace the development of the poet's own mind and imagination as it is affected by education, custom, and nature. The hero of the poem is therefore Beattie himself:

. . . in Edwin, I have given . . . a picture of myself, as I was in my younger days. . . . I have made him take pleasure in the scenes in which I took pleasure, and entertain sentiments similar to those, of which, even in my early youth, I had repeated experience. The scenery of a mountainous country, the ocean, the sky, thoughtfulness, and retirement, and sometimes melancholy objects and ideas, had charms in my eyes, even when I was a schoolboy; and at times when I was so far from being able to express, that I did not understand my own feelings, or perceive the tendency of such pursuits and amusements.[1]

In *The Minstrel*, Beattie assigns, therefore, the re-creation of his own experiences to "the character . . . of an itinerant poet and musician"; and he thereby attempts to show "the Progress of [his] Poetical Genius . . . from the first dawnings of fancy and reason" to mature minstrelsy.[2] The unfinished poem pictures Edwin's development only to early manhood, but it achieves a sense of unity from the revelation of Beattie's imaginative view of man and nature. Even though the "Progress" of such "Genius" had to wait for Wordsworth's *The Prelude* to reach its fruition, Beattie's Romantic point of view is important in itself, especially because of his emphasis upon the supreme blessings that nature can bring to man. In fact, he explicitly assigns to nature much greater significance than it had received in earlier nature poetry:

> O how canst thou renounce the boundless store
> Of charms which Nature to her votary yields!
> The warbling woodland, the resounding store,
> The pomp of groves, and garniture of fields;
> All that the genial ray of morning gilds,
> And all that echoes to the song of even,
> All that the mountain's sheltering bosom shields,
> And all the dread magnificence of Heaven,
> O how canst thou renounce, and hope to be forgiven! (I, ix)

This remarkable challenge to the traditional view of nature is followed by the equally notable statement that nature's "charms shall work thy soul's eternal health,/And love, and gentleness, and joy impart" (I, x). Beattie's new doctrine of nature's moral power is dramatically underscored by the context in which it is presented; for the poet proposes it as a poetic antidote to the morbid, melancholic self-indulgence associated with most contemporary expressions of the popular theme of the vanity of human wishes. Beattie's belief in the instinctive and instantaneous impulses of the human conscience as the means by which temporal joy and eternal happiness may be attained is presented in *The Minstrel* as a sacramental view of nature.

· Consequently, the poet boldly asks the central question concerning the futility of human desire: "Shall Nature's voice, to man alone unjust,/Bid him, though doom'd to perish, hope to live?" (I, xxvii). Beattie's answer, which is immediately supplied, asserts the poet's profound faith in the intimations of immortality that he receives from nature:

> No: Heaven's immortal spring shall yet arrive,
> And man's majestic beauty bloom again,
> Bright through th' eternal year of Love's triumphant reign.
>   (I, xxvii).

For Beattie, then, nature is the proof of God's love for man; in fact, nature can "soften and refine the soul for Heaven" (I, xviii) when man believes without question the instinctive suggestions of the divine will that are transmitted to him through natural perception.

Beattie's new kind of poetic vision inspires many fine Romantic images and passages:

> Oft when the winter storm had ceas'd to rave,
> He roam'd the snowy waste at even, to view
> The cloud stupendous, from th' Atlantic wave
> High-towering, sail along th' horizon blue:
> Where, midst the changeful scenery, ever new,
> Fancy a thousand wondrous forms descries,
> More wildly great than ever pencil drew,
> Rocks, torrents, gulfs, and shapes of giant size,
> And glittering cliffs on cliffs, and fiery ramparts rise.
>
> (I, liii)

> The crimson cloud, blue main, and mountain gray,
> And lake, dim gleaming on the smoky lawn:
> Far to the west the long long vale withdrawn,
> Where twilight loves to linger for a while.
>
> (I, xx)

> Dark woods and rankling wilds, from shore to shore,
> Stretch their enormous gloom
>
> (II, l)

> . . . in the dark east, expanding high,
> The rainbow brightens to the setting sun.
>
> (I, xxx).

> While waters, woods, and winds, in concert join.
>
> (I, xix)

> The wild brook babbling down the mountain side.
>
> (I, xxxviii)

> The hollow murmur of the ocean-tide.
>
> (I, xxxviii)

A final example is found in the oak trees that "from the stormy promontory tower,/And toss their giant arms amid the skies" (II, v). Beattie's sensitivity to natural beauty is evident in the eager anticipation and close observation of these lines. *The Minstrel* makes, therefore, a considerable advance on the visionary view of man and nature that Beattie had presented in "Retirement" and in "The Hermit." Moreover, the development of nature poetry was aided and enriched by Beattie's belief in the salutary effects of nature on human sensibility and by his own enthusiastic response to nature.

II   *As a neo-Classical Poem*

Beattie's Romanticism was just one of many elements in *The Minstrel* that appealed to its eighteenth century readers. In fact, its Romantic qualities were probably read merely as the literary recollection of earlier English landscape poetry such as James Thomson's descriptions of the seasons. Edwin was, therefore, considered by such readers as the latest of the many melancholy swains and prophetic bards who haunt much of early English nature poetry. Since Thomson, Gray, and others are the direct ancestors of Edwin and of his view of the world, eighteenth century readers could not perhaps be expected to have even an inkling of the great changes in poetic ideas and sensibility that are anticipated by *The Minstrel.* For them, the poem's main appeal lay in its blending of sentimentalism, melancholy, didacticism, Medievalism, and primitivism with echoes of the Bible, Spenser, Shakespeare, Milton, Ossian, Gray, Blackwell's *Homer,* the Classics, and many other sources. Early readers, therefore, perceived one of the poem's most important achievements to be the union and crystallization of such hitherto disparate poetic elements. Beattie himself stressed this aspect of his poem by stating in his first advertisement that his aim was to present "some topics of instruction both moral and philosophical"[3]; and, as a consequence, the union in the poem of conventional moralizing and descriptions of nature was much enjoyed by many readers. In a word, *The Minstrel* is much more a neo-Classical than a Romantic poem, as its relationship to the *Essay on Truth* also indicates.

Since Beattie began to write both the *Essay* and *The Minstrel* at the same time in 1766, he often incorporates into the poem the ideas and the attitudes that were fostered by his long distasteful struggle with metaphysics. The inclusion in the poem of such "metaphysical considerations" is probably as important a part of its autobiographical nature as are its Romantic concerns. For the many times that he left the composition of the *Essay* in frustration and disgust provided the respites necessary to renew his moral strength and his resolve to finish the essay. By concluding Canto I with the statement that "the leisure hour is all that thou canst claim," Beattie indicates that he found relaxation and "amusement" in writing *The Minstrel* when he was not working on the *Essay*. Even though Edwin's dreamworld of innocence and love was far removed from the "idle speculation" of metaphysical controversy and from the vision of speculative insanity that he expressed at the same time in "The Castle of Scepticism," *The Minstrel* was not a perfect refuge from sophists, sceptics, and infidels. The very thought of them, even in the midst of exciting recollections of boyhood, immediately called forth in the poem the vituperative "warmth" of the *Essay:*

> Hence! ye, who snare and stupify the mind,
> Sophists, of beauty, virtue, joy, the bane!
> Greedy and fell, though impotent and blind,
> Who spread your filthy nets in Truth's fair fane,
> And ever ply your venom'd fangs amain!
> Hence to dark Error's den, whose rankling slime
> First gave you form! lest the Muse should deign
> (Though loath on theme so mean to waste a rhyme),
> With vengeance to pursue your sacreligious crime. (I, xli)

There are in the poem many such religious and philosophical echoes of the *Essay on Truth*. Beattie's fight against the evils of the world underscores the great hope of both the poet and the hermit that Edwin's innocence might not be corrupted. Beattie's relationships with his students, therefore, contributed another autobiographical element to the poem; for both Beattie and the hermit are presented as kind teachers who brood over their pupils with loving care. Even the list of subjects that the hermit provides for Edwin is very similar to Beattie's course of moral philosophy and logic at Marischal College. The concern that Beattie felt both for his own students and for Edwin is reflected in his prayer of thanksgiving in which he rejoices over his own escape from "the wiles of speculative men":

> Blest be the day I 'scap'd the wrangling crew,
> From Pyrrho's maze, and Epicurus' sty;
> And held high converse with the godlike few,
> Who to th' enraptur'd heart, and ear, and eye,
> Teach beauty, virtue, truth, and love, and melody.
> (I, xl).

Such passages scattered throughout *The Minstrel* recalled the *Essay on Truth* for eighteenth century readers who undoubtedly interpreted the poem as a special kind of refutation of metaphysical philosophy. The poem therefore had a strong appeal (since lost) for an age in which metaphysical works were widely read. Moreover, Beattie's preoccupation with protecting his students because of their youthful inexperience from metaphysicians, was surely a major force in the writing of *The Minstrel* itself, for the poet's yearning after the innocence of youth becomes a central theme of the poem.

But such topical aspects of *The Minstrel* as these references to the controversial issues of the time are in effect authorial intrusions into the poem that tend to detract from its artistic unity. For they are impositions on the poem of Beattie's own ideas and feelings that he never really allows his poetic hero to grapple with; and Beattie's inability in Canto II to make Edwin's early manhood in the poet's own image is in significant contrast to the convincing manner in Canto I by which Edwin springs to life in the re-creation of Beattie's own early experiences with nature. Edwin seemed to be an original character to eighteenth-century readers, therefore, mainly because the poem transcends such limitations and achieves a strong sense of unity by its rich allusions to great writing and by its references to many popular literary ideas and feelings.

The opening stanza recalls, for example, the thoughts and the atmosphere of Gray's "Elegy written in a Country Churchyard" (1750) as the means of establishing a somber moralizing tone and of introducing the kind of world into which the young minstrel is to be born:

> Ah! who can tell how hard it is to climb
> The steep where Fame's proud temple shines afar!
> Ah! who can tell how many a soul sublime
> Has felt the influence of maligant star,
> And waged with Fortune an eternal war;
> Check'd by the scoff of Pride, by Envy's frown,
> And Poverty's unconquerable bar,
> In life's low vale remote has pined alone,
> Then dropt into the grave, unpitied and unknown!
>   (I, i)

In proper neo-Classic fashion, then, Beattie indicates at the start that *The Minstrel* is a dependent literary creation that relies greatly for its effects on the wide reading and perspicacity of its audience.

But the poem's beginning also establishes a new use of the traditional literary device whereby the poet yearns after a golden age; for, by placing the action of the poem in Medieval times and by describing his own childhood experiences, Beattie manages not only to recall the golden days of his own life but also to combine the past and the present into those moments of clear insight that were to become an important concern of the Romantic poets. Beattie, therefore, creates a world that is very much like the real world; and, as in the real world, he stresses that life is not equally hard on all people since some never listen "to the voice of praise" and are, consequently, "deaf to made Ambition's call" (I, ii). Such people are "supremely blest, if to their portion fall/Health, competence, and peace." Beattie's young minstrel is born to such parents amid the Romantic countryside where human life still has a dignity and a value long since lost in crowded cities. In this way, Beattie intentionally shifts his attention away from the setting of Stanza I, where even the paths of glory lead to the grave, to a more fitting environment for the nurturing and shaping of the poetic mind and imagination. *The Minstrel* is consequently a coherent and important statement about the poetic life because of the power of Edwin's developing personality and because of the sources of his inspiration—notably nature, great writing, folktales and folksongs, and his own independent spirit.

III *Edwin as a Literary Character*

As a distinct, clearly etched character, Edwin was a revelation to eighteenth century readers, because he embodied a fuller expression of poetic identity than the many disparate, vaguely formed notions about the poet that had been developing in English poetry for a long time. Edwin was so lifelike, that he was often compared to real people; Oliver Goldsmith's sister, for example, remarked about the great similarity between him and her brother.[4] And, of course, those who knew Beattie well realized how successfully he had recreated his own poetic youth in the figure of the minstrel. Like Beattie, therefore, Edwin was born in a remote little village and grew to boyhood amid the simplicity of country life:

> And yet poor Edwin was no vulgar boy,
> Deep thought oft seem'd to fix his infant eye.
> Dainties he heeded not, nor gaud, nor toy,
> Save one short pipe of rudest minstrelsy:

Silent when glad; affectionate, though shy;
And now his look was most demurely sad;
And now he laugh'd aloud, yet none knew why.
The neighbors star'd and sigh'd, yet bless'd the lad:
Some deem'd him wondrous wise, and some believ'd him mad.
(I, xvi)

Edwin never cared "to mingle in the clamourous fray/Of squabbling imps" (I, xvii); instead, he often retired to the forest or to "the lonely mountain's head" where he wandered all through the night among "deep untrodden groves" (I, xvii). He was also different from ordinary boys in that he was not moved to tests of "strength, dexterity, or speed" (I, xviii); detested blood sports; and was convinced that "the silvan reign unbloody joy might yield" (I, xviii). The young lad, "wrapt in wonder," was fascinated by "the precipice o'erhung with pine" and by the "foaming torrents" (I, xix); and he was enthralled when the "waters, woods, and winds" joined "in concert." In this way, Edwin learned "to prize great Nature's charms" (I, xix).

Nature became Edwin's great teacher, as he often "trac'd the uplands, to survey" the rising sun; and one of his favorite scenes was the view from "the craggy cliff" of the world below shrouded in mist (I, xx). As Beattie recalls and relives in imagination his own happy boyhood days, he concludes that Edwin was in truth "a strange and wayward wight" who was

Fond of each gentle and each dreadful scene.
In darkness, and in storm, he found delight:
Nor less, than when on ocean wave serene
The southern Sun diffus'd his dazzling shene.
Even sad vicissitude amus'd his soul:
And if a sigh would sometimes intervene,
And down his cheek a tear of pity roll,
A sigh, a tear, so sweet, he wish'd not to control.
(I, xxii)

As a gifted "visionary boy," Edwin would often seek the solitude and the melancholy of the forest at night where he would sometimes dream

. . . of graves and corses pale;
And ghosts that to the charnel dungeon throng,
And drag a length of clanking chain, and wail.
(I, xxxii)

On one occasion, he found himself near a "haunted stream, remote from man" where he was visited by a vision of fairy-soldiers dancing amid "the echoing forests" (I, xxxiii, xxxiv). This remarkable experience moved him deeply; but, since he was prepared to accept such visions without question as they were presented to him, he wandered home at sun-rise smiling with rapture "through the scenes of morn" (I, xxxvii). In winter, when the "driving snow" kept him away from his beloved hills and valleys, his fancy was fed by imaginative fare of another sort. At such times, he sat near the cheery evening hearth spellbound by the Beldame's tales of knights and feats at arms, of the "moonlight revel of the fairy glade," of witches, fiends, and spectres; and he joined in singing the "gentle strain" of old ballads with their lilting melodies (I, xliii - xlvi). But often, when the winter storms had abated, Edwin would quickly make his way to "the snowy waste at even" and would sometimes even walk all the way "to the sounding shore" and listen "with pleasing dread, to the deep roar/Of the wide-weltering waves" (I, liii - liv).

As Edwin was tutored by nature and by rural amusements, he learned to scan "with curious and romantic eye:

> . . . whate'er of beautiful, or new,
> Sublime, or dreadful, in earth, sea, or sky,
> By chance, or search, was offer'd to his view
> . . . .
> Whate'er of lore tradition could supply
> From gothic tale, or song, or fable old,
> Rous'd him, still keen to listen and to pry.
> At last, though long by penury control'd
> And solitude, his soul her graces 'gan unfold.
> (I, lviii)

Canto I ends with the "lone enthusiast" still a boy; and Beattie's vision of his own boyhood is pretty much spent at the same point in the poem since Canto II recaptures very little of the nostalgic rapture and enthusiastic joys of the first. Instead, Edwin's philosophical education effectively kills the glory and the dream of his boyhood; and, before the end of the second canto, his "infant Muse" will be refined by "time and culture," he will begin to learn "elegance" of expression, and he will develop the ambition to become an itinerant poet and musician. In the early stanzas of Canto II, however, Edwin continues to wander over the countryside as he had in Canto I; and he even discovers occasionally a magnificent natural scene that

enthralls him completely. At this time, for instance, his favorite
place of meditation is a "lonely eminence" above a hidden valley
where he is often "sooth'd by the lulling sound of grove and
stream," so that "Romantic visions swarm on [his] soul" (II, ix). But
Edwin's reverie is interrupted by the sound of a mournful voice that
echoes through the valley:

> Hail, awful scenes, that calm the troubled breast,
> And woo the weary to profound repose!
> Can passion's wildest uproar lay to rest,
> And whisper comfort to the man of woes!
> Here Innocence may wander, safe from foes,
> And Contemplation soar on seraph wings.
> O Solitude! the man who thee foregoes,
> When lucre lures him, or ambition stings,
> Shall never know the source whence real grandeur springs.
> (II, x)

In this extraordinary manner, Edwin meets the hermit, the old
recluse who is to become his friend and tutor. Meanwhile, as if he
were a disembodied voice, the hermit's solemn tale unfolds as
Edwin stands listening "wrapt in wonder" (II, xiii). The sage had
"sought for glory in the paths of guile," but "pangs of keen
remorse" had made him "rue those years of trouble and debase-
ment vile" (II, xiv). Having sought to repent in the solitude of
nature, he felt that he had at least received a little comfort from its
solitary grandeur. But the old recluse still mourns for "virtue lost,
and ruin'd man" (II, xix); and, as he contemplates the "chaos drear
in the mental world," he prays for the "eternal morn" to come (II,
xx):

> O Thou, at whose creative smile, yon heaven,
> In all the pomp of beauty, life, and light,
> Rose from th' abyss; when dark Confusion, driven
> Down down the bottomless profound of night,
> Fled, where he ever flies thy piercing sight!
> O glance on these sad shades one pitying ray,
> To blast the fury of oppressive might,
> Melt the hard heart to love and mercy's sway
> And cheer the wandering soul, and light him on the way!
> (II, xxi)

The hermit concludes his speech with this sober admonition; and Edwin stands confused and troubled in the ensuing silence. He returns home without seeking even a glimpse of the unseen speaker; but, because the hermit's thoughtful pronouncements have darkened his hopes, doubts beset his disturbed mind. Is the world, as it had always seemed to the young minstrel, a place of love, honor, and great joy; or is it, as the hermit had claimed, full of deceit, corruption, and disappointment? As the days pass, Edwin's disillusionment with his life increases: he resolves, therefore, to meet the hermit face to face and to confront him with the dilemma that the old man's speech had forced upon him. Knowing that he will probably never regain "the calm, contented mind" (II, xxix), Edwin is, nevertheless, convinced that he must at least have his doubts confirmed by the hermit.

But, after Edwin finds the hermit in the wilderness and informs him of his perplexing thoughts and feelings, the recluse hesitates to tell the youth "th' extent of human folly," for he hopes that Edwin may still be able to return to "the gay dreams of fond romantic youth" (II, xxx). The hermit relents, however, when he finally realizes that such a hope is futile, especially since he recognizes in Edwin's state of mind the same untutored, undisciplined thoughts and behavior that had led to the dissolute life of his own youth. Since the hermit adopts the attitude that he has "not liv'd in vain" if he can "improve" even "one soul" (II, xxxii), he undertakes to teach Edwin the truth about life that he himself had learned through personal experience and received knowledge. Edwin makes many times thereafter the long journey to the hermit's hidden bower where he listens to the old man's learned discourses about history, art, literature, the sciences, and the Classics of ancient writing. But, the sage is especially anxious to "curb Imagination's lawless rage" (II, xlv) in Edwin because he is convinced that "Fancy enervates . . . the heart/And . . . wounds the mental sight" (II, xli).

Even though Edwin is made both sadder and wiser by the hermit's lectures, the old man's concerted attempts to control the minstrel's imagination and to direct him into more wholesome intellectual considerations are unsuccessful because

> . . . she, who set on fire his infant heart,
> And all his dreams, and all his wanderings shar'd

> And bless'd, the Muse, and her celestial art,
> Still claim th' enthusiast's fond and first regard.
> From Nature's beauties variously compar'd
> And variously combin'd, he learns to frame
> Those forms of bright perfection, which the bard,
> While countless hopes and boundless views inflame,
> Enamour'd consecrates to never-dying fame.
> (II, lviii)

Edwin continues, therefore, to write and to rework his poems; and, in the process, he learns to cure his tendency to deface "his flowery rhyme" with ornate and conventional ideas by paying proper attention to nature which assigns "ornament [to] the second place" and gives priority "to intrinsic worth and just design" (II, lix). While "he owns [Nature's] charm divine,/And clears th' ambiguous phrase and lops th' unwieldy line," (II, lix) Edwin's lyre is also "taught to modulate the artful strain" (II, lxi). But Edwin is never to practice the art of minstrelsy in the world, for at this point Beattie concludes Canto II with his own formal lament for a dead friend; and, when he later wrote a third canto, he was so dissatisfied with it that he destroyed it and never again wrote poetry.

Beattie's failure to continue Edwin's career does not belittle his achievement in making the minstrel an important, original character. For Edwin is not only a lover of solitude and a dreamer who finds exquisite delight in indulging his melancholic and sentimental traits, he is also a pure and innocent person who is profoundly shocked when he learns the truth about human existence. But, like the Romantic poets after him, his strong belief in his own instincts and emotions enables him to compensate for the great blow to his idealistic hopes. His devotion to nature and to his imagination grows stronger, and he is thereby better prepared to become a poet in the distressing world of men. Beattie was forced to end Edwin's career and his own at this point, however, because the great model for Edwin's life, Beattie's own experiences, provided no hint for further poetic development that Beattie could discover. And yet, Edwin is not only a realistic portrait of the Romantic type of poet; he is also a convincing representation of the early stages of the progress of a poetical genius as recollected in the poet's nostalgic and tranquil reminiscence.

While *The Minstrel* was regarded as an original poem in the eighteenth century, it is doubtful, as has been indicated, whether any pre-Romantic readers interpreted it as a foretaste of future poetry. Since the poem is usually regarded at present as merely an interesting pre-Romantic fragment, it is important to stress that in its own time it was much praised because it conformed to neo-Classical principles of poetic composition. What was regarded as new in it was also judged by these standards, as is indicated in Thomas Gray's remarks about the poem after Beattie had sent him most of Canto I and an outline of his proposal for the rest of the poem. Gray replied on July 2, 1770, that he liked the poem very much and wished to see more of it. While Gray's praise is focused on the poem's "simple design" and many "poetical ideas," he astutely notes its major fault as the difficulty in finding for the young minstrel "some great and singular service to his country . . . such as no general, no statesman, no moralist, could do without the aid of music, inspiration, and poetry."[5]

Gray is anxious for Beattie to provide for Edwin "a full answer to all the Hermit has said when he dissuaded him from cultivating these pleasing arts." The result will be, Gray continues, to "throw more of action, pathos, and interest into [the poem's] design, which already abounds in reflection and sentiment."[6] Beattie probably tried to use Gray's suggestions in the third canto that he suppressed, for he seems to indicate that intent in a letter that he wrote to Lord Hailes after he had published Canto II in 1774: "Its great fault is want of fable, but that is a fault in the plan, and now irremediable. My intention from the beginning was to give rather a philosophical or didactic than a narrative poem. Whether I did right in this I know not; but were it in my power I believe I should alter my design"[7].

In pointing out the greatest deficiency in *The Minstrel*, therefore, Gray was merely reminding Beattie of the major problem that had concerned the poet from the start; and, since both writers also indicate clearly that they consider it to be a very sound neo-Classical poem, its Romantic aspects are viewed by them as acceptable adaptations of approved models. Consequently, Gray's letter continues with the predictable comment that he has "always thought . . . [description to be] the most graceful ornament of poetry, but never ought to make the subject." He concedes, however, that Beattie's "ideas are new, and borrowed from a mountainous country, the only one that can furnish truly picturesque scenery"[8]; and he seems thereby to recognize the originality of Beattie's presentation of

nature. But the thought does not occur to Gray that *The Minstrel*
shows the development of the poet's own mind and imagination;
and his silence on this matter indicates that Beattie himself
probably had only a vague notion at best that by writing about his
own disguised thoughts and experiences he was helping to create a
new type of poetry. Gray's pointed comments, therefore, emphasized as they are by his silence concerning Beattie's concept of
poetic identity, provide a conclusive statement about the view of
The Minstrel that was prevalent in the neo-Classical Age.

IV   *The Spenserian Stanza*

After James Thomson's *The Castle of Indolence* (1748), the
Spenserian stanza declined in quality, so that, by the mid-
eighteenth century, its frequent appearances were often met by the
scorn of the critics. On May 14, 1751, in *The Rambler*, Number 121,
for example, Dr. Johnson dismissed the stanza as a poetic form
because it "is at once difficult and unpleasing; tiresome to the ear
by its uniformity, and to the attention by its length."[9] Johnson's
criticism was not aimed at the stanza as it had been written by great
poets such as Spenser and Thomson, but at those many eighteenth
century imitations that failed to capture the spirit and atmosphere
of the Spenserian model. But Johnson's unqualified praise for *The
Minstrel* indicates that he had changed his mind about the
Spenserian stanza, at least as it had been used by Beattie. The popularity of the poem was probably the major cause of the great
revival of interest in Spenser in the second half of the eighteenth
century. For this reason, Beattie was often linked in readers' minds
with Thomson, the Scotsman who had earlier written the stanza so
well. Shortly after Canto I of *The Minstrel* was published in 1771,
for instance, Lord Lyttelton read it "with as much rapture as
poetry, in her noblest, sweetest charms, ever raised in my soul. It
seemed to me, that my once beloved minstrel, Thomson, was come
down from heaven, refined by the converse of purer spirits than
those he lived with here, to let me hear him sing again the beauties
of nature, and the finest feelings of virtue, not with human, but
with angelic strain."[10] Since most readers of the time shared this
enthusiasm for Beattie's Spenserian imitation, his own remarks
about the stanza are important to an understanding of *The
Minstrel*, especially since they were particularly influential on later
writers.

Beattie's first public statements about the Spenserian stanza, which were contained in his 1771 preface, show the caution of a conscious innovator that is not unlike Wordsworth's tentative claims and proposals in his 1800 preface. The deliberate apology for choosing the form, for example, indicates the disrepute it had gained and the calculated risk in using it. One senses behind every statement the certain knowledge that it will be attacked. Beattie's parting shot is typical of his prepared defense: "What some critics have remarked, of its uniformly growing at last tiresome to the ear, will be found to hold true, only when the poetry is faulty in other respects."[11] Beattie's almost exact repetition of the wording of Johnson's complaint indicates not only that he was deliberately answering the great critic as the spokesman for all those who deplored the proliferation of poor Spenserian imitations but also that he was attempting to prepare the way against great odds for a reasonable hearing of his own imitation. But, having chosen the stanza because of his admiration for Spenser's poetry, Beattie discovered that he had considerable facility in writing it; in fact, no one since Thomson had used it so well. The universal praise that *The Minstrel* received, therefore, enables one to pass over Beattie's fears of failure and to concentrate on what is really valuable in the preface.

For Beattie's preface shows his excitement over the possibilities that he saw in using the stanza. He therefore sets out "to imitate Spenser in the measure of his verse, and in the harmony, simplicity, and variety of his composition," but he avoids "antique expressions," admitting only a few "old words where they seemed to suit the subject" to make the poem "intelligible to a reader of English poetry." He chooses "to write in so difficult a measure" because it pleases his ear and seems "from its Gothic structure and original, to bear some relation to the subject and spirit of the Poem." "It admits both simplicity and magnificence of sound and language, beyond any other stanza . . . [and] allows the sententiousness of the couplet, and somtimes too the more complex modulation of blank verse."[12]

It is interesting to compare these public statements with some private remarks in a letter to Dr. Blacklock on September 22, 1766, in which Beattie reports that he has written one hundred and fifty lines of *The Minstrel* and is surprised that he is having so little difficulty with "the structure of that complicated stanza": " . . . not long ago I began a poem in the style and stanza of Spenser, in which I propose to give full scope to my inclinations, and be either

droll or pathetic, descriptive or sentimental, tender or satirical, as
the humour strikes me; for, if I mistake not, the measure which I
have adopted admits equally of all these kinds of composition."[13]
Lord Byron quotes this statement in the preface to the first edition
of Cantos I and II of *Childe Harold* as his main authority for his
own use of the stanza, thereby indicating the powerful appeal of
Beattie's influence.[14]

Byron found Beattie's enthusiasm contagious, as he continues to
tell Blacklock that he has always been fond of the stanza, for "I
think it the most harmonious that was ever contrived. It admits of
more variety of pauses than either the couplet or the alternate
rhyme; and it concludes with a pomp and majesty of sound, which,
to my ear, is wonderfully delightful. It seems also very well adapted
to the genius of our language, which, from its irregularity of inflex-
tion and number of monosyllables, abounds in diversified ter-
minations, and consequently renders our poetry susceptible of an
endless variety of legitimate rhymes."[15] In addition to its influence
on Byron, *The Minstrel* encouraged the writing of other Spenserian
poems, notably Wordsworth's "Guilt and Sorrow," Shelley's "The
Revolt of Islam," and Keats's "Imitation of Spenser" and "The Eve
of St. Agnes." Beattie was, therefore, not only "the most serious and
extensive handler, up to his time, of the Spenserian stanza,"[16] but
he was also an important theorist and practicing critic of Spenserian
verse.

CHAPTER 8

The Influence of The Minstrel

I *As a Seminal Work*

The Minstrel certainly fascinated the poets of the early nineteenth century; and, the many records of similarities between Edwin and real people suggest that he was much like the young Byron, Scott, or Shelley. The agitator John Thelwall "saw in the character of Edwin 'the faithful delineation of [his] own boyish years' ";[1] Samuel Rogers in "his imaginative boyhood . . . thought himself to be not unlike [the] hero of his favourite poem";[2] and Dorothy Wordsworth wrote the following about her brother William: "In truth he was a strange and wayward wight,/Fond of each gentle, etc., etc. . . . . That verse of Beattie's Minstrel always reminds me of him, and indeed the whole character of Edwin resembles [William] much."[3] Such evidence has prompted one critic to claim that Beattie had created "the character of a type of poet who was even then beginning to be born in the world,"[4] and another even suggests that Wordsworth "was . . . modelling himself on Beattie's hero."[5] But the truth is that Beattie himself was the very poet who came into the world in the 1770s; and, consequently, *The Minstrel,* as the record of the poet's own imaginative insights and experiences that are expressed by the personality and adventures of his fictitious hero, became for the Romantic poets a useful model of the poetic life.

The young Romantic poets were particularly enthralled by Edwin's purity, his innocence, his complete trust in his instincts and emotions, and, above all, by his devotion to nature and imagination. Edwin was the central figure in a vision of youthful promise, and his abruptly ended existence is not only a comment on Beattie's

limitations as a poet but also a harbinger of the great Romantic
dilemma of being a poet among men. These Romantic qualities
reflected the hopes and the fears of the young poets and helped to
shape their responses to experience, for Edwin seemed to give voice
to their inmost reflections. One must conclude from the wealth of
evidence, therefore, that the poem affected them significantly and
that they themselves considered its influence important. As a result,
one of the main values of *The Minstrel* is its creative power to fer-
tilize the growth of other poets. Echoes of the poem are consequently found in abundance in both minor and major poets who repeated
its phrases and cadences, who often derived their ideas about nature
from it, who used it as a model for their poems, and who even to an
extent developed their attitudes and lived their lives according to its
theories. This influence gets by far its best example in Beattie's
effect on Wordsworth, whose published poems and manuscripts,
particularly some parts withheld from print by the poet, contain
conclusive proof of the profound and lasting power of *The Minstrel*.

II *Wordsworth's Early Poems*

Even though similarities between Beattie's *The Minstrel* and
Wordworth's poetry have often been noted, credit is usually given
to Beattie for supplying a felicitious phrase here and there and for
little else. The fact is that Wordsworth's originality is often illustrated with notions that come from Beattie. Critics sometimes
quote as original Wordsworth's lines on sound which show that one
can sometimes hear the noise of a mountain stream more distinctly
at night; but Beattie wrote in *The Minstrel* of waterfalls heard from
afar in the lonely night and in "The Hermit" of the quiet evening
when "nought but the torrent is heard on the hill"(3). Of greater
significance is Beattie's doctrine, credited to Wordsworth, that rural
people, because of their closeness to nature, have a finer sense of
moral worth than the poor of a city. Even more important is the fact
that the informing principle of *The Minstrel*—the growth of the
poet's own mind—is a fundamental link with Wordsworth in its
emphasis on the influence of the natural world. The importance of
Beattie's pre-Wordsworthian attitude to nature is well-illustrated by
a remark in his "Essay on Poetry" (1776): "If [the poet] would paint
external nature . . . he must first be enamoured of her himself"
(*Essays*, p. 57).

The truth of Dorothy Wordsworth's close identification of William with Edwin is amply demonstrated in the early books of *The Prelude* and elsewhere. In 1802, for example, Wordsworth wrote a poetic portrait of himself in his copy of Thomson's *The Castle of Indolence* which shows clearly that he was aware of his striking resemblance to Edwin:

> Thus often would he leave our peaceful home,
> And find elsewhere his business or delight;
> Out of our Valley's limits did he roam:
> Full many a time, upon a stormy night,
> His voice came to us from the neighboring height:
> Oft could we see him driving full in view
> At mid-day when the sun was shining bright;
> What ill was on him, what he had to do,
> A mighty wonder bred among our quiet crew. . . .
> And his own mind like a tempest strong
> Came to him thus, and drove the weary wight along.[6]

The time of the composition of this passage is significant, for it was then that Wordsworth had abandoned for two years the first two books of *The Prelude*, which cover almost exactly the period of Edwin's career, and also the "Intimations Ode," which shows his inability to answer the problem posed by the fading of the "celestial light" of his youthful innocence and freedom. The story of Edwin epitomizes recollections of Romantic youth, and Wordsworth's early attempts in "An Evening Walk" (1787), "Descriptive Sketches" (1792 - 1793), and especially in "The Vale of Esthwaite" (1787) to deal with the problem of poetic identity show his great dependence on *The Minstrel* for inspiration.

The great extent to which he followed Beattie's lead is proved by Christopher Wordsworth's small notebook to which William added some entries.[7] The notebook, which contains an outline of "Descriptive Sketches" and also several specific references to *The Minstrel*, including two stanzas copied directly, shows clearly that Wordsworth used Beattie's poem to aid his composition. In an attempt to write of the difficult role of the poet in coping with life, for example, Wordsworth copied onto the manuscript of "The Vale of Esthwaite" the valedictory lines of *The Minstrel*: "Adieu, ye lays, that Fancy's flowers adorn,/The soft amusement of the vacant mind!" (II, lxii). By copying Beattie's farewell to poetry,

Wordsworth indicated his intention to sing a higher theme, the exploration of the growth of his own mind and imagination.

This was also the period when Dorothy saw so much of Edwin in William. But these poems were so unsatisfactory that Wordsworth abandoned poetry altogether, only to be plunged into the far deeper despair that was bred in him by the French Revolution. Coleridge and Dorothy no doubt helped him prevent a mental breakdown, but it was largely his return to poetry in 1795 that enabled him to regain his slipping stability. This revival of interest was marked by his again reading *The Minstrel;* not only did Edwin express better than even Wordsworth's own juvenile poems the poet's growing awareness of his relationship to the universe but he also seemed to Wordsworth to hold the key to his poetic future.[8] Wordsworth's scribbling of his Edwinlike portrait on the flyleaf of his copy of Thomson, as if he doubted his own ability or even his sanity, indicates, therefore, that Edwin was still the central figure in Wordsworth's inability to proceed with the investigation of his imagination. But it is even more remarkable that Edwin is prominent in the solution to this problem as recorded in *The Prelude.*

III   The Prelude

The similarity of design, aim, and scope of the published texts of *The Prelude* to *The Minstrel* underscores Wordsworth's frequent use of themes, images, and scenes from Beattie.[9] A good example is the experience on Mount Snowdon above the misty moonlight, the well-known episode that begins Book XIII. One is struck by its resemblance to one of Edwin's experiences—the same adventure that Wordsworth had used years earlier as the basis for a scene in "Descriptive Sketches." Both poets describe the view from an eminence of a huge sea of mist enshrouding all except protruding mountain tops. Both indicate the effect of the experience on the imagination: Beattie exclaims, "What dreadful pleasure!" (I, xxi); Wordsworth sees it as "the emblem of a mind/That feeds upon infinity" (70 - 71).[10] Beattie hears "the voice of . . . waterfalls" (I, xxi) rebounding; Wordsworth, the sound "of waters" as "torrents" roar "with one voice" (59 - 60).[11] Beattie's reaction to the solitary, disturbing experience is to be overawed, standing "sublime/Like shipwreck'd mariner on desert coast" (I, xxi). Wordsworth, in his well-known statement about the function of imagination, recaptures the scene in memory as the "perfect image of a mighty Mind"

(70).[12] Both poets have caught something of the grandeur and solitariness that Wordsworth saw in the statue of Newton at Cambridge: "The marble index of a mind forever/Voyaging through strange seas of Thought, alone" (62 - 63).[13] Both Beattie and Wordsworth are clearly trying to convey what it is like to be a poet at such times.

Proof that the many resemblances in *The Prelude* to *The Minstrel* were a direct influence is found in the manuscripts of Wordsworth's poem. In them one finds evidence of Wordsworth's remarkable dependence on Beattie that ranges from expunged verbal echoes considered too close to the original to the omission from the printed text of arrangements of adventures and illustrations that are too reminiscent of Edwin's experiences. That Beattie's vision of the poet who is confounded by the circumstances of his life still haunted Wordsworth long after he became a great poet is seen, for example, in "MS. Y," a notebook written in the autumn of 1804, which contains the first draft of Book VIII ("Retrospect. Love of Nature leading to Love of Man").[14] Canto I of *The Minstrel* rejoices in nature's supremacy in every charm, but Canto II shows the negation of the doctrine. Wordsworth learned to see himself as a meditative and creative soul largely through nature's influence. *The Prelude* is therefore the affirmation of what Beattie knew by instinct in Canto I and the rebuttal of the hermit's belief in Canto II that the poet should be trained in art, industry, and science alone. But "MS. Y" is much more important relative to Beattie's influence on Wordsworth because of a passage rejected from the poem by Wordsworth, a rough summary of Book VIII.

In this suppressed passage, similarities to *The Minstrel* abound; but some lines recall Beattie's poem very closely. Both have, for example, an enormous snake, fairies and fairy lore, spirits in armor, giant shapes, and dancing spirits. Still other parts show great reliance: Wordsworth's "plumes"(25) and "peacock's fan," (28)[15] for example, correspond to Beattie's "peacock's plumes" (I, v); and his "microscope of metaphysic lore" (I, li) is used in Wordsworth's "optic tube of thought" (149) and in "the glass of Galileo" (151)[16] It seems clear that the rejected part of "MS. Y" is an outline of the growth of Wordsworth's mind through infancy and boyhood, that combines recollections of Edwin's experiences with memories of his own. But Wordsworth finds himself so dependent on *The Minstrel* for the exploration of his early development that he must set it aside, not so much because Edwin's song no longer confronts him

with its sense of unfulfilled promise but because even a private account of his early experiences that shows him to be almost a replica
of another man's hero might some day be embarrassing. Consequently, he is led in the printed text to cover his tracks: "Not with
these began/Our Song, and not with these our Song must end"
(XII, 7 - 8)[17]

While *The Minstrel* offers no solution to the dilemma of the
poetic life, it does show the polarity of the problem in the figures of
the minstrel and the hermit. Both figures become prominent in
Wordsworth's solution to his difficulties with the retarding yet
restorative effect of life on the imagination and taste; Wordsworth
himself becomes a kind of Edwin grown up, and the recluse recurs
in several places. *The Minstrel* had indicated to Wordsworth the
possibility of new concepts and new directions in poetry. The results
in both *The Prelude* and *The Minstrel* are poetic journeys into the
solitude of nature; and these create in turn an imaginative
landscape of the mind to be explored and defined. Moreover, both
accounts show the need for the youthful poet to be disciplined by
the wisdom of the sage. For Beattie, the two figures remain
separate; but the young Wordsworth matures into the wise
"philosophical" poet: Beattie's "Progress of Poetic Genius" is
fulfilled in the growth of Wordsworth's mind. It is clear, therefore,
that for a long time Wordsworth thought, and, could not help thinking, a great deal about *The Minstrel*—an experience that forced
him to face and resolve the problems of the poetic life. It is
remarkable that Beattie's poem is such a seedbed of "genius." This
influence was so extensive and pervasive that one would expect to
find it, or something like it, in the work of the other young poets of
the early nineteenth century who were preoccupied with the nature
of the poet.

IV *Shelley's Early Poems*

"The Retrospect: Cwm Elan, 1812" illustrates the fact that
Shelley often used *The Minstrel* as a source of ideas, scenes, and images for his early poems.[18] As an attempt to record his thoughts
about his first year of marriage, Shelley's poem describes his
feelings about Cwm Elan a year earlier in contrast to his present
response and uses the grandeur of the natural setting as
background. The poem marks a significant advance in Shelley's
ability to imbue his poetry with intense personal emotion. The

debts the poet owes to Beattie are therefore quite remarkable, for they show the considerable extent to which Beattie's natural landscape and his picture of the youthful poet impressed themselves on Shelley's mind. There are numerous striking similarities of scene: loving the moonlight better than the day, for example, Shelley's "lingering on the wild brook's shore/To hear its unremitting roar" (11 - 12)[19] corresponds to Edwin's "Listening, with pleasing dread, to the deep roar/Of the wide-weltering waves" (I, liv). All of Shelley's descriptions have their counterparts in the settings of Edwin's adventures; and the great resemblance between Edwin and Shelley himself as he appears in his poem seems to indicate a direct debt. Like Edwin, Shelley finds exquisite joy in storms, the night, the mountains, and the roaring ocean. Like Edwin also, he expresses frustration and distain toward ambition, courtly life, and success in the world.

But the moralizing tone of "The Retrospect" is perhaps the clearest indication of its dependence on *The Minstrel*, especially since Shelley's contemporary poem, "A Retrospect of Times of Old," shows the same effects whereby its visionary elements help to create a mood of uplifting spirituality which is supported by descriptions of the mountains and the sea. These Edwinlike experiences are coupled with themes common to both poets, such as the vanity of human wishes and the paths of glory leading to the grave, that also show marked similarity to the early parts of *Queen Mab* (1813). It seems likely, therefore, that the moralizing tone and the treatment of civilization of *Queen Mab* may be traced to some extent to *The Minstrel*. Consequently, the experiences and the views of both Edwin and the hermit appear to have played an important role in Shelley's search for his own poetic identity in his early poems.

V Alastor

Alastor (1815) is a good example of the fact that Beattie had an effect on Shelley's mature poetry. The poem's relationship to Wordsworth and the whole problem of poetic identity show that *The Minstrel* was its direct ancestor and that it was a useful model of the poetic quest that provided Shelley with a valid statement about man's relationship to nature and imagination. "Shelley's Nature-poetry was a plant slow to mature . . . and it was not until late in 1815 that Wordsworth's influence became important."[20]

Before the writing of *Alastor* Shelley's nature poems were largely modeled on such poets as Thomson, Gray, and Collins, as well as on Beattie. One's feeling that Beattie was more important than the others is supported by the fact that *The Minstrel* was the only eighteenth century poem to play a significant role in Shelley's mature poetry. The fundamental connection between Beattie and Wordsworth may therefore be seen to be at work in Shelley's composition, for Shelley's excitement and disappointment over Wordsworth's poems drew *The Minstrel* strongly to his mind as he wrote. After 1815 the Wordsworthian impress on his poetry was often accompanied by the memory of Edwin's poetic pilgrimage.

Alastor not only gives symbolic expression to the great dilemma of Romanticism—the inevitable failure of the human mind to comprehend what it is compelled to create and contemplate—but also celebrates Wordsworth's youthful, revolutionary greatness and bemoans and shows symbolically the death of his poetic greatness. Consequently, in the sonnet "To Wordsworth" that he published with *Alastor* in 1816, Shelley deplores Wordsworth's desertion of his "Songs consecrate to truth and liberty—/Deserting these, thou leavest me to grieve,/Thus having been, that thou shouldest cease to be" (12 - 14).[21] In spite of Wordsworth's greatness, however, Beattie was the first Romantic poet of nature to contemplate, in Shelley's words, "Childhood and youth, friendship and love's first glow" and to weep at the knowledge that "things depart which never may return" (2 - 3).[22] Beattie was also moved to despair about his failing poetic creativity, which the unfinished state of *The Minstrel* represents. In effect, Beattie discovered the basic pattern of the hopes and the frustrations of Romantic idealism that Wordsworth and Shelley were compelled to follow.

Beattie and Edwin, Shelley and the poet of *Alastor*, are, therefore, poets who are searching for a unique poetic vision. As a result, the many similarities of scene, image, personality, and attitude between *The Minstrel* and *Alastor* are underscored by numerous verbal echoes. Beattie's "rainbow [which] brightens to the setting sun" (I, xxx), for example, becomes in Shelley "the beams of sunset [which] hung their rainbow hues" (334)[23] and the "wild brook babbling down the mountainside" (I, xxxviii) recurs as "the wild babbling rivulet" running down a mountain (524).[24] Such similarities emphasize that both poets attempt to define the poet's relationship to the world that he lives in and his visionary concept of it. Since Shelley adopts and adapts Beattie's hymn to nature as a kind of inspirational muse, his poet has the same training as Edwin. Both poets are educated by "solemn vision, and bright silver dream," by nature, by philosophy, and by the study of "the sacred past/In truth and fable" (*Alastor*, 67, 73).[25] Both poets are idealized youths who epitomize the traditional virtues of gentleness, bravery, and generosity. Led by nature's "choicest impulse," both youths exhibit the growth of the poet's mind in its active and passive moods; for, at one time, they are gleaning impressions from life and from books; at another, they are actively pursuing experience. The figure of the poet searches continually for "Nature's most secret steps" (*Alastor*, 81):[26] "O Nature, how in every charm, supreme!" (*The Minstrel*, I, xl). Both poets are also nurtured alike by vision and dream.

While Shelley's vision of the veiled maiden seems to bear very little resemblance to Edwin's vision of the dancing fairy-soldiers, she is at least sent by the "spirit of sweet human love" (203)[27] just as Edwin is taught by the hermit that "the pure passions prove/How sweet the words of Truth breath'd from the lips of Love" (II, liii). Both poets gain "Knowledge and truth and virtue" (*Alastor*, 158)[28] from such experiences. Following Beattie's path toward the truth of the imagination, Shelley seems to cast the maiden in a role similar to that of the hermit. As both visions fade away, each poet awakens to the reality of the world and pursues in vain the sense of perfection that had been lost in the process. Each poet is consequently delivered a severe shock that kills him: Edwin "dies" because Beattie cannot solve the dilemma posed by the hermit's revelation of the truth about earthly life; and Shelley's poet wanders inevitably to his death when the vision of perfection has vanished. Edwin and Shelley's poet both travel in their own ways back through time and civilization to seek the primordial source of being, and both discover not love or life but a form of death. This confrontation, which is the climax to the symbolic pilgrimage in *Alastor*, is merely hinted at in what Edwin learns from the hermit and from his own experience; but the discovery is in effect embodied in Beattie's inability to finish his poem.

In *Alastor*, then, Shelley has transformed and completed Beattie's vision of the poet's search for truth. But even when Shelley leaves Edwin's world far behind in his poem, his poet continues to resemble Edwin. For example, the cottagers, who minister to his "human wants, behold [him] with wondering awe" (256) as he compulsively wanders over the countryside all through the night.[29] The presence of *The Minstrel* in Shelley's mind, even toward the end of *Alastor*, may be seen by the repetition of Beattie's trees that "from the stormy promontory . . . toss their giant arms amid the skies" (*The Minstrel*, II, v) in Shelley's "trees that stretched their giant arms/In darkness over [the mountains]" (383 - 84).[30] Such evidence is supported by Shelley's direct allusion to Wordsworth's "too deep for tears" passage at the end to associate him with the death of the idealistic poet; for Shelley considers the decline in quality of Wordsworth's poetry to be a form of death, just as Beattie's farewell to poetry marked his own "death," as well as Edwin's. It may even be claimed that, as Shelley's poet grows old and world-weary, he becomes very much like Beattie's hermit who, near to death himself and desiring that Edwin might return to the innocence of youth, knows that the only hope lies in seeking recompense in nature's solitude, and in being "made one with Nature" (370) as Shelley writes in "Adonais."[31] Such a result is precisely what happens in the symbolic death of the poet of *Alastor*. In his own way, then, Shelley has taken Beattie's version of the polarity of poetic identity in the figures of the minstrel and the sage and has shaped a unique vision out of it.

VI   The Revolt of Islam

Many of Shelley's poems after *Alastor* show a similar dependence on *The Minstrel*. *The Revolt of Islam* (1817), for example, not only contains images, thoughts, scenes, and characters similar to Beattie's but also indicates that Shelley was influenced in his decision to write the poem in Spenserian stanzas by Beattie's example in *The Minstrel*. The appearance of such similarities throughout Shelley's poetry, which is remarkable in itself, merely underscores the great importance of Shelley's reliance on Beattie's presentation of the poetic pilgrimage through life. *The Minstrel* shows a marked advance on the tendency of earlier poets, such as Milton and Dante or Thomson and Gray, to allegorize personal experience. The poem is therefore seen as a seminal statement about the poetic life which filled an important need in Shelley's attempts to symbolize the poet's role as part of his grand design to show the necessity for humanity to choose between good and evil. The figure of the poet is, consequently, profoundly important to much of Shelley's poetry; and the image of Edwin is everpresent to remind Shelley of the innocent hopes of youth, of the compulsive pursuit of knowledge, and of the inevitable disillusionment and sadness with experience. For Beattie had created and had tried his best to explore the fundamental pattern of the Romantic search for poetic identity.

It is not surprising, therefore, to find Edwinlike, fictional characters who haunt poem after poem by Shelley and who are like spirits to be exorcised before the poet can reconcile himself to the facts of human life. In his frequent appearances, for example, the figure of the failing poet who is dedicated to the pursuit of "beautiful idealisms of moral excellence" (preface to *Prometheus Unbound*)[32] follows "Nature's moral path" as did Edwin (*The Minstrel*, II, xxxvi); and he eventually realizes, like Edwin, that he is incapable of recreating "the gay dreams of fond romantic youth" (II, xxx). Similarly, Shelley's self-dramatizations, which range between the fictional heroes of *Alastor* and *The Revolt of Islam* and the idealized self-portraits of "Adonais" and "Epipscychidion," may be traced in part to Edwin, Beattie's autobiographical, idealized alter ego. The fact that the "self-portraits exemplify that complex relationship between the personal and the traditional at the heart of [Shelley's] poetry"[33] helps one to realize how essential *The Minstrel* was to the progress of Shelley's vision. Even the autobiographical figure of the poet in Shelley's "Ode to the West Wind" owes something to Beattie, especially since one needs to view the figure in relationship to Shelley's poetry as a whole and to his beliefs about the role of poetry—just as Edwin is more fully understood in the light of Beattie's other Romantic poems, of his theories of poetry, and particularly of his own life.

VII   *Byron's* Childe Harold's Pilgrimage

While Wordsworth was inspired in *The Prelude* to recall and recreate his childhood experiences in the image of *The Minstrel*, Lord Byron actually lived several years of his youth roaming over the very landscape of the valley of the River Dee, the glen of Kincardineshire, and the rugged sea coast of Eastern Scotland that had influenced Beattie's poem. During these formative years, *The Minstrel* was available to Byron as an exciting revelation of Beattie's new presentation of nature that the young lad could use as a kind of literary guidebook to his wanderings. Perhaps, too, Byron sometimes saw the famous poet on the streets of Aberdeen at this time when Beattie must have been to him a fascinating celebrity as well as a thrilling kind of new poet. The importance of these ex-

periences to Byron's writing is seen in *Childe Harold's Pilgrimage,*
which records the poet's recollections of many of them and which
was a source of vicarious adventures with nature for many readers
just as *The Minstrel* had been in its own time. In fact, some aspects
of Beattie's vision are illustrated by many scenes, themes, and
characters in Byron's poetry, as well as by verbal echoes of *The
Minstrel.*

On the strength of such evidence, critics, until shortly after 1900,
used to assume that Beattie had influenced Byron greatly, especially
in the use of Edwin as a model for Manfred, Childe Harold, and
even for Byron himself. Basing this belief on the fact that Byron had
acknowledged Beattie's influence on his choice of the Spenserian
stanza for *Childe Harold's Pilgrimage,* such critics did not attempt
to prove the debt. In 1911, for instance, H. E. Cory wrote that in
Childe Harold Byron's "dependence in general scheme upon *The
Minstrel* was absolute and has never been sufficiently
emphasized."[34] Even though no one has since taken such claims
seriously, Cory's brief statement about Byron's indebtedness is an
important assessment of Beattie's influence:

In the sentimental Edwin roaming the solitude [Byron] saw a vast opportunity. He created the wayward Child Harold who was to have the same
irresponsible career. His travels gave him a treasure of material for a
vagrant hero of this sort who had nothing to do but wander everywhere and
express himself. For the great burst of eloquence in *Childe Harold* there
were . . . some notably suggestive passages in Beattie. . . . Beginning
with a sentimental spoiled child for a hero . . . Byron abruptly cast off the
few remaining shackles of Augustan imitation and became true to his own
fiery romanticism. . . . Thus the spirit of *The Faerie Queene* came
through tortuous paths to become metamorphosed into the spirit of *Childe
Harold.*"[35]

The unexplored implications of such suggestions hold the truth
about Beattie's considerable influence on Byron's poetry.

Aside from Beattie's popular revival of the Spenserian stanza as
an important preparation for its use by Byron, as well as by others,
the great significance of Byron's reliance on *The Minstrel* is
centered on the relationship of the poet to his fictional hero.
Because of the neo-Classical prescription to avoid placing oneself in
a poem, Beattie lightly disguised himself as a Medieval bard and
chose the poorly used Spenserian stanza as appropriate poetic dress.
His enthusiasm for the stanza and his skill in writing it provided a

stirring incentive for Byron; and the possibilities that Byron saw in Edwin encouraged him to create his own wanderer, who would recall his own adventures in Europe. In this way, he introduced the Byronic hero in Cantos I and II of *Childe Harold* in 1812 and he continued to develop the character in Cantos III (1816) and IV (1818); and Byron's attempts to maintain the fiction of Harold's identity until Canto IV corresponds to Beattie's invention of his hero who was from the beginning widely interpreted as being Beattie himself.

Since these autobiographical links between *Childe Harold* and *The Minstrel* indicate only a superficial similarity to Wordsworth's search for his poetic identity in *The Prelude*, it is quite remarkable that Edwin, who had grown into the mature Wordsworth, also developed into the most unWordsworthian of creatures, the Byronic hero. This paradox may be explained by the fact that the pervasive melancholy of *The Minstrel* drew very different responses from Wordsworth and Byron. Wordsworth, who cured himself very early of Beattie's complaint, scorned it in his journal and in *The Prelude;* but he did learn from it the need to cultivate the sense of solitude in *The Minstrel*. But Byron made the most of Beattie's hints about poetic melancholy by transforming it in *Childe Harold* into the great confessional poem of Romantic autobiography.

The crystallization of Byronic melancholy occurred as Byron was forced in the poem to focus more and more on his own poetic identity. Canto I shows that, even though Byron's alter ego, Harold, begins his pilgrimage as a more mature observer of the melancholic state of humanity than Edwin, he is still an Edwinlike fictional character, the "wandering outlaw of his own dark mind" (III, iii).[36] One suspects that Byron chooses in Stanza iii not to reveal the source of Harold's name, even though it was famous and "had been glorious in another day,"[37] because his model, *The Minstrel*, shows the poet and his alter ego only in separation. And, in the first two cantos, Byron has no more success than Beattie in reconciling the poet to his literary persona. The great difficulty of the problem, as J. C. Collins has claimed, is seen in the fact that "the first two cantos of *Childe Harold* . . . are modelled on *The Minstrel* . . . [with] the concluding stanza of the second canto . . . [bearing] a very striking resemblance to those concluding the second canto of Beattie's poem."[38] This marked return to the world of *The Minstrel* may indicate Byron's Edwinlike yearning after his Romantic youth. Since *The Minstrel* offers no solution to this dilemma, it may be claimed that, just as Wordsworth was forced to abandon the unfinished "Intimations Ode" and *The Prelude,* so Byron could not proceed with Harold's pilgrimage without a clearer definition of the relationship of the Childe's role to the author.

At any rate, after Byron had set aside his poem for four years, his Canto III (1816) showed his invention of other poetic figures to aid the exploration of his own melancholic personality. Critics have long agreed, for instance, that in writing about "the self-torturing sophist, wild Rousseau," Byron was really describing himself.[39] But it is in the Promethean qualities of Harold that one may see the increasing likeness between Byron and "the child of [his] imagination."[40] In a sense, Byron here departs forever from the child of Beattie's imagination; for he is about to surrender the pretense of the fictional hero, as Beattie never could. Byron's writing of Canto III helped him to create his own unique poetic identity, the true Byronic hero. In writing Canto IV, therefore, Byron moved "from fiction to truth. . . . [so that] the pilgrim [is not] separate from the author speaking in his own person."[41] Byron's discovery of his proper role in Cantos III and IV is marked by his inspired use of the Spenserian stanza as opposed to his competent imitation of Beattie's verse in the first two cantos. Byron is no longer dependent in any way upon Beattie's natural descriptions or upon Edwin; but, nevertheless, Byron's basic themes, such as melancholy, love, freedom, nature, imagination, and the vanity of human wishes, remind one of *The Minstrel.* Childe Harold's pilgrimage ends at the ocean where Edwin's had begun; once again the youthful poet has been disciplined by the sage.

Just as Beattie had confronted his poetic existence in terms of the minstrel and the hermit, so Byron's struggle with his own poetic insecurity is presented in the relationship between the Childe and the narrator of his poem. For, as Oliver Elton has noted, Beattie's hermit "delivers himself, as critics have remarked, strangely in the manner of Childe Harold"[42]; and Byron himself, in his role of narrator, is much like Edwin, especially in his fascination with natural beauty and human behavior. But it is even more remarkable that Byron was probably no more successful than Beattie in attempting to combine the roles of the two figures into a coherent statement about the poetic life. That supreme achievement was left to Wordsworth in *The Prelude* and to the later Byron in *Don Juan,* in which the Romantic narrator and the satiric commentator on life become one.

VIII   *Burns*

From the start, *The Minstrel* had a special appeal in Scotland, especially for those Scottish writers who tried to emulate Beattie as one of the most successful Scotsmen in gaining fame as a writer in English. Robert Burns's admiration for the poem and for Beattie's reputation, for instance, is reflected in many flattering remarks about him in both his prose and verse, in a wealth of verbal echoes, and in similar scenes and themes from *The Minstrel* in his own poems. In addition, Burns's personal life shows that his preoccupation with the problematic poetic life follows the pattern of Edwin's career; and his union of poetry and music, as will be shown in Chapter 9, was directly influenced by Beattie's views about the poet as musician in *The Minstrel* and in "An Essay on Poetry and Music" (1776). While Burns admired Beattie's example as a popular writer and moralist, Burns was affected significantly by Beattie's writings, especially by *The Minstrel,* which had a seminal effect on his composition. For, Burns "looked to such poets as . . . Beattie as to inaccesible masters . . . [and was] helped . . . inwardly . . . [so that] his originality came into its own."[43]

IX   *Scott*

Since Sir Walter Scott was also an admirer of Beattie as a man as well as a writer, his poems are often reminiscent of *The Minstrel,* as critics have noted. When *Rokeby* was first published, for example, the claim that Edwin was the prototype of Wilfred, a main character in the work, was made in *The Critical Review* for March 1813[44]; and, over a hundred years later in 1924, Eric Partridge wrote that "*The Minstrel . . .* forestalled [all of] Scott's long narrative poems of romance."[45] Such claims for influence are substantiated by Scott's poems, such as "Marmion" and "The Lady of the Lake," and especially by his metrical romance "The Lay of the Last Minstrel." For example, Scott's minstrel, who is "infirm and old," has "wither'd cheeks, and tresses gray," and has a "harp" that is "his sole remaining joy" (I, 1 - 5)[46] is modeled upon Beattie's Gothic minstrel, who has "locks and beard all hoary gray," a "bending shoulder," and a "harp" that is "the sole companion of his way" (I, iii). Scott himself was not only aware of many such debts to Beattie, but also considered the problem of developing poetic personality as expressed in the unfinished state of *The Minstrel:* " . . . I conceive one reason of his deserting the task he had so beautifully commenced, was a suspicion that he had given his hero an education and a tone of feeling inconsistent with the plan he had laid down for his subsequent exploits."[47] The type of hero and the thrilling action that Scott wrote about indicate the great extent to which he supplied his own solution to Beattie's dilemma.

It is significant, therefore, that the character of Scott himself that he reveals in his journal bears a striking resemblance to Edwin. On March 28, 1826, for example, during a rare break in the procession of visitors, Scott asks himself: "Do you love this extreme loneliness?"; and he answers: " . . . I *do*. The love of Solitude was with me a passion of early youth when in my teens I used to fly from company to indulge visions and airy Castles of my own, the disposal of ideal wealth and the exercise of imaginary power."[48] Scott's ability to perceive an accurate introspective view of himself enabled him to create, as well as many appealing heroes of action, an important public character for himself as a defender of Scottish nationality. In trying to command public opinion by painting a picture of Romantic Scotland that would amuse Scotsmen and strengthen their patriotic sense that they were both Scots and Britons, Scott was following the formula laid down by Beattie in his life and works.

X *Keats*

Robert Gittings claims that *The Minstrel* had an important impact on John Keats: "Its method and its message were adopted by Keats, particularly the latter; in fact, the general idea of the poem is one repeated again and again by Keats in poetry and prose."[49] Keats himself hinted that the poem could have had such an effect on his poetry when he recalled in January 1819 how much it had once delighted him and when he also remarked that many readers were still delighted by it.[50] But Gittings makes no attempt to prove his belief; and all other critics who mention Beattie in relationship to Keats denigrate *The Minstrel* as an example of the weakness of Keats's juvenile literary taste. Among them, however, the critics mention enough verbal echoes, similar scenes, and themes from Beattie in Keats's poetry to indicate that *The Minstrel* often came to Keats's mind as he wrote his poems. In fact, Keats's poetry reveals a much greater reliance on Beattie's poem than even Gittings realized.

XI *Spenserian Imitation*

An abundance of echoes of *The Minstrel* fills Keats's early verse, as his "Imitation of Spenser" (1817) indicates; and it also illustrates the importance of Beattie's renewal of interest in Spenser and in the Spenserian stanza. While Keats's poem drew its form, ideas, images, and temper from many sources, its main inspiration came from his reading of epics, especially *The Faerie Queene*, and from Beattie's poem. As a result, Keats's "Imitation" reflects his newfound fascination with Spenser and his long-held joy in *The Minstrel* as a Spenserian poem. But Keats's poem is as different and distinct from Beattie's as it is from Spenser's; in fact, it is more characteristically Keatsian than most critics consider it to be. The poem therefore shows Keats's powers of assimilation to bring together many recollections and allusions that begin to coalesce into a glimpse of the vision that is to be the source and subject of his great odes of 1819. One of the most important features of the poem is the way in which its accurate images of the real world emerge from and blend with its imitations of the ornate descriptions of the Spenserian mode. The opening personification of morning, for example, with "her orient chamber" and "her first footsteps" crowning the crest of "a verdant hill . . . with amber flame" quickly gives way to "many streams" that fill "a little lake" which in turn reflects the landscape and the "sky that never lowers" (1 - 9).[51] This realistic scene provides the contemporary setting that dominates the rest of the poem.

Apart from the probability that the Spenserian decorousness of Keats's poem owes as much or more to Beattie's imitation of Spenser as to *The Faerie Queene*, Keats's Romantic view of nature is the direct heir of his own experience and of *The Minstrel* which introduced such a view into English poetry. And Keats's awareness of Beattie's role in his composition is proved by direct allusion. Just as Edwin "scann'd with curious and romantic eye" whatever "was offered to his view in earth, sea, or sky" (I, lviii), Keats ends his poem with a vision of an island which is fairer than "ever charmed romantic eye" (24).[52] Clearly the hints in the poem of Keats's awareness of himself as a poet influenced by literature and life are controled and to an extent shaped by Beattie's handling of the poet's "romantic eye." The poem follows *The Minstrel* closely in its imitation of acceptable neo-Classical models, but it also distinctly

establishes the poet's own view of nature. In addition, the effects of
Beattie's exploration of poetic identity seem to be supported by
those critics who view the "Imitation of Spenser" as an unconscious
allegory of Keats's own childhood.

A similar influence of *The Minstrel* on other early poems by
Keats, such as "Ode to Apollo" (1815), "O Solitude" (1816), and
"How many bards gild the lapses of time" (1817), may be seen as a
kind of index to Keats's development while it also demonstrates his
adaptation of Beattie's major theme of the great difficulty of gaining poetic fame. It is important to note, therefore, that, when Keats
decided to write his only other Spenserian poem, he produced one
of his greatest works, "The Eve of St. Agnes" (1820), and that this
choice of the stanza was influenced by his rereading of *The
Minstrel*. But Keats's claim that at this time he could find only
weakness in Beattie's poem belies the role played by it in the composition of the St. Agnes ode. For, as Robert Gittings claims, "*The
Minstrel* . . . contributed to the new poem many echoes, and even
one character, the Beldame—the same word used by both Beattie
and Keats—who in both poems instructs the young hero in
traditional superstitution and folk-lore."[53] In addition, both poems
are imaginative and often fanciful tales about the joys and difficulties of adolescent experience; and both poems show the poet's
distinct awareness of his quickening ability to write poetry. "The
Eve of St. Agnes," therefore, records Keats's search for the truth of
the imagination in much the same way that Beattie had shown his
own and Edwin's growth.

XII   Hyperion

Keats wrote "The Eve of St. Agnes" during a respite from the
writing of *Hyperion* (1820) which was giving him considerable difficulty. One element of his dissatisfaction with the long poem
appears to have been associated with the use of *The Minstrel* as an
unfinished model of the poetic quest; for Keats's poem contains
several passages that are reminiscent of Beattie's poem:

> . . . where their own groans
> They felt, but heard not, for the solid roar
> Of thunderous waterfalls and torrents hoarse,
> Pouring a constant bulk, uncertain where.
> Crags jutting forth to crag, and rocks . . . (II, 6-10).[54]

Such recurrences of remembered scenes from Beattie reflect the fundamental link between the two poems: *The Minstrel* is the record of the poet's spiritual journey, and "the theme of *Hyperion* is the struggle of spiritual growth itself."[55] One also expects, therefore, to find evidence of Beattie's influence on *Endymion* (1818), for it is very similar to Shelley's *Alastor* as the tale of the visionary poet searching for perfection, as well as to Wordsworth's *The Prelude* as the record of the growth of the poet's mind in the form of a narrative. But, while Keats was greatly influenced by *Alastor,* he wrote *Endymion* without the benefit of reading *The Prelude;* one must therefore assign considerable importance to *The Minstrel* as the poem that laid down the basic pattern for the poet's exploration into self-knowledge.

XIII   Endymion

Keats's retelling of the Greek myth about the love of the Moon-Goddess for the youthful Endymion seems to follow the form of Beattie's poetic quest in which experience enables the imagination to progress from mere fancy to knowledge. Each hero is prepared for his destiny by wanderings that significantly affect his growth: Edwin becomes a poet, and the poetic Endymion is united with the goddess. As he writes of his hero, Keats, like Beattie before him, finds himself recalling the landscapes of his childhood and thereby begins to comprehend the meaning of the world around him. One suspects that Beattie's exploration of literal and mental landscapes helped to shape this important element in Keats's poem. It is likely, indeed, that Edwin is a model for Endymion, as Keats himself seems to indicate in describing Endymion in a letter to Fanny Keats on September 10, 1817: " . . . he was a very contemplative sort of Person and lived solitry among the trees and Plains. . . ."[56] As the need arises to describe Endymion's responses to experience, Keats often draws on Edwin's adventures and translates them into his own poetic idiom. The following impassioned speech of Endymion to the moon, for example, is a good example of passages that are indebted to Beattie:

> Yes, in my boyhood, every joy and pain
> By thee were fashion'd to the self-same end;
> And as I grew in years, still didst thou blend
> With all my ardours; thou wast the deep glen;

> Thou wast the mountain-top—the sage's pen—
> The poet's harp—the voice of friends—the sun;
> Thou wast the river—thou wast glory won;
> Thou wast my clarion's blast—thou wast my steed—
> My goblet full of wine—my topmost deed:—
> Thou wast the charm of woman, lovely Moon!
> O what a wild and harmonious tune
> My spirit struck from all the beautiful!
> On some bright essence could I lean, and lull
> Myself to immortality: I prest
> Nature's soft pillow in a wakeful rest (III, 160 - 74)[57]

There are many such passages in *Endymion* in which Beattie's "visionary boy" plays a similar role; but of greater significance to this claim about Beattie's direct influence are those places where, in spite of the differences in idiom, there are clusters of words that show direct borrowing. The following lines from Keats's work provide a good example:

> my sweet *dream*
> Fell into nothing—into stupid *sleep*.
> And so it was, until a gentle *creep*,
> A careful moving caught my waking *ears*. (I, 677 - 80)[58]

The general similarities and the italicized words in this passage and in the following lines from *The Minstrel* seem to indicate that Keats actually had Beattie's stanza before him, or in his memory, as he wrote:

> And there let Fancy roam at large, till *sleep*
> A *vision* brought to his entranced sight
> And first, a wildly murmuring wind 'gan *creep*
> Shrill to his ringing *ear*. (I, xxxiii)

Similarly, one finds Keats reworking many lines from Beattie: "Where twilight loves to linger for a while" (I, xx) becomes "Where sleepy twilight dreams/The summer time away" (II, 73 - 4)[59]; the "Soul sublime" who has "felt the influence of malignant star,/And waged with Fortune an eternal war" (I, i) is rendered by Keats in terms of Endymion's "rage," "no longer did he wage/A rough-voiced war against the dooming stars" (II, 863 - 64)[60]; and Beattie's "dim gleaming lake" (I, xx) is coupled with the love of Edwin's

father for "blameless Phoebe" (i, xiii) and with Beattie's concept of
the poet in Keats's lines where

> . . . the forest told it in a dream
> To a sleeping lake, whose cool and level gleam
> A poet caught, as he was journeying
> To Phoebus' shrine (II, 832 - 35).[61]

Keats also used Beattie's hermit as one of the models for Glaucus,
the aged recluse who has been condemned by the enchrantress
Circe to the misery of premature old age. In accord with the magic
prescription, Endymion delivers him from his wretchedness and in
turn is taught by him. In this way, Endymion learns that he may
have to suffer to be deserving of love, and he does so in much the
same way that Beattie's hermit tries to control Edwin's imagination
to fit him for the trials of life. In writing these scenes in which Endymion meets with and is taught by Glaucus, Keats seems to follow
the pattern of the meeting and the dialogue between the hermit
and Edwin. Endymion discovers the white-haired Glaucus "sitting
calm and peacefully/Upon a weeded rock" in a kind of glen under
the sea where he is resting "his cold thin feet" on "a mat/Of
weeds" and has his "pearly wand" lying beside him. (III, 192 -
217).[62] Edwin finds the hermit "seated on a mossy stone . . . in a
flowery nook" with "his harp" lying beside him as a stag licks his
"wither'd hand" (II, xxv). The fateful meeting of the ancient sage
and the poetic youth is introduced thus by Keats: "The old man
raised his hoary head and saw/The wilder'd stranger" (III, 218 -
19)[63]; and by Beattie: "And now the hoary sage arose, and
saw/The wanderer approaching" (II, xxvi). Thereafter, the
speeches of Glaucus and Endymion seem in part to be paraphrases
of the conversations between Edwin and the hermit. Glaucus's
remark to Endymion, for example, "Thou openest/The prison gates
that have so long opprest/My weary watching" (III, 295 - 97),[64]
echoes the hermit's description of "the dark shades of melancholy":
"For solitude has many a dreary hour" (II, xxxii). Glaucus even
seems to describe his own youth in terms of Edwin's life:

> I was a lonely youth on desert shores.
> My sports were lonely, 'mid continuous roars,
> And craggy isles, and sea-mew's plaintive cry. (III, 339 - 41)[65]

From such similarities, it seems clear that Beattie's presentation of the poet amid his new view of nature made a deep impression upon Keats, as did his thoughtful, melancholic musings about literature and life. In creating his first poetic hero, therefore, Keats consciously used *The Minstrel* as a convenient model of appropriate characters, scenes, themes, ideas, and images. The fact that he drew on many other authors to aid his composition underscores the importance of Beattie's contribution, for he first suggested the basic pattern of the poet's quest that is symbolized by changing landscapes. Just as Edwin alternates between elation and despair and thereby begins to confront his poetic nature, so Keats's contemplation of his solitary hero, Endymion, becomes more and more an image of himself. Only vaguely aware while writing *Endymion* that his best poetry was to be about himself, Keats finds that both Edwin and the hermit fit his present needs; and he thereby indicates his preoccupation with the problems of his poetic life, even in the midst of a long narrative poem based on a Greek myth.

XIV   *The Great Odes of 1819*

The fact that Keats could not solve in *Endymion* the poetic problems that had defeated Beattie emphasized the need to find another kind of solution. The culmination of that search, as recorded primarily in the five great odes of 1819, demonstrates the remarkable extent to which Keats surpassed Beattie's poem in quality of technique and vision. But the odes are, nevertheless, linked fundamentally with *The Minstrel* as the poet's quest after beauty and truth; indeed, they are in effect the kind of poems Edwin might have written if Beattie could have managed it. There are, therefore, many echoes of *The Minstrel* in the odes. One of Beattie's favorite words, for example, is *forlorn* ("that rugged heart forlorn" [*The Minstrel,* I, lvi] "Melancholy strays forlorn" ["Retirement" (13)]): and Keats's recent reading of *The Minstrel* with its fairy tales told by the Beldame, its dance of fairy soldiers in Edwin's vision, and its "Fairyland" where Edwin's ancestors dwelled, may have suggested "fairy lands forlorn" in the Nightingale ode, especially since a "simple bell" marks the end of Edwin's vision which "Fancy . . . [had] brought to his entranced sight" (I, xxxiii) as the "very word [Forlorn] is like a bell/To toll [Keats] back . . . to [his] sole self" (70 - 72).[66] Even if there is no significance to such similarities, Beattie's poetic pilgrimage was, nevertheless, completed in the growth of Keats's mind and imagination as he gave shape and form to the great odes.

Throughout his poetry, then, Keats takes up Beattie's major themes concerned with poetic melancholy, with the poet's quest as a spiritual pilgrimage that is reflected in his wanderings over varying landscapes and in his meetings with various persons, with the imagination as the means of becoming a poet even while it promises more than it can deliver, and, above all, with "the distinction between the true poet and the mere dreamer."[67] The frequency of verbal echoes from *The Minstrel* in Keats's poems bears a special relationship to his adoption of Beattie's themes, scenes, and characters; for they underscore the essential connection between Beattie's pattern of the poetic life and the poet's life and work as seen in Keats's poems and letters. The remarkable nature of Beattie's influence is emphasized and confirmed by the fact that Keats's reading of Wordsworth and Shelley, as well as of Chaucer, Spenser, Shakespeare, Milton, and Dante, could not relieve him of the need to recall the career of Beattie's minstrel from time to time.

XV *Coleridge*

Coleridge's poetry reveals the same kind of reliance on *The Minstrel* as that of the other Romantic poets, for one may find in his poems many verbal echoes of it, as well as similarities of scene, theme, and verse patterns. Like Wordsworth and the others, therefore, Coleridge also used *The Minstrel* as a model for his poems; but of greater significance is the fact that Coleridge himself was much like Edwin. And also like the other Romantic poets, Coleridge, it is important to note, never made a comment that has been recorded concerning the great similarity between Edwin and himself. Since it seems inconceivable that these poets were all unaware of their Edwinlike qualities that were so often noticed by others, one may assume that their silence indicates a deep-rooted preoccupation with Edwin as the personification of the largely unspoken fears and hopes of their own early poetic lives. Only in retrospect could they know with certainty how to solve the dilemma of poetic identity that had confounded Edwin. It is not surprising, therefore, even in the absence of any such comment by Coleridge concerning Edwin, that similarities between the two have been noted from time to time. Eric Partridge, for instance, writes that Beattie "managed, in a moment of keen insight, to present [in *The*

Minstrel] an attitude of mind and a disposition of the artistic temperament that might well have formed the motto of Coleridge."[68] There is even the possibility, therefore, that Coleridge was to some extent modeling himself on Edwin. At any rate, there is ample evidence that Beattie's verse often came to Coleridge's mind when he was writing his poems.

XVI *"Monody on the Death of Chatterton"*

Even though Coleridge's "Monody on the Death of Chatterton" (1794) is a good example of his indebtedness to *The Minstrel*, no critic has given any prominence to Beattie's poetry as a source.[69] It is claimed that the "Monody" is most notably indebted for inspiration to Thomas Wharton's ode, "The Suicide"; to Bowles's sonnet on poverty; and to Gray's odes, "The Bard" and "The Progress of Poesy," as well as to his "Elegy." Coleridge was clearly influenced by these poems, but Beattie was obviously also in his mind in such lines as the following:

> Is this the land of song-ennobled line?
> Is this the land where Genius ne'er in vain
>   Poured forth her lofty strain?
> Ah me! yet Spenser, gentlest bard divine,
> Beneath chill Disappointment's shade . . . (33 - 36)[70]

The model for this passage is Beattie's satiric poem about Charles Churchill:

> Is this the land where Gray's unlabour'd art
> Soothes, melts, alarms, and ravishes the heart;
> While the lone wanderer's sweet complainings flow
> In simple majesty of manly woe . . .
> Is this the land, o'er Shenstone's recent urn
> Where all The Loves and gentler Graces mourn? (29 - 36)

Consequently, in quoting the following lines as Coleridge's direct reply to Wharton and the others concerning suicide, critics of Coleridge's poem have missed its main source of inspiration:

> Is this the land of liberal hearts!
> Is this the land, where Genius ne'er in vain
> Pour'd forth her soul-enchanted strain? (13 - 15)[71]

The form, ideas, metaphors, and many of the words in Coleridge's passage are clearly derived from Beattie's poem, which itself makes much of the liberty of England, the "land that owns th' omnipotence of song," (21) and of its genius soaring "unbounded to the skies." (56) More important, however, is the claim of the critics that "the whole conception of the Minstrel 'far from Men' and gazing distractedly from a precipice on the waves below is a blend of the melancholic recluse of the 'Elegy' and the frenzied 'Bard' standing

> On a rock, whose haughty brow
> Frowns o'er old Conway's foaming flood."[72]

But a glance at *The Minstrel* shows that this description of the Chatterton of Coleridge's poem also fits Edwin remarkably. In Canto I, xix, for instance, Edwin "roves/Beneath the precipices o'erhung with pine [as]/From cliff to cliff the foaming torrents shine"; and, in Canto II, xxi, he climbs "the craggy cliff . . . /When all in mist the world below was lost . . . /[to] view th' enormous waste of vapour, tost/In billows." Coleridge's "conception of the Minstrel" seems, therefore, to draw from Beattie's poem much of its vitality and power, as well as many of its scenes, themes, and images.

XVII *Coleridge's Poetry Compared with* The Minstrel

Of even greater significance to the understanding of Beattie's influence on Coleridge, however, is the fact that the nature of much of Coleridge's poetry leads one to claim that he knew considerably less about nature and poetic identity than any of the other Romantic poets. He may be seen before 1797 as a minor poet who wrote typical eighteenth century verses; but, when he suddenly came under the influence of Wordsworth's genius, his own mimetic talent began to produce great Romantic poems. Thereafter, his separation from Wordsworth brought reversion to the type of his early verse; his reunion with Wordsworth produced his last few fine poems. This pattern in the writing of Coleridge's poems suggests not only that Wordsworth's stimulation had a profound effect on Coleridge's best poems but also that, in the absence of Wordsworth's influence, Coleridge found it very difficult to write poems that improved and transcended the sources that had inspired them. His "Religious

Musings" (1796), for example, is little better than the gathering
together in verse form of many popular religious thoughts and
feelings of the late eighteenth century. *The Minstrel* and its impact
on Wordsworth offer an interesting contrast to the relationship
between Coleridge and Wordsworth; for Beattie's poem, as it unified its neo-Classical elements with its new view of the poet in the
real world, gave voice and focus to the inevitable growth of Romanticism.

One may see in some of Coleridge's poems a similar reliance on
his neo-Classical roots and in others the brilliant manifestation of
the new Romantic spirit of the age. At its best, therefore,
Coleridge's poetry shows the poet's imaginative quest for perfection
in the friendship poems, the poet's despair over fading inspiration
in "Dejection: An Ode," the poet's journey into the supernatural
world of vision and dream, especially in "The Rime of the Ancient
Mariner," and the poet's perception of the exciting exploration of
poetic ability in "To William Wordsworth"—all themes also han-
dled by Beattie and Wordsworth. While such similarities give Beattie no claim to a place in the company of Coleridge and Wordworth
when they are at their best, they do indicate the importance of his
seminal role as an early Romanticist; and one may claim that in his
Romantic passages he wrote better poetry than some of Coleridge's
verse. For, when not at its best, Coleridge's poetry sometimes was
very much like the lifeless type of late eighteenth century verse that
shows little sign of the insistent need for change so evident in Beattie's poem. One should not be surprised, therefore, to discover that
Coleridge was not completely aware of the qualities in *The Minstrel*
which so profoundly affected Wordsworth and others; for Coleridge
remarked: ". . . I was rather surprised to hear him speak so well of
. . . Beattie's 'Minstrel'. . . . Wordsworth seemed to be endeavor-
ing to direct my taste towards the best models in our language."[73]
Such remarks are important not only because they show Coleridge's
possible misunderstanding of *The Minstrel* but also because they
clearly indicate that Wordsworth was aware of the poem's implications for his own poetry.

It is, however, much more difficult to find Coleridge's meaning
when he claims that "the title [of *The Minstrel*] ought to have been
the *Decay of Genius*, instead of the *Progress of Genius*."[74] If
Coleridge means that the poem is one of the worst models in the
English language, one must cite his use of it in the "Monody on
Chatterton" and elsewhere to show that he did not always seem to

think so. It seems almost as if he is more interested in repudiating Wordsworth's attempts to teach him than in delivering a just verdict about Beattie's poem. In either case, the evidence seems to indicate that Coleridge did not understand Beattie's vision of the poet and his world as well as Wordsworth did. Coleridge's response to *The Minstrel* also helps one understand why it has lost even its accustomed place in the latest anthologies of eighteenth century literature. For such denigration of the poem has found its counterpart in twentieth century criticism where the poem has rarely been properly understood and discussed. Even though the neglect of *The Minstrel* has been largely caused by the response to similar poems of the great Romantics, one may nevertheless, trace the roots of the present disregard for Beattie's poem to the misreading by literary critics of the casual remarks of Coleridge and Keats.

CHAPTER 9

Literary Essays

I The Evolution of Romanticism

BEATTIE published his literary essays, "On Poetry and Music" and "On Laughter and Ludicrous Composition," in a companion volume to a new edition of the *Essay on Truth* in 1776; and in 1783 he added three more literary compositions to *Dissertations Moral and Critical:* "Of Memory and Imagination," "On Fable and Romance," and "Illustrations on Sublimity." One of the most important aspects of these popular essays is the fact that they were influential in the evolution of Romanticism. In fact, they contain ample proof that many so-called Romantic ideas and trends were in wide circulation long before the Romantic poets and critics adopted and adapted them for their own uses. In addition to Beattie's advocacy of such Romantic notions, his reputation as a literary critic gained for these concepts wider acceptance than they would otherwise have received; for his influence as a critic was largely bound up with the public estimation of him as a fine poet, especially in *The Minstrel* in which he became the first English poet to recognize the importance of investigating his own mind and imagination as a legitimate poetic activity. While it is likely that no early readers of the poem realized the implications of that Romantic aspect of the work for the development of poetry, each Romantic poet grew toward maturity as he perceived the importance of Beattie's discovery that the poet could fit himself into his poetic landscape and could therefore use the traditional peregrination across the countryside as an invitation to create and explore his own mental landscape.

By 1800, however, when Wordsworth and Coleridge published the second edition of the *Lyrical Ballads* with its important preface in which Wordsworth argues persuasively for the public acceptance of poetic innovation, it seems likely that more and more readers, like the Romantic poets themselves, were realizing the seminal im-

134

portance of the Romantic elements in *The Minstrel*. Meanwhile, Beattie himself had done much in his literary essays to train readers to perceive the poem in this way; and, as a consequence, he helped prepare the reading public to accept later critical statements such as Wordsworth's views in the 1800 preface. Beattie's essays and *The Minstrel* worked in concert, for the poem prepared readers for Beattie's literary ideas, which in themselves strike the same balance as the poem between the imitation and the crystallization of earlier models and trends and the suggestion of a new visionary view of man and nature. Readers of the preface to the *Lyrical Ballads* in 1800, therefore, would probably not have had as much difficulty as readers of Beattie's "An Essay on Poetry" in 1776 in understanding Beattie's remark that " . . . if a man under the influence of any passion were to compose . . . a poem . . . [it] would exhibit an image of his own mind" (*Essays*, p. 179). Such isolated remarks scattered throughout Beattie's essays not only illustrate his concept of the poet in *The Minstrel* but also indicate his importance as the purveyor of ideas that have long been believed to have originated with the Romantic poets.

II   *Natural Description*

In much the same way, Beattie's essays reflect the great emphasis in *The Minstrel* on the power of nature to shape character. His theory of sympathy in "An Essay on Poetry," for example, which accepts as its basis the principles laid down by Adam Smith in his *Theory of Moral Sentiment* (1759), called wide attention to important notions about the emotional response to art, and probably shaped significantly current taste, and thereby prepared the way for Wordsworth and others to emphasize the "moral" influence of nature on human sensibility. But Beattie's "Essay on Poetry" provides even better examples of such effects in its descriptions of natural scenes. The Highlands of Scotland, for example, are described as

a picturesque, but in general a melancholy country. Long tracts of mountainous desert, covered with dark heath, and often obscured by misty weather; narrow vallies, thinly inhabited, and bounded by precipices resounding with the fall of torrents; a soil so rugged, and a climate so dreary, as in many parts to admit neither the amusement of pasturage nor the labours of agriculture; the mournful dashing of waves along the firths and lakes that intersect the country; the portentous noises which every change of the wind, and every increase and diminution of the waters, is apt to raise, in a lonely region, full of echoes, and rocks, and caverns; the grotesque and ghastly appearance of such a landscape by the light of the moon:—objects like these diffuse a gloom over the fancy, which may be compatible enough with occasional and social merriment, but cannot fail to tincture the thoughts of a native in the hours of silence and solitude (*Essays*, pp. 181 - 82)

On the other hand, some of the southern provinces of Scotland "present a very different prospect. Smooth and lofty hills covered with verdure; clear streams winding through long and beautiful vallies; trees produced without culture, here straggling or simple, and there crouding [*sic*] into little groves and bowers;—with other circumstances peculiar to the districts . . . render them fit for pasturage, and favourable to romantic leisure and tender passions" (*Essays*, p. 186). A final example is Beattie's claim that

persons of lively imagination, immured in deep solitude, and surrounded with the stupendous scenery of clouds, precipices, and torrents . . . dream, even when they think themselves awake, of those few striking ideas with which their lonely lives are diversified; of corpses, funeral processions, and other objects of terror; or of marriage, and the arrival of strangers, and such like matters of more agreeable curiosity. Let it be observed also, that the ancient highlanders of Scotland had hardly any other way of supporting themselves, than by hunting, fishing, or war, professions that are continually exposed to fatal accidents. And hence, no doubt, additional horrors would often haunt their solitude, and a deeper gloom overshadow the imagination even in the hardiest native. (*Essays*, pp. 182 - 85)

These kinds of prose description that were published for their own sake are not to be found in eighteenth-century criticism before Beattie; and they anticipate by over thirty years Wordsworth's attempts to show the effects of landscape on the mind in his *Guide to the Lakes* (1810). There had been accounts of natural scenes earlier than Beattie's, such as Thomas Gray's letters that describe his tours of Scotland and the Lake District, but Beattie was the first to publish such passages as legitimate parts of public literary essays. But of greater importance in these descriptions is the emphatic expression that they give to Beattie's sympathetic involvement with man and nature and to the brooding sense of gloomy dreaming that pervades the landscape and controls the imagination. Beattie's "Essay on Poetry," therefore, may be seen as an attempt by the poet to explain and illustrate the poetic impulse that had inspired

The Minstrel. As such, the essay and the poem complement each other, thereby giving important evidence of the state of Romanticism when its foundations were being laid.

III *Transition to Romanticism*

One of the most distinctive features of the growth of Romanticism in the latter part of the eighteenth century was the marked increase in the tension between the established neo-Classical view of literature and life and the growing need to find ways of modifying that view. When a poet like Thomas Gray, for example, tried to write about the poet and nature, he produced poems such as "The Bard" (1757) and "The Progress of Poesy" (1757) in which the traditional idealized figure of the poet is presented in stylized settings that are foreign to Gray's own experience. Gray's failure to create a proper poetic landscape that would entice him to explore fully his own poetic identity may be seen as an unsuccessful attempt at responding to the growing pressure to investigate the poetic life in the context of the real world. Since the type of poetry to satisfy such needs had not yet been invented, Gray had to be content to write his remarkably enthusiastic and accurate prose descriptions of nature in his letters where, as Graham Hough remarks, "we see him as an earlier and less adventurous explorer of the path that Wordsworth was to follow."[1] But Beattie was also to follow that path much more extensively than Gray in both *The Minstrel,* where he invented an appropriate form for his own poetic development, and in his literary essays, where he publicized and explored his thoughts about the poet and where he described his poetic view of the world. This kind of response by Beattie to the literary tensions of the time made him a valuable poet and critic in the transition to the Romantic mode. Beattie's flexibility in using new ideas to suit his literary purposes was a main reason that he was more successful than greater writers like Gray in dealing with the insistent pressure for change during his era. A good example of Beattie's adaptability may be found in his use of scientific knowledge.

IV *The Literary Use of Science*

Beattie's writing reflects closely the tendency of the period to see in the precept and the example of the scientific spirit of inquiry a means of improving on, or even replacing, earlier critical approaches to literature. Beattie seemed to think more and more that criticism could be improved to the extent that it might be considered perfect or "scientific." One sees in his criticism, therefore, an interesting and probably typical response of the time to the ageless yearning after permanence in art and consequently for rules to judge it. As a result, in drawing frequent illustrations from science and in accepting only those rules arrived at by rational analysis, he attempts to state the final criteria of literary judgment. In his "Essay on Poetry," for example, he tries to prove that critical taste can be stable and to name the distinguishing characteristics of poetry. Finally, he gives the terms "reason," "nature," and "truth" as the main criteria of excellence; and he then offers his proof of the longstanding maxim that the poet is to imitate nature in a reasonable way if he is to glimpse truth.

Since Beattie's great aim was to emphasize the need to strive for the kind of stability that had been accepted as an ideal of neo-Classical literature and criticism since the Restoration, his literary essays often indicate that he was trying to ease the tension between the "old" and the "new" that confronted him as a critic. His application of the scientific model of reasoning to literary criticism was, therefore, an exercise that was necessary to the development of literary thought, especially since he demonstrates the futility of such a union. For the time was almost at hand when Wordsworth, in writing of the poet and the scientist in his 1800 preface, was to make the sudden yet conclusive statement about the relationship between literature and science. For Wordsworth, there is no difference between the "truth" of the poet and that of the scientist. "The knowledge both of the poet and the man of science is pleasure," Wordsworth states; only the methods of arriving at it differ: "The Man of Science seeks truth as a remote and unknown benefactor; he cherishes and loves it in his solitude: the Poet, singing a song in which human beings join with him, rejoices in the presence of truth as our visible friend and hourly companion."[2] In spite of Beattie's shortsightedness, his willingness to choose scientific examples in illustrating literary principles must have helped to prepare the way for the acceptance of Wordsworth's views.

V   The Union of Poetry and Music

Beattie's "Essay on Poetry and Music" was also important to another aspect of developing Romanticism, for it exerted a direct influence on Robert Burns's attempts to unite poetry and music. With dramatic suddenness, Beattie's "Essay" revived wide interest in the problem that had long been consigned to the theorists by serious critics who charged that most unions in the age were vulgar and unskilled. The "Essay," as the culmination of the long debate over the conditions and principles that might best unite poetry and music, shows the complexity of the problem that forces Beattie to draw upon new developments such as the notion of music as a means of communication and the theory of the association of ideas. Beattie's basis for argument is an accurate estimate of the current attitude toward the sister arts:

Is not good music set to bad poetry as unexpressive, and therefore as absurd, as good poetry set to bad music, or as harmonious language without meaning? Yet the generality of musicians appear to be indifferent in regard to this matter. If the sound of the words be good, or the meaning of particular words agreeable; if there be a competency of hills and rills, doves and loves, fountains and mountains, with a tolerable collection of garlands and lambkins, nymphs and cupids, *bergerés* and *tortorellas*, they are not solicitous about sense or elegance. (*Essays*, pp. 162 - 63).

In spite of the apparent hopelessness of this situation, Beattie presents his arguments for the reunion of poetry and music; and he describes enthusiastically the benefits he foresees from it because he hopes that the expression of new knowledge will help to solve the problem. In this way, he proceeds to the firm statement that "Poetry is the most immediate and most accurate interpreter of Music" (p. 161). When poetry and music are well united, therefore, one can expect "pathos, sentiment, and melody, and in a word every gratification that the tuneful art can bestow" (p. 166). In fact, after such a union, music is even capable "of being improved into an instrument of virtue, as well as of pleasure" (p. 167).

Beattie's fresh, forceful approach to this difficult problem brought joy and hope to his fellow Scot, Burns, who was particularly interested in Beattie's views about Scottish pastoral music in his essay. Consequently, Burns, Beattie, and George Thomson collaborated on a collection of Scots airs: Beattie was to submit songs in manuscript and to rewrite his remarks on pastoral music as an introduction to the volume; and Burns was to "draw up an appendix to the Dr's essay [itself a treasure], containing [his] stock of anecdotes, &c of our Scots Airs & Songs."[3] Beattie's ill-health and Burns's death thwarted these plans, but Burns's letters about the proposal, which were written between 1787 and 1793, show clearly that he regarded Beattie as an inspiring authority. Moreover, Beattie's "Essay" has many ideas about the union of poetry and music that were realized in practice by Burns. There is Beattie's authoritative statement that Scottish music arose from the native folk, "who actually felt the sentiments and affections whereof it is so very expressive" (*Essays*, p. 189), and that it was not an importation from the Continent as was widely believed. One can imagine Burns's nationalistic pride swelling at such a declaration, as well as his enthusiasm over Beattie's emphasis on the virtue of tender feelings in song and his thoughts about the "wild irregularities" of ancient "fragments" (p. 189). But Beattie's insistence that music "never appears to the best advantage but with poetry for its interpreter" (p. 129) must have struck Burns as the most important critical statement ever written about the two arts. This notion of the ability of poetry to interpret music is an informing principle in the composition of Burns's songs.

Aside from Beattie's knowledge of poetry, he was able to make such important statements about the union of poetry and music because he was himself a skilled musician and an accomplished singer. In addition to his fine singing voice and his facility on the violincello and other stringed instruments that placed him in great demand as a performer at public concerts and at family gatherings, Beattie was also quite knowledgeable about the theory and history of music. The cultivation of his natural gifts as a poet, a musician, and a singer enabled him to bring new ideas and a new perspective to the longstanding problems associated with the sister arts and to provide thereby important hints for further development by Burns. Burns immediately recognized an authoritative note of promise in these hints because he sensed that Beattie possessed, as he himself did, the proper combination of knowledge and skill as both a poet and a musician to supply new insight to and new hope for the solution of the disunion of the two arts. Burns's great success was thereby built in the image of Beattie's prophetic suggestions for reuniting poetry and music.

VI *Imagination*

An even more impressive example of Beattie's contribution to the development of Romantic criticism may be found in his remarks about the imagination in his essay "Of Memory and Imagination" (1783). Taking his lead from William Duff's *Essay on Original*

Genius (1767), Beattie became one of the most important pre-Coleridgean critics of the imagination by assigning much greater powers to it than earlier writers had. Beattie also added to the knowledge about the changing concept of imagination by arguing strenuously against the statements of some earlier critics; he disagrees with Addison, for example, that sight alone "furnishes the Imagination with its ideas" (*Dissertations*, p. 73). He claims that Addison's expression is too loose in seeming to use idea and image synonymously: ". . . we cannot have a single image in the fancy, that did not make its first entrance through the sight" (p. 73). This statement is nonsense, Beattie claims, for it denies imaginative power to blind persons; and he then cites the case of the Scotsman, Thomas Blacklock, who had lost his sight as a baby but who became a very imaginative poet. Beattie also tries to refute Hume's notion that memory and imagination may be distinguished "according to the liveliness or faintness of the ideas suggested by the one, or by the other" (p. 6).

Beattie disagrees with some of his contemporaries, notably Edmund Burke, Alexander Gerard, and Lord Kames, over the scope of imaginative activity. Like them, Beattie follows Hobbes and Locke in assuming that the imagination is governed by the laws of association; but, unlike them, he investigates other possibilities and then claims that the imagination has two important functions that are based on the way ideas are associated in the mind. Imagination's first role is the conceiving of ideas "as they are in themselves without any view of their reality," (p. 71) and the second is the creation of new forms from the ideas and notions derived from experience. Even though Beattie had started this general account of imagination by stating that "Imagination and Fancy are not perfectly synonymous" (p. 72), he ascribes both descriptions to "the Imagination or Fancy" (p. 74); and he then seems to contradict himself by emphasizing the "combining power" of the second as more important. But years later, in Volume I of *Elements of Moral Science* (1790), he corrected this discrepancy in summarizing his essay on imagination: "Imagination [as] employed in its more trivial exertions is often called Fancy" (p. 104). In assigning the role of the conceiving of ideas as they really are to fancy and the creation of new forms to imagination, Beattie was merely echoing the distinction between the two powers of the mind that had been perceived vaguely throughout the neo-Classical era and that had had its first distinctive crystallization in Duff's *Essay*.

It seems clear that long before Coleridge's celebrated definition

of imagination and fancy in his *Biographia Literaria* (1817), the two
terms were not always used synonymously, as Coleridge seemed to
think. In fact, Beattie's remarks show that the distinction was widely circulated while Coleridge was still a child. Even though fancy
and imagination are often the same, Beattie writes, they sometimes
perform differently. They are therefore names for the same faculty;
but imagination is applied to its more solemn use: "A witty author
has a lively Fancy; but a sublime poet is said to possess vast
Imagination" (*Dissertations*, p. 72). In this way, Beattie preserved
and explained the common eighteenth century theory about the imaginative and fanciful powers of the poetic mind; and, as a consequence, he provided a remarkably accurate forecast of Coleridge's
distinction between fancy and imagination.

VII   *Anticipation of Wordsworth's Criticism*

The anticipation of Coleridge's ideas is one of the many ways in
which Beattie's literary essays foreshadow the thoughts of Romantic
critics. There are, for example, many similarities in the essays to
Wordsworth's statements about literary theory and practice that indicate that Wordsworth, in shaping the attitudes of his readers,
called attention to many more notions already implanted in their
minds than has been realized. Beattie's doctrine of sympathy—the
power that enables one to appreciate and enjoy art—is prophetic of
Wordsworth's poet who finds everywhere "objects that immediately
excite in him sympathies . . . accompanied by an over-balance of
enjoyment."[4] For both critics the power of sympathy permeates the
poetic process, affecting even inanimate objects. "We sympathize
. . . even with things inanimate," Beattie writes (*Essays*, p. 195);
and Wordsworth echoes: "Things inanimate speak to the social
reason's inner senses, With inarticulate language."[5] The fact is that
both critics cover much the same ground and arrive at much the
same conclusions. A good example of their overall affinities may be
seen in their lists of the powers of the poetic mind:

Beattie's List (*Dissertations*, p. 166)	Wordsworth's List (1815 preface)[6]
1. Distinct apprehension	1. Observation and Description
2. Sympathy, or sensibility of heart	2. Sensibility
3. Acuteness of taste	3. Reflection
4. A lively and correct imagination	4. Imagination and fancy
5. Judgment	5. Invention
	6. Judgment

Both Beattie and Wordsworth reacted strenuously against the elaborate diction of neo-Classical poetry. Wordsworth delivered a severe shock to so-called "poetical language" in his 1800 preface: ". . . the language of a large portion of every good poem . . . must necessarily, except with reference to metre, in no respect differ from that of good prose. . . . Some of the most interesting parts of the best poems will be found to be strictly the language of prose when prose is well written."[7] But Beattie had made much the same statement in his "Essay on Poetry" in 1776: "Many passages there are of exquisite poetry, wherein not a single phrase occurs, that might not be used in prose" (*Essays*, p. 247). Consequently, Beattie and Wordsworth both stress that rhythm is the most characteristic feature of poetry. "Prose and Verse are opposites, but Prose and Poetry may be consistent," Beattie writes (*Dissertations*, p. 518); and Wordsworth claims that the "antithesis to Prose is Metre."[8] The poet must therefore search for "the most appropriate language," which for Wordsworth is that "really used by men"[9] and for Beattie "the universal language of men," for "common people speak and look what they think . . . [and] affect no sympathies which they do not feel" (*Essays*, p. 287).

For Wordsworth, the poet is a man of extraordinary sensibility, enthusiasm, and tenderness who recollects emotion in tranquility and recaptures its spontaneous overflow in poems. The language that is appropriate to these "passions . . . must necessarily be dignified and variegated, and alive with metaphors and figures."[10] Beattie's views about the writing of poetry, which he first delivered to his students in 1762 and then published in his "Essay on Poetry" in 1776, are remarkably similar to Wordsworth's. When the "pathos of composition" arises in Beattie's poet, he cultivates "a peculiar liveliness of fancy and sensibility of heart," which heightens his excitement and pleasure, "as long at least as he employs himself in framing of words for them" (p. 57). This process directs the poet's thoughts and gives "a peculiar colour to his language" that awakens "corresponding sympathies in the reader" (p. 56). Proper images and figures consequently present themselves to his mind because they are so "*natural* . . . that it would be impossible to imitate the language without them" (p. 264).

It is clear from *The Minstrel* and his "Essay on Poetry" that Beattie agrees in general with Wordsworth's beliefs concerning the proper subject matter of poetry. Both writers stress the natural world and its ability to mould character and both try to preserve the "particular" while depicting "general" nature. Wordsworth's poet, who rejoices "more than other men in the spirit of life that is in him," looks for "passions and volitions" similar to his own "in the goings-on of the Universe" and is "habitually impelled to create them where he does not find them."[11] Beattie too believes that "our affections are . . . the medium through which we may be said to survey ourselves and everything else" (*Dissertations*, p. 521). Wordsworth sees the universe as dynamic and organic, while Beattie writes that "everything in nature is complex in itself, and bears innumerable relations to other things" (*Essays*, p. 52).

For both Beattie and Wordsworth, the imagination, the judgment, and the moral sense combine to create poetry that shows man as its main preoccupation. Beattie anticipates almost exactly Wordsworth's statement that the poet's "passions and thoughts and feelings are the general passions and thoughts and feelings of man"[12]: ". . . the true poet addresses himself to the passions and sympathies of mankind, which, till his own be raised, he cannot hope to do with success" (*Essays*, p. 287). But, when he is successful, the poet shows that "nothing in nature so powerfully touches our hearts, or gives so great variety of exercise to our moral and intellectual facilities, as man" (p. 36). Wordsworth considers "the mind of man as naturally the mirror of the fairest and most interesting properties of nature."[13] Such remarkable similarities of attitude, ideas, and aims indicate not only that Beattie possessed sound literary taste and judgment but that he also demonstrated a significant awareness of and influence on the developing concept of eighteenth century Romanticism, as well as the considerable ability to give popular expression to important current notions. There is even the possibility that some of these thoughts may have originated with Beattie.

It is an interesting fact that, aside from the criticism of Coleridge and Wordsworth, the prose of the other Romantic critics shows little direct reflection of Beattie's ideas. The reason for this fact, however, is clear; for the knowledge that Wordsworth was the great pioneer of Romantic criticism in his many pronouncements in the 1800 preface and elsewhere enabled the others to assume public awareness of such ideas and consequently to proceed with the important task at hand—the discussion of current poetry. What has been lost sight of is the extent to which Beattie had prepared readers for the acceptance of the statements of Wordsworth and the others. In this sense, one may claim considerable importance for Beattie's public instruction in literature and criticism. One can only wonder, indeed, how much more opposition Wordsworth and the others would have met if Beattie had not published his literary essays.

VIII   *Other Important Literary Concerns*

It is characteristic of Beattie's literary essays as pre-Romantic documents that all of his hints that anticipate later Romantic attitudes and ideas are scattered apparently at random wherever they occur to Beattie as appropriate comments on or illustrations of the matter at hand. While this situation reflects the incipient state of eighteenth century Romanticism, it is also characteristic of the essays that they present Beattie's predominantly orthodox, neo-Classical thoughts and principles in a logically ordered, amply illustrated, and clearly conceived pattern. Beattie's main aim as a critic, therefore, was to guide his readers by expressing his considered judgments of the best literary works and opinions of the past and to use such judgments as the basis for the study of contemporary works. As such, his essays are dominated by his orderly, thoughtful presentation of familiar, accepted beliefs and assumptions. His studied expression of his literary views in which new ideas and attitudes appear to grow naturally out of his otherwise orthodox opinions and principles is entirely consistent with the proper role of the critic as Beattie defined it in the chapter entitled "Of Taste, and its Improvement" in his essay "Of Memory and Imagination" (1783).

IX   *The Role of the Critic*

For Beattie, the critic had to possess sound taste and an active imagination so that he could quickly comprehend an author's purpose and thereby follow "the connection of his thoughts, [form] the same view of things which he had formed, and clearly [conceive] the several images or ideas which the artist describes or delineates" (*Dissertations*, p. 166). While Beattie believes that the best critics are those "who think with precision," he stresses that all critics must strive to preserve "the native vigour of the mind" from the "superficial medley of knowledge" that is inevitably produced when the critic allows his own "lively imagination" to blind him to the greatness of the creative artist (p. 170). Only by knowing his humble place and keeping it, therefore, can the critic hope to develop the "capacity of being easily, strongly, and agreeably affected with sublimity, beauty, harmony, and exact imitation" (p. 173). But he must also take care not to be too discriminating: "If an author abound in beauties, let his blemishes be forgotten" (p. 178). The true poet touches the heart, Beattie claims, and the true critic "has a heart capable of being touched . . . and of feeling the full effect of . . . [an author's] composition" (p. 182). The true critic is one in whom sympathy, imagination, taste, and judgment unite to produce writings that perceive "the reality of things" and thereby show "the truth." This well-balanced view of the proper relationship between criticism and literature is maintained by Beattie throughout all of his own writings.

X   The Eighteenth Century Novel

Aside from the importance of Beattie's pre-Romantic passages and of his admirable persistence in defining the role of the critic, and of playing it himself, as subservient to the creative artist, his essays are notable for his treatment of eighteenth century writers. In fact, he was among the first to write extensively about the novel in "On Fable and Romance" (1783) in which one may find opinions about Miguel de Cervantes, Daniel Defoe, Samuel Richardson, Tobias Smollett, and Henry Fielding that are still valid and that in their own time influenced the improvement of popular attitudes toward the new genre. "On Fable and Romance" also illustrates the balance in Beattie's criticism between established views and the presentation of new topics, the tension between the didactic moralist and the enthusiastic discoverer of novel ideas, and the contention between the intense preacher and the gentle teacher. As Beattie's contribution to the many eighteenth century theories about the origin of romance, his essay uses Richard Hurd's *Letters on Chivalry and Romance* (1762) as the basis for tracing the development of chivalry from the fall of the Roman Empire to its great flowering in feudal Europe and for evaluating the Romantic epics of the Renaissance, such as Spenser's *Faerie Queene*, as well as for assessing the value to poetry of chivalry, knight-errantry, and Medieval superstition.

In this way, Beattie pays tribute to Hurd as the first eighteenth century critic to recognize the importance of reopening the controversy concerning romantic subject and epic form; but Beattie goes much farther than Hurd by showing that "Modern Romance" is the direct heir of the old fable and romance and by devising categories for the new works of romance that are derived from the treatment of the older literary forms. But Beattie's use of such terms as "serious historical romance," "poetical comical romance," and other variations is not nearly as important as are his discussions of the actual works that fit these classifications; for, by devoting much of his essay to the "New Romance," he became in his own time one of the most important critics of the novel.

XI   *Cervantes*

Beattie believes that the era of the "New Romance" may be dated from the publication of Cervantes' *Don Quixote* (1605) which revealed with dramatic finality the absurdity of the "wild dreams of chivalry" that had "intoxicated all of Europe" both in prose and verse for a very long time:

[*Don Quixote*] no sooner appeared, than chivalry vanished, as snow melts before the sun. Mankind awoke as from a dream. They laughed at themselves for having been so long imposed on by absurdity; and wondered they had not made the discovery sooner. It astonished them to find, that nature and good sense could yield a more exquisite entertainment, than they had ever derived from the most sublime phrenzies of chivalry. For, that this was indeed the case: that Don Quixote was more read, and more relished, than any other romance had ever been. (*Dissertations*, p. 563)

The great significance of *Don Quixote* as a new form of fiction, Beattie claims, lies not only in the fact that the book helped fiction to divest itself of its "gigantic size, tremendous aspect, and frantick demeanour," but also in the way that later writers learned from Cervantes "to avoid extravagance, and to imitate nature" (p. 564). Beattie views Cervantes' fiction, therefore, not only as very important to the development of prose fiction but also as one of the great incentives to the creation of the novel in the eighteenth century.

XII   *Defoe*

While Defoe's *Robinson Crusoe* (1719) is not properly a novel but a fiction based on fact, Beattie nevertheless believes it to be "one of the most interesting narratives that ever was written" (*Dissertations*, p. 566). Beattie admires the "air of humanity" in the book and the treatment of its central theme concerning "the desire of self-preservation" (p. 556); but he is most impressed by Defoe's presentation of Crusoe's strong sense of moral purpose and by the book's usefulness as a means of teaching strong character, proper behavior, and the adaptability to solve great problems:

. . . Robinson Crusoe must be allowed, by the most rigid moralist, to be one of those novels, which one may read, not only with pleasure, but also with profit. It breathes throughout a spirit of piety and benevolence: it sets in a very striking light . . . the importance of the mechanick arts, which they, who know not what it is to be without them, are so apt to undervalue: it fixes in the mind a lively idea of the horrors of solitude and, consequently, of the sweets of social life, and of the blessings we derive from conversation, and mutual aid: and it shows how, by labouring with one's own hands, one may secure independence, and open for one's self many sources of health and amusement. I agree, therefore, with Rousseau, that this is one of the best books that can be put in the hands of children. (pp. 566 - 67)

But it is, nevertheless, an imperfect book, Beattie concludes, for its style is "plain," inelegant, and sometimes ungrammatical, and "the second part of the story is tiresome" (p. 567). True to his own ideal, therefore, Beattie points out the "beauties" of *Robinson Crusoe* at some length, and he merely notes its "blemishes" in one sentence.

XIII *Richardson*

In preparing to discuss Richardson's novels, Beattie presents what is probably the first discussion of the epistolary novel to be published in the eighteenth century. Having described the way that the technique works, Beattie concludes that the epistolary method has both advantages and disadvantages. To its credit, it "prevents all anticipation of the catastrophe," it builds suspense well, and it permits "varieties of style, suited to the different tempers, and sentiments of" the letter writers; but, to its discredit, it tends "to run out into an extravagant length, and to be encumbered with repetitions" (*Dissertations*, p. 567). Even the greatest epistolary writer cannot avoid such difficulties with the form, Beattie argues; for even Richardson, in spite of his great imaginative powers, "is apt to be tedious, and to fall into minuteness of detail, which is often unnecessary" (pp. 567 - 68). In addition, Beattie continues, Richardson often makes his scenes too long and too "pathetic," and he gives "too much prudery to his favourite women, and something of pedantry or finicalness to his favourite men" (p. 568). In spite of these major faults, however, Beattie is convinced that Richardson "is an author of uncommon merit": "His characters are well drawn, and distinctively marked; and he delineates the operation of the passions with a picturesque accuracy, which discovers great knowledge of human nature. His moral sentiments are profound and judicious; in wit and humour he is not wanting; his dialogue is sometimes formal; but many of his conversation-pieces are executed with elegance and vivacity. For the good tendency of his writings he deserves still higher praise; for he was a man of unaffected piety, and had the improvement of his fellow-creatures at heart" (p. 568).

By expressing great admiration for Richardson as a novelist, Beattie feels justified in devoting the whole of his discussion of *Clarissa Harlowe* (1747 - 1748) to an examination of the serious faults of characterization that he thinks the epistolary method of writing, and perhaps all novel writing, tends to encourage. Beattie cites Lovelace, the villain of Richardson's novel, as 'a wicked character who is presented as a more attractive figure than is necessary to the author's plan. Beattie's moral sense is disturbed by the possible harm to young readers who may try to emulate Lovelace's actions because they admire the charming qualities that the novelist has given to him; but his argument that the depiction of Lovelace's character, and especially of his death, constitutes a literary blunder is much more convincing and much more important to the history of literary criticism. For Lovelace's death was the result not of the proper progression through his wickedness to a just punishment for the villain's actions or through the self-realization that leads inevitably to his repentance; instead, it was caused by Lovelace's inability to defeat his antagonist in a swordfight. If he had been a better swordsman, Beattie argues, Lovelace would not only have conquered Clarissa's avenger but he would have also experienced no more guilt or remorse than he had felt when he was still alive. Beattie concludes, therefore, by suggesting how Richardson's error in characterization and plot might have been avoided: "Had [Lovelace's] crimes been represented as the necessary cause of a series of mortifications, leading him gradually down to infamy, ruin, and despair, or producing by probable means an exemplary repentance, the fable would have been more useful in a moral view, and perhaps more interesting" (p. 569).

XIV *Smollett*

Tobias Smollett's novels, *Roderick Random* (1748) and *Peregrine Pickle* (1751), both arouse Beattie's moral consternation, for Smollett "is often inexcusably licentious" in making his favorite characters into "profligates, bullies, and misanthropes" (*Disser-tations*, p. 571). But Beattie's good sense as a critic enables him to praise the novels as "humourous and entertaining" and to perceive Smollett's excellence "in drawing the characters of seamen" and the great "vivacity and energy of expression" with which he relates his "vast number of merry stories" (pp. 570 - 71). There is, nevertheless, a great imbalance in his writing, Beattie complains, for "his style often approaches to bombast; and many of his humourous pictures are exaggerated beyond all bounds of probability" (p. 571). Because Beattie is aware of the tension between the moralist and the critic in these remarks, or perhaps because he wishes at least to balance his censure with praise, he concludes his treatment of Smollett's writings by mentioning two novels, *Count Fathom* (1752) and *Sir Lancelot Greaves* (1762), to which he can direct praise that is only slightly qualified. *Sir Lancelot Greaves* in particular he believes to be a "truly original" imitation of *Don Quixote*. In spite of his moral disapproval of Smollett's novels, Beattie's comments leave the strong impression that he approved of them more than he cared to admit.

XV *Fielding*

When Beattie writes about Henry Fielding's novels, *Joseph Andrews* (1742), *Tom Jones* (1749), and *Amelia* (1751), he finds much more to praise and much less to blame than in any of the other novelists he has read. In fact, Beattie believes that, in modern times, only Shakespeare was superior to Fielding in wit, humor, and "knowledge of mankind." Fielding achieved such greatness as a novelist, Beattie explains, because he had refined his "great natural abilities . . . by studying the best authors of antiquity" (*Disser-tations*, pp. 571 - 72). While Beattie does give Fielding a mild rebuke for his occasional ostentatious display of learning and wit, for the "indelicacy" of some passages, and for the moral incon-sistency of some characters in *Joseph Andrews*, he directs most of his attention to the remarkable qualities that he finds in *Amelia* and especially in *Tom Jones*: "Since the days of Homer, the world has not seen a more artful Epick fable" (p. 573). Beattie praises the novel for its marvelously diversified characters and adventures and for its masterful combinations of events that build to the catastrophe of the action by continually stimulating the reader's curiosity "till at last it becomes downright anxiety" (p. 573): "And when we get to the end, we are amazed to find, that of so many incidents there should be so few superfluous; that in such variety of fiction there should be so great probability; and that so complete a tale should be so perspicuously conducted, and with perfect unity of design" (p. 573).

XVI *Defects of Popular Fiction*

Apart from such discerning remarks about eighteenth century novelists, Beattie's essay on fable and romance is notable also for its reflection of his strong moralistic disgust at the display of immoral behavior and licentious thoughts in popular fiction. Since, however, the essay was originally written for his college students at the time when Beattie was devising the arguments found in his *Essay on Truth* against the irresponsibility and amorality of scepticism, it is remarkable that, in contrast to the polemical violence of the *Essay*, his comments about indecency in novels are very few and quite mild. One's impression, therefore, that Beattie greatly enjoyed the novels he recommends indicates in his essay an admirable supremacy of artistic taste that transcends his pious rage at public immorality. For example, Beattie does not condemn the characterization of Tom Jones as a loveable rogue; rather, he praises Tom for his consistency and probability as a character in the development of Fielding's fable. But the moralist in Beattie has his own kind of triumph at the end of the essay, which Beattie hastily concludes by claiming that, since Fielding's death in 1754, the "Comick Romance" has declined "from simplicity and nature, into improbability and affectation," and by issuing a solemn warning to "young readers" to avoid "Romance" as "a dangerous recreation" (*Dissertations*, p. 573). While one may wonder whether Beattie considered Laurence Sterne's *Tristram Shandy* (1760) as representing a decline "into improbability and affectation" when he revised his essay on fable and romance for publication in 1783, it is likely that Beattie had not read either Sterne or any other novelist after Fielding. In fact, only the novels that he treats in his essay are noted in the list of his large library that he compiled in 1785. In effect, then, the moralist has the last word.

XVII *English Satirists*

Beattie's remarks about the great English satirists, Chaucer, Samuel Butler, Alexander Pope, and Jonathan Swift, in "An Essay on Laughter and Ludicrous Composition" (1776), which he had written in 1764, also shows his cultivated affinities with the moral issues of his time. The fact that he decided to publish this essay instead of his treatment of the novel when he needed another literary piece to complete the companion volume to the *Essay on Truth* in 1776 indicates that he was more comfortable with the satirist's righteous indignation toward human stupidity and vice than he was with the novelist's apparent recommendation of human folly and cupidity. But Beattie's very comfortable familiarity with the great satirists would not allow him to perceive the composition of an essay on laughter and its relationship to satirical writing as an opportunity to give his own opinions of specific works, such as Pope's *The Dunciad* (1742) or Swift's *Gulliver's Travels* (1726), as he was to do in discussing the origin and development of the novel. Instead, he seems content to drop hints about satirical works that tantalize the twentieth century reader into wishing for more of the kind. Consequently, Beattie writes of the kind of laughter "which arises on reading the Tale of a Tub" (*Essays*, p. 328), and he later refers to Swift's book as one "of the most laughable . . . pieces of ridicule that ever [was] written" (p. 468). He similarly notes the "laughable peculiarities that distinguish Don Quixote, Parson Adams, Sir Roger de Coverley, Squire Western, and many other heroes of the Comic Romance" (p. 467); but in no case does he explain or illustrate his opinion.

But, in spite of the fact that analytical comments on literary works did not form part of his plan to show the historical development of the concept of laughter, Beattie indicates at the end of his essay that he recognizes the need for such a treatment of satiric writings: "To a full examination of the present topic, it would be further necessary, to give a critical analysis of our most celebrated works in wit and humour, and of the human characters displayed in them; and to inquire, from what external causes the laughable peculiarities in each character arise; and how far the same or similar causes could take place in ancient times" (p. 477). Beattie's essay is notable, nevertheless, for giving modern satirists greater respectability than they had had and for instructing readers in a proper approach to their writings. For, even if Beattie's eighteenth century readers forgot immediately his long-winded arguments and his complicated categories for the different types of laughter and "ludicrous composition," they would recall vividly his great claim that the English satirists such as Chaucer, Butler, and Swift were superior even to the ancients in wit and humor.

XVIII   *Dryden and Pope*

Beattie's literary essays do not always disappoint the wish that he had published critical analyses of writers or works; and, on such occasions, he writes some of his most satisfying criticism. In his "Essay on Poetry" (1776), for example, he sets forth his opinion of Dryden's poetry: "There is no modern writer, whose style is more distinguishable. Energy and ease are its chief characters. The former is owing to a happy choice of expressions, equally emphatical and plain: the latter to a laudable partiality in favour of the idioms and radical words of the English tongue; the *native* riches and *peculiar* genius whereof are perhaps more apparent in him, than in any other of our poets . . . his English is pure and simple, nervous and clear, to a degree which Pope has never exceeded, and not always equalled" (*Essays*, p. 16). At this point, Beattie's discussion leads naturally to a comparison of Dryden to Alexander Pope:

Dryden's verse, though often faulty, has a grace, and a spirit, peculiar to itself. That of Pope is more correct, and perhaps upon the whole more harmonious; but it is in general more languid, and less diversified. Pope's numbers are sweet but elaborate; and our sense of their energy is in some degree interrupted by our attention to the art displayed in their contexture: Dryden's are natural and free; and, while they communicate their own sprightly motion to the spirits of the reader, hurry him along with a gentle and pleasing violence, without giving him time either to animadvert on their faults, or to analyse their beauties. Pope excels in solemnity of sound; Dryden, in easy melody, and boundless variety of rhythm. (pp. 18 - 19).

These remarks are also important for the circumstances under which they occur in "An Essay on Poetry." Since Beattie had committed himself as a critic to establishing and illustrating the rules of literary judgment, he rarely decides, or the idea does not occur to him, to publish his personal response to literary works. In this case, however, since he had attacked Dryden's translations in his essay, he felt obliged to declare such faults to be minor blemishes and to tell by contrast what he believes about the rest of Dryden's work. As a result, Beattie justified what he thought might be considered a breach of proper literary behavior by arguing that it is salutary to criticize bad passages in a great writer and by printing his comments about Dryden and Pope in a footnote. The twentieth century reader is perhaps a little saddened that the neo-Classical prescription to write general and not minute criticism exerted such a powerful influence on Beattie.

XIX *Illustrations*

Beattie manages to compensate somewhat for the lack of close scrutiny of literary works in his essays by supplying a great many illustrations of his ideas and principles. He always considered his greatest obligation as a prose writer to be the search for striking examples and allusions to enliven and explain clearly those truths that have stood the test of time. As some of the more pleasing effects in his literary essays, Beattie's illustrations are often invented stories or imaginative reconstructions of his own experiences, as well as analogies from the fine arts, from science, and especially from literature. The discussion of the emotional response to poetry in his "Essay on Poetry," for example, is illustrated by a description of Beattie's experience as a young man at Fordoun: "A melancholy man walking in a grove, attends to those things that suit and encourage his melancholy; the sighing of the wind in the trees, the murmuring of waters, the darkness and solitude of the shades: a chearful man in the same place, finds many subjects of chearful meditation, in the singing of birds, the brisk motions of the babling stream, and the liveliness and variety of the verdure" (*Essays*, p. 53).

Beattie invigorates a ludicrous situation in "An Essay on Laughter and Ludicrous Composition" by inventing the following scene: "If Pope and Colley Cibber had been so squeezed by a croud [*sic*] in the playhouse, as to be compelled to sit with their heads contiguous, and the arm of one about the neck of the other, expressing at the same time in their looks a mutual antipathy and reluctance, I believe the sight would have been entertaining enough, especially if believed to be accidental" (*Essays*, pp. 339 - 40). A final example is drawn from science to prove a point about the essential rules of poetic composition: the poet who ignores nature's directions is comparable to a mechanic who wishes to construct an engine on principles inconsistent with the laws of motion and who excuses himself by rejecting the authority of Newton. Many such illustrations scattered throughout Beattie's prose have the pleasing effect of creating a sense of thoughtful, eager anticipation in the reader, who soon learns that Beattie can be relied upon again and again to produce impressive new perspectives and expressions that make obvious and simple the authenticity of the author's beliefs.

XX   *Relationship to Eighteenth Century Criticism*

While most of Beattie's critical statements are not in themselves remarkable, the fact that he gave popular expression to so many ideas that became part of received criticism, and that he formulated them long before modern criticism was created during the Romantic period, is of considerable importance to the development of eighteenth century literary theory and practice. Beattie was clearly a representative and an influential critic; for, by combining new ideas with proven doctrines, he seems to have provided a useful model for the impending transition to the new literary view soon to flower with the Romantics. As such, he may be considered to be a member of the School of Taste, a group of late eighteenth century writers who believed that those literary effects that are completely free from external authority can be defined and judged only by individual taste. Beattie and the other champions of this notion of taste, notably Hugh Blair, Oliver Goldsmith, Alexander Gerard, and Sir Joshua Reynolds, contributed to the development of the concept by attempting to define the nature and function of taste more precisely than the term had been used by earlier critics for whom it had remained a vague, indecisive "something" in art that was not subject to the established rules that more conservative critics claimed should govern its composition.

The great authority for the School of Taste was Longinus, the Greek rhetorician who had written with great energy and personal conviction about sublimity in literature as the combination of qualities that give consummate artistry to a literary work. Beattie not only borrowed many of his ideas from Longinus, such as the belief that pleasure is the end of literature, but also published a kind of continuation of Longinus' "On the Sublime" in his essay "Illustrations on Sublimity" (1783) which is an attempt to present a clearer distinction between sublimity and beauty than any other critic had made. Beattie also demonstrates the validity of Longinus' ideas, and of some of his own, about sublimity by collecting many illustrations of the various types of the sublime from nature and from literature. For Beattie, therefore, the great writer always establishes his own rules of composition by the very act of creating a great work of art. As a result, Beattie defines taste as the union of the imaginative and the intellectual powers of the mind by which the individual perceives accurately intuitive knowledge about what is elegant, sublime, or beautiful in art and in nature. Beattie's belief in the soundness of this theory of art—one that was to become central to the Romantic ideal of individuality—was largely responsible for the many vivid pre-Romantic insights that are sprinkled liberally into his essays and that helped the growth of Romantic assumptions about life and literature.

The representative value of Beattie's essays is also indicated by the fact that he deals with all the important and with many of the minor literary considerations of the time. In all his essays, for instance, he gives strict adherence to the current, predominant principles of rationalism; for example, he insists in his "Essay on Poetry" that true poetry is perfectly rational, that emotion should be controled within rational limits, and that the writer should discard everything that does not conform to rational tests. As a consequence, Beattie, like the other adherents to the School of Taste, often challenged earlier critical judgments that he felt were not in tune with reason; and this new point of view, in Beattie as in the others, resulted not only in a relaxation of the rules of literary, and of critical composition, but also in the reexamination of earlier literary works in the context that had produced them. Among the best results of this growing sense of historical relativity was the rediscovery of chivalry and romance, and Beattie's "On Fable and Romance" was one of the most important essays to develop from it.

An offshoot of this new interest in the past was the increased emphasis on the editing of texts that was strong enough to entice even a general critic like Beattie to publish first-class texts of Gray's poems and Addison's prose. In addition, the excitement generated by the development of the historical approach to literature stimulated the exploration of many current topics; and Beattie became in these matters perhaps the most prolific critic of his time. In his many remarks about poetry, for example, he dealt with most contemporary poetic forms, such as verse-satire and the Spenserian stanza, with poetic diction and composition, with such problematical concepts as the role of fancy and imagination, and with such longstanding problems as the relationship of poetry to music and the use of natural description in poetry. Similarly, he wrote about the neo-Classical doctrine of the inviolateness of the "kinds" and the "rules" of poetic composition, and of the growing tendency to invent new poetic forms and subjects and to publish them as serious poems. In addition to Beattie's discussions of such topics as the sympathetic or emotional response to art, the need to establish durable standards of literary judgment, the prose-satire, and the novel, his essays also reflect the eighteenth-century preoccupation with primitivism, sublimity, sentimentalism, melancholy, didacticism, and Medievalism.

Eighteenth century readers often expressed their admiration for the pleasing flow of ideas, the clearness of reasoning, and the artistic penetration that they found in Beattie's literary essays. They admired the perspicuity, simplicity, grace, strength, and harmony of his prose style; and they especially appreciated his authoritative sense of judgment that, for them, was infused with imaginative insight. Beattie's early readers believed that he had measured up to the ideal of proper criticism that he himself had laid down in his essay "Of Memory and Imagination." As such, these widely accepted views on the nature and function of criticism did much, one may argue, to prepare readers to accept the new ideas and attitudes soon to be presented to them by the new generation of writers. Taken as a whole, then, Beattie's literary essays are an impressive body of criticism that had an effect much like John Dryden's a century earlier in demonstrating a fine taste for literature and in promoting the strong desire to share the joy that the critic perceives in great writing. Mainly through the power of Beattie's own pleasure in literature and through his enthusiastic attempts to teach his public audience to become better readers, his essays seem to have given a sharper focus and a sense of direction to the changing literary ideas and beliefs of the time when the clarification of the role of criticism was a necessary as well as a salutary exercise. As such, Beattie must be considered to be one of the soundest and most important critics of the late eighteenth century.

CHAPTER 10

Assessments of Writings

I *Minor Poems*

THE contemporary assessment of Beattie as a major writer was even hinted at in the response to *Original Poems and Translations* (1761), his first published work. Writing in *The Monthly Review* for May 1761, Robert Lloyd stated that he had "not met with, since Mr. Gray . . . a poet of more harmonious numbers, more pleasing imagination, or more spirited expression"[1]; and the reviewer in *The Scot's Magazine* for April 1761 declared that Beattie's *"original poems"* were distinguished by "the indisputable mark of true genius."[2] In addition, Thomas Gray himself told Beattie that he was very impressed with the poems, and John Wesley considered Beattie to be "one of the best Poets of the age."[3] Meanwhile, in 1765, "Verses occasioned by the Death of the Rev[d] Mr. Charles Churchill" gained him the reputation as a vigorous verse-satirist; and the second edition of his poems in 1766, including the poem about Churchill, strengthened the assessment that he was an original poetic genius.

Beattie served his apprenticeship with the composition of these poems; and he thereby demonstrated that his mind was well-stocked with poetic images and thoughts, that he possessed uncommon talent as a versifier, and that his imaginative insight was versatile enough to produce an energetic, traditional satire, such as the poem about Churchill, and occasionally to inspire poems such as "Retirement" and "The Hermit" that break new ground by transcending the limitations of their models. The extent to which these poems and their enthusiastic reception encouraged Beattie to reshape and revitalize other old ideas and verse forms is indicated by the fact that he had already started to write *The Minstrel* when the second edition of his poems was published in 1766.

II   The Minstrel

The publication of Canto I of *The Minstrel* in 1771, followed by Canto II in 1774 when Beattie acknowledged being the author, seemed to convince most readers that they had been presented with the work of a new, major poet. Mrs. Montagu's friend, Lord Lyttelton, considered the poem to be a refinement of James Thomson's treatment of "the beauties of nature, and the finest feelings of virtue."[4] Dr. Johnson told Beattie that "there is not a line in *The Minstrel* which one would not wish to have written"[5]; and the periodical reviewers spread the word of Beattie's success to all their readers. *The Critical Review* for February 1771 considered that Beattie's use "of Spenser's stanza animates it with the true spirit of poetry"[6]; and John Langhorne greeted the publication of Canto II with the acknowledgement in *The Monthly Review* for September 1774 that he found "the same style of harmony, and the same spirit of enthusiasm in this book, which distinguished the first."[7]

For the rest of the century, as more and more editions of the poem were published, high praise for *The Minstrel* continued to be recorded. William Cowper, for example, wrote to his friend, William Unwin, about the poem in 1784: "If you have not his poem called the Minstrel, and cannot borrow it, I must beg you to buy it for me; for though I cannot afford to deal largely in so expensive a commodity as books, I must afford at least the poetical works of Beattie."[8] Even though Samuel Rogers, the English poet, was only eight years old when the first canto of *The Minstrel* was published, he recalled years later his introduction to the poem: "I remember taking Beattie's *Minstrel* down from my father's shelves, on a fine evening, and reading it for the first time with such delight! It still charms me."[9] An aspiring young poet in the 1780s, Robert Burns declared that he dared not hope for "distinguished fame . . . in a language where . . . Beattie [has] painted the landscape."[10] Later, when he presented a copy of *The Minstrel* to a friend, Burns remarked that he had given her "more than India boasts/In Edwin's simple tale."[11]

In the early nineteenth century, most new editions of the poem were favorably reviewed by all the major periodicals; and individuals continued to record their assessments of *The Minstrel* as a great poem. As a consequence, a writer in *Blackwood's Magazine* for August 1824, in reviewing the literary situation of 1812, estimated that at that time "Beattie was the man of highest and most deserved reputation" and that "the Minstrel was . . . incomparably the best work from the hand of any [contemporary] writer."[12] In 1819, when poet and prose writer Robert Southey was in Aberdeen, he visited Beattie's grave in St. Nicholas' churchyard to pay posthumous homage to the Scottish minstrel and to copy the inscription on his tombstone[13]; and, a year later, John Clare, another poet, called *The Minstrel* "a sweet poem."[14] In fact, aside from the remarks by Coleridge, Byron, and Keats that have been noted, most of the other major Romantic writers also recorded opinions about the poem that indicate its reputation as an influential work during the Romantic period. William Hazlitt, for example, printed a passage from the poem as an excellent example of poetry that shows the love of the countryside;[15] and Thomas de Quincey placed Beattie on his list of "the twelve best poets of all time."[16]

In the 1820s, when Tennyson was a young boy, his mother often read to him from *The Minstrel;* and it not only became one of his favorite poems but contributed many echoes to his own poems. While Beattie was probably not regarded by many readers during the Romantic period as a major poet, it is clear not only that his reputation as an important minor poet was widespread but also that the influence of *The Minstrel* was immense for more than sixty years after the publication of both cantos in 1774. Throughout most of the nineteenth century, readers of the poem regarded its great similarities to the poems of the Romantic poets as evidence of a seminal influence; and it was, therefore, considered to be a very important poem. John Wilson (Christopher North) gave voice to such beliefs by writing in *Blackwood's Magazine* for October 1838 that Wordsworth "must . . . forego the praise of originality" for *The Excursion* because he had taken so many ideas, scenes, and characters from *The Minstrel.*[17] Such comments were repeated by others, some as late as the early years of the twentieth century; but in 1913, when Volume X of *The Cambridge History of English Literature* was published, George Saintsbury pronounced that *The Minstrel* retained only "a historic interest" as a serious Spenserian poem,[18] and this estimate of the poem has determined to the present time its reputation.

It was inevitable, therefore, that *The Minstrel* would have less and less attention for its own sake and that mention of it would be made merely to illustrate weakness or bad taste in a major poet. Indeed, Geoffrey Tillotson's pronouncement in 1951 effectively rang the death knell for Beattie's reputation as an important minor poet: "It is characteristic [of the Romantic poets] that they did not plead their being poets as a ground for exemption from the common lot. They did not accept the version of the poet . . . puffed out by Beattie in his much-read poem *The Minstrel* . . . . Beattie's Edwin certainly fascinated them . . . but they rejected him for the painful world of men."[19] As has been demonstrated in this review of the reactions of such Romantic poets, they did not reject Beattie's version of the poet; they did, however, modify it, add to it, and even transform it. As each Romantic poet contemplated *The Minstrel* as a model for the poetic life, he became a kind of Edwin, took up the challenge of Beattie's dilemma, and thereby grew into a mature poet. One may claim, therefore, that Romantic poetry would not have developed precisely as it did without Beattie; indeed, it may even be argued that the Romantic poets cannot be studied properly without consideration of *The Minstrel.*

Latter-day critics would, therefore, do well to heed Shelley's assessment of his great contemporaries and the influences on them. He found it impossible, he wrote in *A Defense of Poetry* (1821), "to read the compositions of the most celebrated writers of the present day without being startled with the electric life which burns within their words."[20] As astute as this remark was at the time, it would now be considered commonplace if Shelley had not followed it with an equally sound statement about the source of their "comprehensive and all-penetrating" insight into human nature: " . . . they are themselves perhaps astonished . . . [by the power of their poetry,] for it is less their spirit than the spirit of the age."[21] But long before any of the Romantic poets, Beattie sensed this spirit in his youthful experiences with nature; he recreated it in *The Minstrel* where it is personified in Edwin and expressed philosophically by the hermit; and Beattie thereby provided a powerful and irresistibly incomplete pattern of the poetic life for the young poets during the new dawn of Romanticism.

III   An Essay on Truth

In view of the phenomenal response to *The Minstrel,* it seems incredible that Beattie was considered during the eighteenth century as being a greater philosopher than poet. In fact, the initial reaction to Canto I in 1771 was largely caused by the great popularity of the *Essay on Truth* which had just had a second edition when the canto was anonymously published. But word spread quickly that the important new philosopher, who had refuted the whole posture of sceptical reasoning, was also a brilliant poet. Indeed, most of the praise during the early 1770s for *The Minstrel*, as well as for the *Essay*, was reported to Beattie by word of mouth, especially during his journeys through Edinburgh and the Scottish countryside and then to London in the summers of 1771 and 1773. A great many people were particularly eager to pass along to Beattie their assessments of the *Essay*, and they were overjoyed if they could report to him that a famous person thought highly of the book. Such people were encouraged to do so by the fact that all the early reviews in English and Scottish periodicals recommended the book as an excellent safeguard against scepticism. A review in *The Annual Register* for 1770 that was written by Edmund Burke "immediately proclaimed [the *Essay on Truth*] true philosophy."[22] In May 1772, Beilby Porteus, who was to become the bishop of London and a close friend of Beattie, wrote to him that "in London your book has been received with universal applause";[23] and it was reported that John Wesley thought "that Beattie had refuted Hume."[24]

Similarly, James Boswell wrote to Beattie in October 1772 to report Dr. Johnson's opinion of the *Essay:* "I had a letter not long ago from Mr. Samuel Johnson, in which he says, 'Beattie's book is, I believe, every day more liked; at least I like it more as I look upon it.'"[25] A year later, David Garrick reported that Johnson had strongly supported his praise for the book: "Why, sir, there is in it a depth of reasoning and a splendour of language which make it one of the first-rate productions of the age."[26] On another occasion, Johnson was heard to exclaim that "Beattie has confuted Hume."[27] Beattie continued to receive many such reports for years after his celebrity as a writer had been established; in 1777, for instance, James Williamson, a former student at Marischal College, wrote to Beattie from Oxford that William Pitt the Elder, Lord Chatham, thought the *Essay* to be the "best book written for years."[28] Even well into the nineteenth century, the eminent Scottish divine, Thomas Chalmers, "recommended it as the book to which he was most indebted for his deliverance from philosophical scepticism."[29]

IV *Evidences of the Christian Religion*

But long before this statement Emmanuel Kant had, in 1783, announced his opinion that the *Essay on Truth* was not a proper work of philosophy; and he had thereby inadvertently indicated that the book was really a very effective exercise in Christian apology, as eighteenth century readers had always known. For this reason, Beattie's *Evidences of the Christian Religion* (1786) met with a large audience that was eager to receive assurances of the validity of Christianity and to inform Beattie that his efforts were much appreciated. Dr. Duncan of Smallholme, for example, wrote to Beattie in November 1787 to acknowledge "the just sense I have long had of the great service of which you have been to the interest of truth and virtue and the cause of the religion of Jesus";[30] and John Gillies, the minister at Paisley, wrote in October 1798 to ask whether Beattie would permit the book to be published in a cheaper edition so that poor people might read it.[31] Because Beattie had received such encouragement ever since the first publication of the *Essay on Truth*, he never missed an opportunity to insert recommendations of the Christian life into his other books. Beattie must, therefore, be considered to have been one of the most successful writers who ever attempted to justify and make popular the Christian religion in opposition to the sceptical, intellectual concerns of pure philosophy. But the very fact that he was acclaimed in his own lifetime for being both a philosopher and a Christian apologist in the same works led inevitably to the decline in his reputation until the present time when he has been forgotten or is not regarded seriously by historians of either philosophy or Christianity.

V   *Literary Criticism*

Greatly encouraged by his success as a public moralist in the *Essay on Truth* and in *The Minstrel* and by the many requests that he write more books, Beattie decided by 1775 that he should take advantage of his reputation by publishing with his moral essays some of his literary ones as a means of instructing readers in proper literary taste and judgment. As a result of this decision, he published his first literary essays with a new edition of the *Essay on Truth* in 1776 and included three others in *Dissertations Moral and Critical* in 1783. The response to these literary essays was precisely what Beattie had hoped for, as the review of *Dissertations* in the July 1783 issue of *The London Magazine* indicates: "The reputation which Dr. Beattie has so deservedly acquired as a writer, will not be lessened by these dissertations . . . . [for they] are well calculated for the entertainment and instruction of youth . . . . Few writers,

indeed, appear to be more desirous of promoting the interests of virtue and literature than Dr. Beattie, and there are very few who
possess, in so considerable a degree, the happy talent of blending
critical knowledge with useful and practical truths."[32] A year later,
William Cowper praised Beattie's "critical researches" with great
enthusiasm, for they were the "most agreeable and amiable" that
he had ever read.[33] By the turn of the century, therefore, Beattie's
reputation as an important critic seems to have been well established; in 1804, for example, the Scottish critic, David Irving, considered that Beattie was the best critic of his time: "Dr. Beattie dis-
plays a more elegant vein of criticism than any of his predecessors
. . . as a critic his merit is conspicuous."[34] Consequently, Sir Walter
Scott was merely echoing a long-held belief when he praised Beattie
in *The Edinburgh Review* for April 1807 as "the most pleasing and
ingenious writer on the *Belles Lettres* of his day."[35]

But Wordsworth had published by this time the 1800 preface to
the *Lyrical Ballads;* and the Romantic movement was so well advanced that Englishmen were paying less and less attention to the
writings of Scotsmen who, like Beattie, had once been famous.
Thereafter, it seems that only Scotsmen read his literary essays; and
even shortly after Beattie's death in 1803, when the Scotsman Alexander Bower published a hasty biography of Beattie, there were
clear implications that the neglect of the literary essays had started
earlier in England, since Bower states that Beattie's writings about
literature and criticism "have long been considered oracular and
decisive" in Scotland.[36] It was, therefore, not very far into the
nineteenth century before Wordsworth, Coleridge, and the other
Romantics were given full credit in England as the originators of
ideas that had been propagated by Beattie; and, as a result, he was
denied, even at the time of his death, any influence as a critic on
English letters.

By 1829, John Wilson's disgust and nationalistic pride moved him
to write in *Blackwood's Magazine* that, up to his own time, Beattie
was "the best writer on Literature and the Fine Arts Britain ever
produced—full of feeling and full of genius."[37] Such extravagant
praise is difficult to support, of course; but it does indicate the need
to give Beattie the credit due him. As late as 1880, a writer in the
July issue of *Blackwood's Magazine* considered Beattie the most important writer in the development of Scottish criticism.[38] Beattie's
literary essays, it seems, were read, at least in Scotland, long after
the *Essay on Truth* ceased to be published; and these publications

rivaled *The Minstrel* in popularity until the early years of the twentieth century. Since then, they have been largely ignored even by historians of Scottish criticism, just as *The Minstrel* has received less and less attention from Scottish as well as English critics.

It should be stated, therefore, that Beattie was not only the most important writer up to his time in the evolution of Scottish literary criticism but that he was also very influential in the development of English criticism, especially in helping to prepare for the coming of Romanticism. Beattie's originality as a pre-Romantic critic should be measured not so much in terms of his ideas and his attitudes that were later to be espoused by the Romantics as by the great number of them that appeared in his essays. While one may claim another kind of originality for Beattie's direct influence on Burns, his essays are just as remarkable for the way in which his strong advocacy of the historical method of criticism and his use of other new developments, such as scientific knowledge, gave a sense of authority and prestige to his role as originator, especially in his remarks about the novel, the satire, and the Spenserian stanza, and in his treatment of such topics as taste, imagination, and the use of natural objects in the poetic landscape. One great strength of Beattie's criticism is an inclusiveness that enables one to read his views as an index to the major and minor literary happenings and ideas of the time. In addition, Beattie was a particularly fine critic when he felt the need to publish critiques of individual writers, such as his treatment of Dryden and Pope; and he was also very good at providing the necessary information for the understanding of his topics; but he was at his best in choosing literary passages for close commentary. Above all else, however, the freshness of Beattie's approach made him both a pleasing and an important critic.

VI *Prose Style*

Beattie's Addisonian prose style was perhaps the most pleasing element in all of his essays. After he had chosen Addison's essays as his model, Beattie perfected his own distinctive style; but he was never satisfied with it. When many readers were commenting about his fine style in his essays of 1776, Beattie himself complained that his prose had "nothing of that accuracy, that ease, or that simplicity which it ought to have. Nay, in the prose I have printed, my expression, after all the pains I have taken about it, is not what I wish it to be: it is too pompous, and, I fear, too visibly elaborate; and there is often a harshness and stiffness in it, which I would fain avoid, but cannot."[39] Beattie was, however, his own most severe critic; for all readers seem to have considered his style to be lively and interesting.

William Cowper wrote that Beattie's "critical and philosophical researches are diversified and embellished by a poetic imagination, that makes even the driest subject, and the leanest, a feast for an epicure in books. He is so much at his ease too, that his own character appears in every page, and which is very rare, we see not only the writer, but the man: and that man so gentle, so well-tempered, so happy in his religion, and so humane in his philosophy, that it is necessary to love him, if one has any sense of what is lovely."[40] Beattie's prose reflected accurately his style of life and thought, as well as his preoccupations of the moment and his characteristically positive response to the human need for edification. His style was, in effect, the mirror of the man and his principles, so that he appears in his own essays as a kind of literary character who gives an entirely convincing performance as the intelligent, well-informed, imaginative man of trustworthy beliefs that Beattie himself was in real life. For this reason, Beattie's writing, called by Dr. Johnson "a splendour of language," earned him the reputation as one of the finest eighteenth century prose stylists.

VII   *The Importance of Beattie and His Writings*

In all of Beattie's publications, he spoke to and for his age in a unique way; in fact, the extent to which he was a writer primarily of his own time is indicated in his great contemporary reputation and in its equally great decline. His work also reveals such a clear reflection of literary, philosophical, religious, and educational beliefs and practices that they present perhaps the most complete index to the temper of his era of any contemporary writer. In addition, they give a reliable indication of these matters, for one is impressed by Beattie's consistently high standard of judgment and execution; everything that he recommends or emulates is invariably the best from earlier writers; and his strain of originality led him to explore and strengthen the most important aspects of developing trends. The best example of his originality is his poetry, with which his literary essays share the fundamental pattern of transition; but a similar appeal to the proven principles of the past, while the acceptance of new points of view is being recommended, is the main aim of his moral and educational essays and of his Christian apology. Since everything that he published was almost universally believed in his own time to be true and important, his enormous popularity must be viewed as evidence of great influence on his contemporary readers.

Beattie's main value as a writer, therefore, lies in the considerable extent to which he prepared his readers for later writers by teaching them to trust the precept and the example of great writing and to be receptive to innovation and change. Because his books give not only the last popular expression to the Augustan Age but also early important intimations of inevitable change, they therefore stress the proper value to be put on the too often neglected minor writer. For it is usually he, and not the great writer, who more nearly painted the times as they were and thereby gained popular acclaim and support. As such a writer, Beattie provides an important view of the background against which the dependence upon tradition and the originality of great writing may be judged.

When one acknowledges the extent of Beattie's influence on Wordsworth, for instance, one perceives more clearly the importance of Beattie's seminal role and the greatness of Wordsworth's achievement. The special relationship between these two men needs to be emphasized, for it is much more extensive and important than has been indicated in the discussion of their poetry and criticism. There are many other quite remarkable similarities in their styles of living and in their feeling, thinking, and writing. Because of Beattie's place of birth and upbringing, as well as his temperament, education, and inclination, he was particularly suited to play his Wordsworthian role. For both Beattie and Wordsworth were moral, dedicated, Christian, church-going men of great common sense who were greatly affected by the deaths of brothers and sons but who nevertheless developed attitudes of optimistic stoicism relative to the hardships of life. Both were also forced to endure the pain of mental breakdown, for Beattie lived in fear of an insane wife and Wordsworth watched helplessly over Dorothy's debility; both had lifelong financial and physical difficulties; and, in addition, both were interested in many diverse matters—traveling, the teaching of the young, politics, nature, books, science, Classical writers, literature, and many others—and both wrote excellent, impassioned prose when the need arose.

Such marked similarities indicate the nature and scope of

Wordsworth's evolution as a writer, just as Beattie's great popularity underscores his important role in providing inspiration and in preparing an audience for Wordsworth. Unlike Beattie, Wordsworth was not content with merely mirroring his age by recording what he saw. One measure of Wordsworth's greatness, therefore, is the extent to which he improved Beattie's Romantic vision, but remained true to his own deep eighteenth century roots. It seems clear that Beattie had a similar effect on other Romantic writers such as Burns, Byron, Scott, Shelley, and Keats, as well as on innumerable minor writers such as Robert Southey, William Lisle Bowles, John Clare, Mary Tighe, Samuel Rogers, and the American poets William Cullen Bryant and Fitz-Greene Halleck. Beattie must be considered, therefore, not only as one of the most representative but also as one of the most influential minor writers of the late eighteenth and early nineteenth centuries.

Notes and References

Chapter One

1. J. M. Lothian, *Adam Smith: Lectures on Rhetoric and Belles Lettres* (London, 1963), p. xxxix.
2. *Ibid.*, p. xxxviii.
3. See D. D. McElroy, *Scotland's Age of Improvement: A Survey of Eighteenth-Century Clubs and Societies* (Washington, 1967).
4. "Rules and Minutes of the Philosophical Society of Aberdeen," MS. 539, King's College Library, University of Aberdeen. For a discussion of the nature, function, and importance of the Philosophical Society, see my article "A Scottish Philosophical Club in the Eighteenth Century," *Dalhousie Review*, L, 2 (Summer 1970), pp. 201 - 14.
5. James McCosh, *The Scottish Philosophy* (London, 1875), p. 268.
6. Gladys Bryson, *Man and Society: The Scottish Inquiry of the Eighteenth Century* (New Jersey, 1945), p. 4.
7. Item B.342 in the collection of Beattie manuscripts in King's College Library, University of Aberdeen. Hereafter cited as Beattie MSS. See Bibliography for a description of the collection.
8. Alexander Chalmers, "Life of James Beattie," in *The Works of the British Poets* (London, 1810), XVIII, pp. 532 - 33.
9. Alexander Dyce, "Memoir of James Beattie," in *The Aldine Edition of the British Poets* (London, 1831), LXIV. Unless otherwise noted, all quotations from Beattie's poems are from this edition. Hereafter cited as Beattie's *Poems*.
10. William Forbes, *An Account of the Life and Writings of James Beattie* (Edinburgh, 1807), III, p. 147.
11. *Ibid.*, p. 149.
12. Beattie's *Poems*, p. 155.
13. James Boswell, *Life of Johnson*, ed. G. B. Hill (Oxford, 1934), II, p. 148.
14. Samuel Johnson, *The Lives of the English Poets*, ed. G. B. Hill (Oxford, 1905), III, p. 428.
15. Margaret Forbes, *Beattie and his Friends* (Westminster, 1904), p. 243.
16. Thomas Miller, "Memoirs of James Beattie" in *The Poetical Works of Beattie and Collins* (London, 1846), p. xxiv.
17. Chalmers, p. 529.
18. W. Forbes, I, pp. 118 - 19.

19. Beattie MSS., C. 62

20. Boswell, II, p. 148.

21. W. Forbes, II, pp. 253 - 54.

22. Fanny Burney, *Diary and Letters of Madame D'Arblay*, ed. Austin Dobson (London, 1905), III, p. 280 f.

23. *Correspondence of Thomas Gray*, eds. Paget Toynbee and Leonard Whibley (Oxford, 1935), II, pp. 895 - 96.

24. W. Forbes, I, p. 261.

25. Gray, III, p. 975.

26. All quotations are taken from the sixth edition of *An Essay on Truth* (hereafter cited as *Truth*) which was published in Edinburgh in 1776.

Chapter Two

1. These are also the three essential qualities of excellent teaching that are suggested by Gilbert Highet, *The Art of Teaching* (London, 1963), p. 11 f.

2. James Rennie, "A Compendious System of Pneumatology comprehending Psychology, Moral Philosophy & Logic. Taken at the Lectures of Mr. Js Beattie P. P. At the Marischal College & University of Abdn by J. Rennie. Anno 1767" (Library of the University of Glasgow).

3. Beattie MSS., B. 16.

4. W. Forbes, I, pp. 384 - 85.

5. M. Forbes, p. 17.

6. William Rose, *The Monthly Review*, LXIX (July 1783), p. 31.

7. W. Forbes, III, pp. 44 - 45.

8. *Ibid.*, p. 108.

9. *Ibid.*, pp. 60 - 61. A manuscript in Beattie MSS. entitled "A List of Books and Pamphlets relative to the Slave Trade" confirms Beattie's study of the subject.

10. W. Forbes, I, p. 129.

11. Archibald Arthur, *Discourses on Theological and Literary Subjects* (Glasgow, 1803), p. 541.

12. Lothian, p. xiii.

13. *Ibid.*, p. xiv.

14. *Ibid.*, p. xxix.

15. Beattie MSS., B. 136.

16. Chalmers, pp. 525 - 26. Beattie's "Journal of Sessions" records other indications of his great emphasis on language. On Saturday, December 22, 1764, for example, he lectured concerning the "Direction for reading in Public given at the desire of the class." Thereafter, Beattie added instruction on public speaking and devoted two to four periods a year to the topics.

Chapter Three

1. W. Forbes, II, p. 295.

2. *Ibid.*, I, p. 102.

3. McCosh, pp. 267 - 68.

4. Terrence Martin, *The Instructed Vision: Scottish Common-Sense Philosophy and the Origins of American Fiction* (Bloomington, Indiana, 1961; New York, Kraus Reprint, 1969), pp. 14, 19. This book gives a good indication of the wide influence of common sense in America. The manner "in which the Scots influenced American writers on mental and moral philosophy . . . . [for instance, may be seen in] a typical treatise, Ezra Stiles Ely's *Converssations on the Science of the Human Mind* (1819). The Rev. Dr. Ely, a Presbyterian pastor in Philadelphia, selects what he 'deems true and most important' from a number of 'celebrated authors', among them Locke, Hume, Kames, Reid, Stewart, and Beattie" (p. 6).

Some of Martin's specific references to Beattie illustrate the extent of this influence: "Between 1805 and 1825, [the Farmer's Library in New York] acquired [among several Scottish philosophical and critical books] . . . . James Beattie's *Elements of Moral Science*"(p. 32). This book was one of Beattie's lesser known prose works; and yet its effects seem to have been considerable: in an edition of Lord Kames's *Elements of Criticism* (New York, 1868), for example, the editor, the Rev. James R. Boyd, "sets out to improve Kames, and in a section on the emotions and passions in which he thinks Kames gives only a partial view of the danger of fiction he buttresses the argument by appealing to 'Dr. Beattie in his Moral Science'. The deficiencies of one Scot are made up for by the excellencies of another" (p. 25).

Since the influence of Beattie's more popular books was probably much greater in America, as in Europe, it seems clear that American readers reacted to his writings in the same way as their contemporaries in Great Britain and in Europe: "The Scottish James Beattie spoke for many Americans when [, for example,] he said that a habit of reading fiction 'breeds a dislike of history' " (p. 73). In a word, it must have seemed to American readers that Beattie wrote what they wanted to read and that he wrote it very well.

5. Beattie tells of the origin and composition of the *Essay on Truth* in a long letter to Thomas Blacklock on January 9, 1769 (W. Forbes, I, pp. 167 - 71).

6. W. Forbes, I, p. 171.

7. *Ibid.*, p. 136

8. *Ibid.*, p. 141

9. *Ibid.*, p. 174.

10. *Ibid.*, p. 223.

11. *The Letters of David Hume to William Strahan*, ed. G. B. Hill (Oxford, 1888), p. 29.

12. N. K. Smith, *The Philosophy of David Hume* (London, 1941), p. 6.

13. Mrs. Piozzi, *Letters to and from Samuel Johnson* (London, 1788), I, p. 186.

14. W. Forbes, III, pp. 49 - 50.

15. *Thraliana: The Diary of Mrs Thrale*, ed. Katherine Balderston (Oxford, 1951), I, p. 82

16. *James Beattie's London Diary 1773*, ed. R. S. Walker (Aberdeen, 1946), p. 55.

17. The painting shows Beattie in his red Oxford Doctor of Laws gown with the *Essay on Truth* under his arm; and he is standing near the allegorical figure of truth as she forces three grotesque persons into submission. Beattie claims that these represent "Sophistry, Scepticism, and Infidelity"; and it has often been suggested that the figures also stand for Hume, Voltaire, and Edward Gibbon. Reynolds said outright that Voltaire was one of them; he laughed knowingly when Hume's large girth was mentioned in regard to the fat figure in the picture; but it is very unlikely that the third figure is Gibbon since he did not have then the reputation that would have placed him in such company. The picture, which now hangs in Marischal College in Aberdeen, is said to bear a striking resemblance to Beattie.

18. Oliver Goldsmith, cited in James Northcote, *Life of Sir Joshua Reynolds* (London, 1818), I, p. 300.

19. (London, 1774).

20. *Ibid.*, p. viii.

21. *Ibid.*, p. 118.

22. *Ibid.*, p. 190.

23. *Ibid.*, pp. 192 - 93.

24. Emmanuel Kant, *Prologomena and Metaphysical Foundations of Natural Science* (London, 1883), p. 5.

25. Joseph Addison, *The Spectator*, ed. D. F. Bond (Oxford, 1965), I, p. 44.

26. *Ibid.*

Chapter Four

1. Alexander Gerard, *A Sermon preached in the High Church of Edinburgh May 31, 1761* (Edinburgh, 1761), p. 3.

2. John Brown, *An Estimate of the Manners and Principles of the Times* (London, 1757 - 1758), I, p. 15.

3. *Ibid.*, p. 83.

4. David Hume, *The Life of David Hume* (London, 1777).

5. *Ibid.*, pp. 5 - 6.

6. *Ibid.*, pp. 14 - 15.

7. (London, 1757).

8. Hume, p. 21.

9. Hurd, pp. 6 - 7.

10. *Ibid.*, p. 8.

11. George Campbell, *A Dissertation on Miracles* (Edinburgh, 1797), I, p. ix.

12. George Campbell, cited in W. K. Leask, *Intermna Borealis* (Aberdeen, 1917), p. 299.

13. Alexander Gerard, *The Influence of the Pastoral Office on the Character examined* . . . (Aberdeen, 1770), p. 6.

14. Beilby Porteus, *Two Sermons preached at the Chapel Royal, St. James's* (London, 1772), p. 22.

15. Burney, III, p. 281.

16. M. Forbes, p. 99.

17. W. Forbes, I, p. 371.

18. Beattie MSS., B. 249.

19. W. Forbes, III, p. 169.

20. Chalmers, p. 526 n.

21. *Evidences of the Christian Religion: briefly and plainly stated* (London, 1821), p. 3. Hereafter cited as *Evidences;* all references are to this edition.

Chapter Five

1. "The Castle of Scepticism" is B. 18 in Beattie MSS. All quotations are from this source hereafter cited as "Castle." The manuscript has been published by E. C. Mossner with a short introductory essay about the fame of the *Essay on Truth* and with some speculation about Beattie's reasons for writing the satire (see "Beattie's 'The Castle of Scepticism': An Unpublished Allegory against Hume, Voltaire, and Hobbes," *Texas University Studies in English*, XXVII, 1 [June 1948], pp. 108 - 45). In his brief sketch, Mossner neither analyzes the satire nor sets it successfully in the proper context of Beattie's life and writings. He does, however, throw out an oblique hint which points to the truth about the work: "More akin to fiction and to poetry than to philosophy, the allegory perhaps does more justice to the genuine genius of Beattie as now recognized than does the once famous *Essay on Truth*" (p. 114). Since no other modern critic has thought of Beattie as possessing "genuine genius," it was perhaps predictable that Mossner would be chastized for suggesting that the satire has some literary value, as, in fact, he was by David Daiches. On the contrary, the "Castle" not only gives an important perspective to Beattie's other writings but also is a better satire than even Mossner realized.

2. W. Forbes, I, p. 196.

3. *Ibid.*, II, p. 188.

4. "Remarks on some Passages of the sixth Book of the Eneid," *Transactions of the Royal Society of Edinburgh*, 11, II (1790), pp. 33 - 54.

5. W. Forbes, I, p. 287.

6. *Ibid.*, p. 288.

7. M. Forbes, p. 12.

8. H. G. Graham, *Scottish Men of Letters in the Eighteenth Century* (London, 1908), pp. 56 - 57.

Chapter Six

1. J. W. Draper, *William Mason: A Study in Eighteenth-Century Culture* (New York, 1924), p. 186. Draper is the only twentieth century critic to mention "Retirement" favorably.

2. W. Forbes, I, p. 24.

3. Wordsworth liked these lines so much that he used them as the conclusion to a cento that he published in 1835.

4. W. Forbes, I, pp. 373 - 74.

5. Helen Darbishire, *The Poet Wordsworth* (Oxford, 1958), p. 14.

6. W. Forbes, I, p. 374.

7. *Ibid.*, II, pp. 178 - 79.

8. Boswell, IV, p. 186.

9. J.M. Beatty, "Churchill's Influence on Minor Eighteenth Century Satirists," *Publications of the Modern Language Association*, XLII (1927), p. 163.

10. Douglas Grant, *The Poetical Works of Charles Churchill* (Oxford, 1956), p. xxi. All quotations are from this edition.

11. W. C. Brown, *Charles Churchill: Poet, Rake, and Rebel* (New York, 1968), pp. 197 - 98.

12. W. Forbes, I, p. 106.

13. Brown, p. v.

14. Grant, p. v.

15. Brown, p. ii.

16. Grant, p. 97.

17. *Ibid.*, p. 197.

18. Grant, p. 126.

19. *Ibid.*, p. 210.

20. Brown, p. 98.

21. *The Poems of Alexander Pope* (The one volume edition of the Twickenham Pope, ed. John Butt [London, 1965]), pp. 362 - 63.

22. *Ibid.*, p. 425.

23. *Ibid.*, p. 351.

24. *Ibid.*, pp. 350 - 51.

25. *Ibid.*, p. 416.

26. *Ibid.*, p. 415.

27. Brown, p. i.

28. George Sampson, *The Concise History of English Literature* (Cambridge, 1953), p. 556.

29. James Laver, *Poems of Charles Churchill* (New York, 1970), p. xxxii.

30. Brown, p. 145.

Chapter Seven

1. W. Forbes, I, pp. 267 - 68.

2. *The Minstrel; or, The Progress of Genius*, I (Edinburgh, 1771), p. v.

3. *Ibid.*

4. A. F. Potts, *Wordsworth's Prelude: A Study of its Literary Form* (Ithaca, 1953), p. 131.

5. Gray, III, p. 1140.

6. *Ibid.*

7. M. Forbes, p. 59.

8. Gray, III, pp. 1140 - 41.

9. Samuel Johnson, *The Rambler*, eds. W. J. Bate and A. B. Strauss (New Haven, 1969), IV, p. 285.

10. W. Forbes, I, p. 249.

11. *The Minstrel . . .* (Edinburgh, 1771), p. v.

12. *Ibid.*, p. vi.

13. W. Forbes, I, pp. 113 - 14.

14. *The Poetical Works of Lord Byron* (London, 1966), p. 179

15. W. Forbes, I, p. 114.

16. George Saintsbury, "Young, Collins and Lesser Poets of the Age of Johnson," in *Cambridge History of English Literature* (Cambridge, 1913), X, p. 155.

Chapter Eight

1. John Thelwall, *The Peripatetic* (London, 1793), I, p. 95.

2. P. W. Clayden, *The Early Life of Samuel Rogers* (London, 1887), p. 59.

3. Dorothy Wordsworth, *Letters of the Wordsworth Family* (London, 1907), I, p. 53.

4. George Douglas, *Scottish Poetry* (Glasgow, 1911), p. 101.

5. F. W. Bateson, *Wordsworth: A Re-interpretation* (London, 1954), p. 63.

6. *The Poetical Works of William Wordsworth*, ed. Thomas Hutchison, revised by Ernest de Selincourt (London, 1965), p. 85.

7. *The Early Wordsworthian Milieu: A Notebook of Christopher Wordsworth with a few entries by William Wordsworth*, ed. Z. S. Fink (Oxford, 1958).

8. On the morning of October 23, 1795, Wordsworth walked over the hills of Lyme to see an old friend; and the sights and sounds along the way reminded him of *The Minstrel*. That night, he wrote to another friend, tell-

ing him of the pleasures of the walk and hinting at his need to be reunited with Edwin: "My walk over the hills was charming. I could hear the murmuring of the sea for three miles, of course I often stopped 'Listening with pleasing dread to the deep roar of the wide weltering waves.' This is from the Minstrel and has reminded me of a request I have to make of you . . . . make me a present of . . . The Minstrel . . . . I know you are possessed of it; so was I once, but one of my brothers lent it to a person who valued it so highly as to deny himself the pleasure of returning it." [*The Letters of William and Dorothy Wordsworth: The Later Years*, ed. Ernest de Selincourt (Oxford, 1939), p. 1334].

9. All quotations are from Ernest de Selincourt's edition of *The Prelude*, 2nd ed., revised by Helen Darbishire (Oxford, 1959).

10. *Ibid.*, p. 483.

11. *Ibid.*

12. *Ibid.*, p. 482.

13. *Ibid.*, p. 75.

14. *Ibid.*, pp. xxxi - xxxii, 569 - 578.

15. *Ibid.*, p. 572.

16. *Ibid.*, p. 575.

17. *Ibid.*, p. 431.

18. All quotations from Shelley's poems are taken from *The Complete Poetical Works* . . . , ed. Thomas Hutchinson (London, 1965).

19. *Ibid.*, p. 874.

20. Desmond King-Hele, *Shelley: His Thought and Work* (Madison, 1971), p. 54.

21. Shelley, p. 526.

22. *Ibid.*

23. *Ibid.*, p. 22.

24. *Ibid.*, p. 26.

25. *Ibid.*, pp. 16 - 17.

26. *Ibid.*, p. 17.

27. *Ibid.*, p. 19.

28. *Ibid.*, p. 18.

29. *Ibid.*, p. 20.

30. *Ibid.*, p. 23.

31. *Ibid.*, p. 441.

32. *Ibid.*, p. 207.

33. Judith Chernaik, *The Lyrics of Shelley* (London, 1972), p. 10.

34. H.E. Cory, "Spenser, Thomson, and Romanticism," *Publications of the Modern Language Association*, New Series, XIX (1911), p. 82.

35. *Ibid.*, pp. 82 - 83.

36. Byron, p. 209.

37. *Ibid.*, p. 181.

38. J. C. Collins, "The Descriptive Poetry of the Eighteenth Century," *Poet's Country* (London, 1907), p. 202.

39. Byron, p. 220.

40. *Ibid.*, p. 179.

41. *Ibid.*, p. 226.

42. Oliver Elton, *A Survey of English Literature* (London, 1928), II, p. 115.

43. Hans Hecht, *Robert Burns: The Man and his Work* (London, 1950), p. 32.

44. *The Critical Review*, III (March 1813), p. 245.

45. Eric Partridge, *Eighteenth-Century English Romantic Poetry* (Paris, 1924), p. 40.

46. *The Poetical Works of . . . Scott*, ed. J. L. Robertson (London, 1931), p. 1.

47. Sir Walter Scott, cited in R. Polwhele, *Tradition and Recollections* (London, 1826), II, p. 645.

48. *The Journal of Sir Walter Scott*, ed. W. E. K. Anderson (Oxford, 1972), p. 121.

49. Robert Gittings, *John Keats* (Boston, 1968), p. 37.

50. *The Poetical Works and Other Writings of John Keats*, ed. H. B. Forman (New York, 1970), VII, p. 175.

51. *The Poems of John Keats*, ed. Miriam Allott (London, 1970), p. 3. All quotations from Keats's poems are from this edition.

52. *Ibid.*, p. 4.

53. Gittings, p. 282.

54. Keats, p. 416.

55. Aileen Ward, *John Keats: The Making of a Poet* (New York, 1963), p. 218.

56. *The Letters of John Keats, 1814 - 1821*, ed. H. E. Rollins (Harvard, 1972), I, p. 154.

57. Keats, p. 213.

58. *Ibid.*, p. 150.

59. *Ibid.*, p. 167.

60. *Ibid.*, p. 199.

61. *Ibid.*, p. 198.

62. *Ibid.*, pp. 214 - 15.

63. *Ibid.*, p. 215.

64. *Ibid.*, p. 218.

65. *Ibid.*, pp. 219 - 20.

66. *Ibid.*, pp. 530 - 31.

67. Gittings, p. 37.

68. Partridge, p. 43.

69. See I. A. Gordon, "The Case-History of Coleridge's 'Monody on the death of Chatterton,'" *Review of English Studies*, XVIII (1942), pp. 49 - 71. See also Norman Fruman, *Coleridge, The Damaged Archangel* (New York, 1971), pp. 245 - 48.

70. *The Poems of . . . Coleridge*, ed. E. H. Coleridge (London, 1960), p. 126.

71. *Ibid.*, p. 13.

72. Gordon, cited in Fruman, p. 248.

73. Coleridge, cited in *The Complete Works of William Hazlitt*, ed. P. P. Howe (London, 1932), XI, p. 373.

74. *Coleridge's Shakespearean Criticism*, ed. T.M. Raysor (London, 1930), II, p. 51.

Chapter Nine

1. Graham Hough, *The Romantic Poets* (London, 1964), pp. 23 - 24.

2. Wordsworth's *Poetical Works*, eds. Hutchinson and de Selincourt, p. 738.

3. *The Letters of Robert Burns*, ed. J. D. L. Ferguson (Oxford, 1931), II, p. 148.

4. Wordsworth, p. 738.

5. Cited in W. J. Bate, *From Classic to Romantic* (London, 1946), p. 145.

6. Wordsworth, p. 756.

7. *Ibid.*, p. 736.

8. *Ibid.*, p. 736 n.

9. *Ibid.*, p. 734.

10. *Ibid.*, pp. 736 - 37.

11. *Ibid.*, p. 737.

12. *Ibid.*, p. 738.

13. *Ibid.*

Chapter Ten

1. *The Monthly Review*, XXIV (May 1761), pp. 393 - 95.

2. *The Scot's Magazine*, XXIII (April 1761), pp. 196 - 97.

3. *The Works of John Wesley* (London, 1872), IV (*Journal*, Friday, January 15, 1766).

4. W. Forbes, I, p. 249.

5. Beattie MSS., B. 31.

6. *The Critical Review*, IV (February 1771), p. 144.

7. *The Monthly Review*, LI (September 1774), p. 189.

8. *The Letters of William Cowper* (London, 1817), II, p. 21.

9. *Recollections of the Table-Talk of Samuel Rogers*, ed. Alexander Dyce (London, 1856), p. 40.

10. *The Letters of Robert Burns*, I, p. 70.

11. M. A. Oliver, "The Scottish Augustans," *Scottish Poetry: A Critical Survey* (London, 1955), p. 146.

12. *Blackwood's Magazine*, XVI (August 1824), p. 162.

13. Robert Southey, *Journal of a Tour in Scotland*, ed. C. H. Herford (London, 1929), p. 72.

14. *The Letters of John Clare*, eds. J. W. and Anne Tibble (London, 1961), p. 48.

15. *The Complete Works of William Hazlitt*, IV, p. 18; V, p. 100.

16. H. A. Eaton, *Thomas De Quincey: A Biography* (New York, 1936), p. 93.

17. *Blackwood's Magazine*, XLIV (October 1838), p. 512.

18. *The Cambridge History of English Literature* (Cambridge, 1932), X, p. 155.

19. Geoffrey Tillotson, *Criticism and the Nineteenth Century* (London, 1951), pp. 215 - 16.

20. *The Complete Works of . . . Shelley*, ed. R. Ingpen and W. E. Peck (New York, 1965), VII, p. 140.

21. *Ibid.*

22. E. C. Mossner, *The Forgotten Hume: Le Bon David* (New York, 1943), p. 35.

23. W. Forbes, I, p. 294.

24. Oliver Elton, *Survey of English Literature: 1730 - 1780* (London, 1928), II, p. 220.

25. M. Forbes, p. 71.

26. *Ibid.*, p. 79.

27. Boswell, V, p. 273.

28. Beattie MSS., C. 49.

29. Henry Laurie, *Scottish Philosophy in its National Development* (Glasgow, 1902), p. 171.

30. M. Forbes, p. 233.

31. Beattie MSS., C. 767.

32. *The London Magazine*, LI (July 1783), p. 50.

33. Cowper, II, pp. 20 - 21.

34. David Irving, *The Lives of the Scottish Poets* (Edinburgh, 1804), II, pp. 175 - 76.

35. *The Edinburgh Review*, X (April 1807), p. 199.   36. Alexander Bower, *An Account of the Life and Writings of James Beattie* (London, 1804), p. 223.

37. *Blackwood's Magazine*, XXV (April 1829), p. 539.

38. *Ibid.*, CXXVIII (July 1880), pp. 20 - 24.

39. W. Forbes, II, pp. 147 - 48.

40. Cowper. II, pp. 20 - 21.

Selected Bibliography

PRIMARY SOURCES

I. Manuscripts

A. The Beattie Collection in King's College Library, University of Aberdeen (Beattie MSS), contains the following material:

1. *Letters*
More than four hundred letters and fragments written by Beattie between 1758 and 1779.
More than eight hundred letters and fragments received by Beattie between 1760 and 1800.
A few letters to and from Mary Beattie and a few to and from James Hay Beattie and Montagu Beattie.
A miscellaneous assortment of letters between Beattie's friends, including some to and from George Glennie, Beattie's successor as professor of moral philosophy at Marischal College, which are mostly about the publication of William Forbes's biography of Beattie.
Of special interest are six letters from James Boswell, two from Dr. Johnson, and seven from Thomas Gray.

2. *Other Manuscripts*
B. 14 and B. 15. Beattie's day-book of accounts and memoranda, in two volumes: the first volume covers the years 1768 to 1777; the second continues to 1798.
B. 16a. The diary of Beattie's visit to London in 1773.
B. 16. "Journal of Sessions," the account of Beattie's classwork from 1762 to 1793.
B. 17. "The Hermit."
B. 18. "Allegory against Hume: Letter in the style of Voltaire," and "The Castle of Scepticism."
B. 19. "Essay on Laughter."
B. 20. "Evidences of Christianity."
B. 21. "An Elegy."
B. 23. "Notes on Hebrew."
B. 31. An account of Beattie's health in 1777 by Dr. John Gregory.
B. 44. Copies of Gray's poems in Beattie's hand.

B. 46. An outline of an unpublished answer to Joseph Priestley's book about the *Essay on Truth.*

B. 47. A list of the books in Beattie's library in 1785.

B. 49a. Beattie's "Lectures on Moral Philosophy and Logic."

B. 49. "Essay on Slavery."

B. The Library of the University of Glasgow

"A Compendious System of Pneumatology comprehending Psychology, Moral Philosophy, & Logic. Taken at the lectures of Mr. Js Beattie P.P. At the Marischal College & University of Abd by J. Rennie. Anno. 1767."

II. *Published Works*

(Chronologically listed with number of editions located)

Original Poems and Translations. Aberdeen: F. Douglas; London: A. Millar, 1761.

"Verses occasioned by the Death of the Rev [d] Mr. Charles Churchill." Edinburgh, 1765.

"The Judgment of Paris." London: T. Becket and P. A. de Hondt, 1765.

Poems on Several Subjects. London: W. Johnson, 1766.

An Essay on the Nature and Immutability of Truth, in Opposition to Sophistry and Scepticism. Edinburgh: A. Kincaid and J. Bell; London: E and C Dilly, 1770 (twenty-six editions up to 1852; and a "Facsimile-Reprint of the first edition . . . With a general introduction . . . by Friedrich O. Wolf." Stuttgart - Bad Cannstatt: Friedrich Frommann Verlag [Günther Holzboog], 1973.)

The Minstrel: or, the Progress of Genius. A Poem. Book the First. London: E and C Dilly; Edinburgh: A. Kincaid and W. Creech, 1771 (five editions up to 1775).

The Minstrel . . . Book the Second. London: E and C Dilly, 1774 (three editions in this year).

The Minstrel . . . in Two Books. London: E and C Dilly; Edinburgh: A. Kincaid and W. Creech, 1774 (thirty-nine editions up to 1858; the poem is also included in all editions of the collected poems after 1776).

Essays: On Poetry and Music as they affect the Mind; On Laughter and Ludicrous Composition; On the Utility of Classical Learning. London: E and C Dilly; Edinburgh: W. Creech, 1776 (seven editions up to 1798).

A Letter to the Rev. Hugh Blair . . . on the improvement of Psalmody in Scotland. Edinburgh: R. Buchanan and J. Stevenson, 1778.

A List of two hundred Scoticisms. With Remarks. Aberdeen: F. Douglas, 1779.

Dissertations Moral and Critical: Of Memory and Imagination; On Dreaming; The Theory of Language; On Fable and Romance; Illustrations on Sublimity. London: W. Strahan, 1783 (three editions up to 1790).

Evidences of the Christian Religion; briefly and plainly stated. Edinburgh: W. Creech, 1786 (eight editions up to 1821).

Scoticisms: arranged in alphabetical order, designed to correct improprieties of speech and writing. Edinburgh: W. Creech, 1787 (three editions up to 1838).

The Theory of Language. London: A Strahan, 1788; "A Scolar Press Facsimilie." Menston: Scolar Press, 1968.

"Remarks on some Passages of the sixth Book of the Eneid." *Transactions of the Royal Society of Edinburgh* II, II (1790), 33 - 54; rpt. *Annual Register* (1790), pp. 109 - 14.

Elements of Moral Science, I. Edinburgh: W. Creech, 1790.

Elements of Moral Science, II. Edinburgh: W. Creech, 1793 (six editions up to 1840).

The Poetical Works of James Beattie In *The Works of the British Poets,* XXXVII. Ed. Thomas Park. London: Charles Whittington, 1805 (twenty-two editions in various collected editions of *British Poets* up to 1881).

Beauties selected from the writing of James Beattie. London: Longman & Co., 1809.

Select Poems of James Beattie. Philadelphia, 1822.

James Beattie, "The Minstrel". Some Unpublished Letters. Ed. Alexander Mackie. Aberdeen: "Aberdeen Daily Journal" Office, 1908.

The Letters of James Beattie. . . . In *British Prose Writers,* V. London: John Sharpe, 1918 - 1921.

James Beattie's London Diary 1773. Ed. R. S. Walker. Aberdeen: Aberdeen University Studies, No. 122, 1946.

James Beattie's Day-Book 1773 - 1798. Ed. R. S. Walker. Aberdeen: Third Spalding Club, 1948.

SECONDARY SOURCES

ALDRICH, E. A. "James Beattie's *Minstrel:* Its Sources and its Influence on the English Romantic Poets." Doctoral dissertation, Harvard University, 1927. Valuable work for pointing to sources and for demonstrating the "memorable" qualities of *The Minstrel.*

BEVILACQUA, V. M. "The Authorship of 'Alexander Gerard's Lectures on Logic and Rhetoric': Edinburgh University Library MS. DC.5.117." *Notes and Queries,* CCX (January-December 1865), 101 - 05. Proves that Beattie was the author of much in these lectures ascribed to Gerard.

BOSKER, AISSO. *Literary Criticism in the Age of Johnson.* Folcroft, Pennsylvania: Folcroft Press, 1969 (Rpt. of the 1930 ed.), Chapter 18 is notable for treatment of Beattie's criticism, especially that concerning the imagination.

BOWER, ALEXANDER. *An Account of the Life and Writings of James Beattie . . .* London: C and R Baldwin, 1804. Hastily written and often ill-informed, this first biography was published shortly after Beattie's death. Since it seems to have been rushed into print to "cash in" on Beattie's fame, it is a good reflection of his great reputation, especially as it makes some extravagant claims for his writings.

CHALMERS, ALEXANDER. "Life of James Beattie." In *The Works of the British Poets*, XVIII, pp. 515 - 33. London: J. Johnson, 1810. Written in 1803 before Bower and Forbes had published their biographies, this work is the best firsthand account of Beattie and his writings. Chalmers, who was the best known of Beattie's students, gives a particularly valuable account of Beattie's teaching and its effect on his own books.

DYCE, ALEXANDER. "Memoir of James Beattie." In *The Aldine Edition of the British Poets*. London: William Pickering, 1831. This often reprinted "Memoir" became the standard short commentary about Beattie and his rank as a writer. It is the best of the many nineteenth century accounts.

EBERWEIN, ROBERT. "James Beattie and David Hume on the Imagination and Truth." *Texas Studies in Literature and Language*, XII, 4 (Winter 1971) 595 - 603. In viewing Beattie's concept of the imagination as a potential means of reaching truth in relation to his attacks on Hume's scepticism, Eberwein argues that Beattie's ideas on the powers of the imagination provide an important corrective to Hume's thoughts.

FORBES, MARGARET. *Beattie and his Friends*. Westminster: A. Constable, 1904. Written by a descendant of Beattie, this centennial book presents the facts of his life with a wealth of detail; at best, however, it merely provides a framework for additional study.

FORBES, WILLIAM. *An Account of the Life and Writings of James Beattie . . . Including many of his Original Letters*. 2 vols. Edinburgh: A. Constable, 1806 (three editions up to 1824). Written by an old friend and confidant, this important work is modeled on Mason's technique in his "Life of Thomas Gray" in which the writer's "story" is told through the printing of many letters that are strung together by the biographer's chronological commentary. Consequently, this book has always been a main source for Beattie's letters, which have yet to be published in a scholarly edition.

GRAY, JAMES. "Beattie and the Johnson Circle." *Queen's Quarterly*, LVIII (Winter 1951 - 1952), 519 - 32. Gray argues convincingly that Beattie's correspondence offers a more realistic view of Dr. Johnson, balancing criticism against praise, than may be found in Boswell and in other recorders of his sayings.

JESSOP, M. A. *A Bibliography of David Hume and of Scottish Philosophy from Francis Hutcheson to Lord Balfour*. New York: Russell and Russell, 1966. This book contains the first published bibliography of Beattie's philosophical writings.

KING, E. H. "James Beattie's *The Minstrel* (1771, 1774): Its Influence on

Wordsworth." *Studies in Scottish Literature*, VIII (1970), 3 - 29. The treatment of Wordsworth in Chapter 8 of this study is a brief indication of Beattie's influence on Wordsworth that relies heavily on this much longer article for detailed proof of the important seminal effects of *The Minstrel*.

———. "James Beattie's *The Minstrel* and the Romantic Poets." *Aberdeen University Review*, XLVI, 3, 155 (Spring 1976), 273 - 87. This article documents the general case for the influence of *The Minstrel* on the Romantic poets that is developed much more fully in Chapter 8 of this study.

———. "Beattie and Coleridge: New Light on the Damaged Archangel." *The Wordsworth Circle*, VII, 2 (Spring 1976), 142 - 51. The considerable debt that Coleridge owes to Beattie's writings provides, the author contends, significant evidence of the quality of Coleridge's thought and writings, as well as of the nature of his l'cerary borrowings.

KINSLEY, JAMES. "The Music of the Heart." *Renaissance and Modern Studies*, VIII (1964) 5 - 52. Presents a convincing account of Burns's debt to Beattie about the union of poetry and music.

KLOTH, KAREN, AND FABIAN, BERNHARD. "James Beattie: contributions towards a bibliography." *The Bibliotheck: A Scottish Journal of Bibliography and Allied Topics*, V, 7 (1970), 232 - 45. This article is supplemental to Jessop's bibliography of Beattie's philosophical writings.

LAND, STEPHEN K. "James Beattie on Language." *Philological Quarterly*, LI, 5 (October 1972), 887 - 904. Excellent article which shows that Beattie's arguments in "On the Theory of Language" (1783) and "On Poetry and Music" (1776) are an important defense of the essentially rational nature of language. Land demonstrates also that Beattie's esthetic and rhetorical approaches to language are more flexible than those of most writers of the time and that he anticipates some of Wordsworth's views on expression and diction.

MOSSNER, E. C. "Beattie's 'The Castle of Scepticism': An Unpublished Allegory against Hume, Voltaire, and Hobbes." Texas University *Studies in English*, XXVII, (June 1948), 108 - 45. This article prints the text of the manuscript with some notes and background.

———. "Beattie on Voltaire: An Unpublished Parody." *The Romanic Review*, XLI (February 1950), 26 - 32. This article prints the text of the manuscript with some notes and background.

POTTS, ABBIE F. *Wordsworth's Prelude: A Study of its Literary Form*. Ithaca, New York: Cornell University Press, 1953. Ch. 3 ("Minstrel and Bard"), pp. 63 - 76. By illustrating Wordsworth's development through the similarities between *The Prelude* and *The Minstrel*, Potts inadvertently indicates that Beattie had an important influence on Wordsworth.

ROUNDTREE, T. J. "Wordsworth and Beattie's Minstrel." *The South Atlantic Quarterly*, LXIX, 2 (Spring 1970), 257 - 63. Article shows in general terms some of the many ideas that Wordsworth may have derived from Beattie.

TAVE, S.M. "Some Essays by James Beattie in the 'London Magazine' (XL-1771)" *Notes and Queries*, CXCVII (1952), 534 - 37. This article shows that these essays published by "J. Rennie" are actually notes taken from Beattie's lectures. In fact, Rennie is the author of the notebook that was written in Beattie's class of 1767 - 1768.

WAGNER, M. J. "An Analysis of the Critical and Philosophical Works of James Beattie." Doctoral dissertation, Northwestern University, 1956. This sound analysis of Beattie's system shows its historical, derivative nature, as well as its anticipation of later writers, especially Wordsworth.

WALKER, R. S. "Introduction." *James Beattie's London Diary 1773*. Aberdeen: The University Press, 1946. This only notable recent account of Beattie's life, writings, and reputation is very competent and useful.

WOLFF, R. P. "Kant's Debt to Hume via Beattie." *The Journal of the History of Ideas*, XXI (June 1961), 165 - 75. Wolff demonstrates the wide effects of Beattie's philosophical writings.

Index

(The works of Beattie are listed under his name)

Addison, Joseph, 36, 48, 62, 73, 141, 156, 165

"Adonais" (Shelley), 116, 117

Aeneid (Vergil), 67, 70

Akenside, Mark, 85, 86

Alastor (Shelley), 113 - 16, 117, 125

Amelia (Fielding), 150

Analogy of Religion, The (Butler), 50, 53, 55

Ars Poetica (Horace), 34

"Bard, The" (Gray), 130, 137

Beattie, James: becomes professor at Marischal College, 18; Christian attitudes, 20; early influences, 17; father dies, 17; graduates with M.A. from Marischal College, 17; grief over the deaths of his two sons, 19 - 20; marital problems and frequent illness, 18 - 20; popularity as a writer, 24 - 25; prose style, 36, 43, 48; publishes first poems, 17; receives honorary LL.D. from Oxford, 46; relationships with students, 17, 26 - 27, 30; responses to Beattie as a person by Dr. Johnson, Fanny Burney and Thomas Gray, 22 - 24; role in the abolition of slavery, 31 - 32; schoolmaster at Fordoun, 17; sense of humor, 21; skill as a singer and musician, 140; teaching career, 26 - 37; teaching of rhetoric and belles lettres, 34 - 37

WORKS—MANUSCRIPTS:

"Castle of Scepticism, The," 60 - 74, 95, 173nl

"Discourse on Slavery, A," 31

"Journal of Sessions," 17, 29 - 30, 34, 35, 37

WORKS—POETRY:

"Epitaph, Intended for Himself," 20

"Hermit, The," 78 - 82, 94, 108, 158

Minstrel, The, 18, 24, 25, 61, 78, 79, 81, 82, 90, 91 - 106, 107 - 33, 134 - 35, 137, 143, 159 - 61, 162, 163, 165

Original Poems and Translations, 23, 75, 158

"Retirement," 75 - 78, 82, 94, 158

"Verses occasioned by the Death of the Revd Mr Charles Churchill," 82 - 90, 130, 158

WORKS—PROSE:

"Dissertation on the Theory of Language, A," 36

Dissertations Moral and Critical, 25, 30, 36, 70, 72, 134, 163

Elements of Moral Science, 25, 29, 31, 37, 141

"Essay on Poetry and Music, An," 37, 108, 121, 134, 135 - 36, 138, 139 - 40, 143, 153, 154, 156

Essay on Truth, An, 16, 18, 24, 25, 31, 32, 33, 39 - 48, 49, 53 - 55, 56, 57, 60, 70, 71, 73, 94 - 96, 151, 152, 161 - 62, 163, 164

Evidences of the Christian Religion, 25, 56 - 59, 162 - 163

"Illustrations on Sublimity," 37, 134, 155

"Of Memory and Imagination," 37, 134, 145, 157

"On Fable and Romance," 37, 146, 156

"On Laughter and Ludicrous Composition," 37, 134, 151 - 52; 154

Beattie, James Hay, 19, 20

Beattie, Mary, 18, 22

Beattie, Montagu, 19, 20

Berkeley, George, 38, 41, 43

Bible, The, 94
Biographia Literaria (Coleridge), 142
Blair, Hugh, 35, 82, 155
Boswell, James, 22, 81, 162
Brown, John, 50
Bunyan, John, 66
Burke, Edmund, 141, 162
Burney, Fanny (Madame D'Arblay), 22 - 23, 53 - 54
Burns, Robert, 121, 138 - 40, 159, 165, 168
Bute, Lord, 83
Butler, Joseph, 50, 53, 55
Butler, Samuel, 66 70, 151, 152
Byron, Lord, 81, 106, 107, 117 - 20, 160, 168

Campbell, George, 33, 41, 42, 52, 53
Castle of Indolence, The (Thomson), 69, 104, 109
Cervantes, Miguel, 70, 146, 147
Chalmers, Alexander, 21
Chalmers, Thomas, 162
Chaucer, Geoffrey, 129, 151, 152
Childe Harold's Pilgrimage (Byron), 106, 117 - 20
Churchill, Charles, 82 - 90
Cibber, Colley, 89, 154
Clare, John, 160, 168
Clarissa Harlowe (Richardson), 149
Coleridge, Samuel Taylor, 110, 129 - 33, 134, 141 - 42, 144, 160
Collins, William, 114
Count Fathom (Smollett), 150
Cowper, William, 159, 164, 166

Dante, 116, 129
Defects of popular fiction, The, 151
Defense of Poetry, A (Shelley), 161
Defoe, Daniel, 146, 147 - 48
Deism, 50 - 51, 53
"Dejection: An Ode" (Coleridge), 132
De Quincey, Thomas, 160
"Descriptive Sketches" (Wordsworth), 109, 110
Dissertation on Miracles, A (Campbell), 41, 52
Don Quixote (Cervantes), 70, 147, 152
Dryden, John, 36, 66, 90, 153, 157, 165
Duff, William, 140

Dunciad, The (Pope), 70, 71, 72, 73, 88, 89, 152

Eighteenth Century Novel, The, 146 - 151
"Elegy written in a Country Churchyard" (Gray), 96, 130
Endymion (Keats), 125 - 28
English Satirists, The, 151 - 53
"Epipsychidion" (Shelley), 117
Essay on Original Genius (Duff), 140, 141
Estimate of the Manners and Principles of the Times, An (Brown), 50
"Eve of St. Agnes, The" (Keats), 106, 124
"Evening Walk, An" (Wordsworth), 109
Evolution of Romanticism, The, 134 - 35
Examination of . . . Beattie's 'Essay on Truth' . . . , An (Priestly), 46 - 47
Excursion, The (Wordsworth), 160

Faerie Queene, The (Spenser), 69, 70, 118, 123, 146
Fielding, Henry, 146, 150 - 51
Forbes, Margaret, 54
Forbes, William, 18, 56

Garrick, David, 162
Gerard, Alexander, 49 - 50, 52, 53, 141, 155
Ghost, The (Churchill), 85, 87
Goldsmith, Oliver, 44 - 46, 97, 155
Gotham (Churchill), 90
Gray, Thomas, 23 - 24, 75, 84, 85, 87, 94, 96, 103 - 104, 114, 116, 130, 131, 136, 137, 156
Gregory, John, 42, 44
Guide to the Lakes (Wordsworth), 136
"Guilt and Sorrow" (Wordsworth), 106
Gulliver's Travels (Swift), 70, 71, 152

Hazlitt, William, 160
Hobbes, Thomas, 64, 65, 72, 73
Homer, 35, 36, 67, 69, 71
"How many bards gild the lapses of time" (Keats), 124
Hudibras (Butler), 70
Hume, David, 38, 40, 41, 42, 43, 44, 47, 49, 50 - 53, 55, 56, 57, 61, 62, 63, 65 - 66, 72, 73 - 74, 162

Hurd, Richard, 51 - 52, 146
Hyperion (Keats), 124 - 25

Illustrations, Use of, 42, 154
Imagination, 140 - 42
"Imitation of Spenser" (Keats), 106, 123 - 24
Inquiry into the Human Mind upon the Principles of Common Sense, An (Reid), 38, 40, 41, 63
"Intimations Ode" (Wordsworth), 109, 120

Johnson, Dr. Samuel, 20, 22, 44, 45, 77, 81, 85, 87, 104, 105, 159, 162, 166
Joseph Andrews (Fielding), 150

Kant, Emmanuel, 44, 47, 162
Keats, John, 90, 106, 122 - 29, 133, 160, 168

"Lady of the Lake, The" (Scott), 121
"Lay of the Last Minatrel, The" (Scott), 121
Letters on Chivalry and Romance (Hurd), 146
Life of David Hume, The (Hume), 51
Literary use of science, The, 137 - 39
Locke, John, 28, 38, 41, 43
Longinus, 155
Lyrical Ballads (Wordsworth and Coleridge), 134, 135, 138

Mandeville, Bernard, 64
Marischal College, 16, 18, 95
"Marmion" (Scott), 121
Milton, John, 35, 36, 85, 86, 87, 88, 89, 94, 116, 129
"Monody on the Death of Chatterton" (Coleridge), 130 - 31, 132
Montagu, Mrs Elizabeth, 23, 29, 31, 32, 55, 56, 68, 78, 159

Natural description, The use of, 135 - 37
Newton, Issac, 111
North Briton, The, 83, 89

Observations on Man (Hartley), 46
"Ode to Apollo" (Keats), 124
"Ode to the West Wind" (Shelley), 117

Odes (Keats), 128 - 29
Odyssey (Homer), 67
On the Sublime (Longinus), 155
"O Solitude" (Keats), 124
"Ossian," 94

Peregrine Pickle (Smollett), 149
Philosophical Society of Aberdeen, The, 15 - 17, 29, 32, 38, 41, 42, 71 - 72
Philosophy of Common Sense, The, 32, 38 - 48, 171n4
Pope, Alexander, 36, 66, 70, 71, 72, 85, 88 - 89, 151, 152, 153, 154, 165
Porteus, Beilby, 53, 162
Portrait of Beattie by Reynolds, 46, 172n17
Prelude, The (Wordsworth), 82, 92, 109, 110 - 12, 117, 119, 120, 125
Priestley, Joseph, 40, 46 - 47, 49
"Progress of Poesy, The" (Gray), 130, 137
Prometheus Unbound (Shelley), 80, 117
Prophecy of Famine, The (Churchill), 83, 85, 87, 90
Pyrrho, 64

Queen Mab (Shelley), 113

Reid, Thomas, 35, 38 - 39, 40, 41, 42, 44, 46, 52, 53, 62, 63
"Religious Musings" (Coleridge), 131 - 32
Remarks on Mr D Hume's Essay on the Natural History of Religion . . . (Hurd), 51
Rennie's "Notebook" of Beattie's lectures, 27 - 29, 32, 33, 34, 35, 36, 37, 41
"Retrospect: Cwm Elan, 1812, The" (Shelley), 112 - 13
"Retrospect of Times of old, A" (Shelley), 113
Revolt of Islam, The (Shelley), 106, 116 - 17
Reynolds, Sir Joshua, 46, 155
Richardson, Samuel, 146, 148 - 49
"Rime of the Ancient Mariner, The" (Coleridge), 132
Robinson Crusoe (Defoe), 147 - 48
Roderick Random (Smollett), 149

Rogers, Samuel, 107, 159, 168
Rokeby (Scott), 121
Role of the literary critic, The, 145 - 46

School of Taste, The, 155 - 56
Scotland's "Age of Improvement," 15 - 17, 29
Scott, Sir Walter, 107, 121 - 22, 164, 168
Scottish universities, 16, 29, 31, 34 - 35, 37
Shakespeare, William, 35, 85, 87, 89, 94, 129
Shelley, Percy Bysshe, 80, 90, 106, 107, 112 - 17, 129, 161, 168
Shenstone, William, 85
Sir Lancelot Greaves (Smollett), 150
Smith, Adam, 16, 34, 135
Smollett, Tobias, 146, 149 - 50
Southey, Robert, 160, 168
Spenser, Edmund, 67, 69, 73, 85, 94, 105, 123, 129, 146
Spenserian Stanza, The, 91, 104 - 106, 118, 120, 123 - 24, 156, 165
Swift, Jonathan, 36, 66, 70, 71, 73, 151, 152

Tennyson, Alfred Lord, 160
Thelwall, John, 107
Theory of Moral Sentiment (Smith), 135
Thomson, George, 139
Thomson, James, 67, 69, 94, 104, 105, 109, 110, 114, 116, 159
"To William Wordsworth" (Coleridge), 132

"To Wordsworth" (Shelley), 114
Tom Jones (Fielding), 150 - 51
Treatise on Human Nature (Hume), 38, 44, 50, 51, 63
Treatment of rhetoric and belles lettres in Scottish universities, 34 - 37
Tristram Shandy (Sterne), 151

Union of poetry and music, The, 138 - 140

"Vale of Esthwaite, The" (Wordsworth), 109
Vergil, 35, 36, 67 - 69
Voltaire, 46, 53, 64, 70 - 71

Warburton, William, 51, 53
Wesley, John, 75, 158, 162
Whitefield, George, 89
Wilberforce, William, 31, 32
Wilson, John ("Christopher North"), 160, 164
Wordsworth, Christopher, 109
Wordsworth, Dorothy, 107, 109, 110, 167
Wordsworth, William, 80, 82, 91, 92, 105, 106, 108 - 12, 113, 114, 116, 117, 119, 120, 125, 129, 131 - 33, 134, 136, 137, 138, 142 - 45, 164, 167 - 68, 174n3, 175n8
Wilkes, John, 83, 87, 89

Young, Edward, 78